Front Cover: photo courtesy of U.S. Marine Corps

NO GREATER LOVE

– *Books by Marion Sturkey* –

BONNIE-SUE: A Marine Corps Helicopter Squadron in Vietnam
ISBN: 978-0-9650814-2-9 (509 pages, published in 1996)

MAYDAY: Accident Reports and Voice Transcripts from Airline Crash Investigations
ISBN: 978-0-9650814-3-6 (461 pages, published in 2005)

Murphy's Laws of Combat (first edition)
ISBN: 0-9650814-4-3 (241 pages, published in 2003)

Murphy's Laws of Combat (second edition)
ISBN: 978-0-9650814-6-7 (366 pages, published in 2009)

MID-AIR: Accident Reports and Voice Transcripts from Military and Airline Mid-Air Collisions
ISBN: 978-0-9650814-7-4 (477 pages, published in 2008)

Military Monuments and Memorials in South Carolina
ISBN: 978-0-9650814-8-1 (575 pages, published in 2012)

Warrior Culture of the U.S. Marines (first edition)
ISBN: 0-9650814-5-1 (207 pages, published in 2002)

Warrior Culture of the U.S. Marines (second edition)
ISBN: 0-9650814-1-9 (212 pages, published in 2003)

Warrior Culture of the U.S. Marines (third edition)
ISBN: 978-0-9650814-9-8 (370 pages, published in 2010

Gone But Not Forgotten
LCCCN: 88-92560 (679 pages, published in 1988)

Gone But Not Forgotten: An Introduction
LCCCN: 88-92649 (42 pages, published in 1988)

PLUM BRANCH: Heaven in South Carolina
ISBN: 978-0-9913011-0-2 (565 pages, published in 2014)

NO GREATER LOVE: The Groucho Marx Battle
ISBN: 978-0-9913011-1-9 (291 pages, published in 2016)

NO GREATER LOVE

NO GREATER
LOVE
The Groucho Marx Battle

Marion F. Sturkey

Heritage Press International

NO GREATER LOVE: The Groucho Marx Battle

First Edition

Library of Congress Control Number: 2015914785

ISBN: 978-0-9913011-1-9

Heritage Press International
204 Jefferson Street
P.O. Box 333
Plum Branch, SC 29845
USA

Manufactured in the United States of America

Table of Contents

The United States Marine Corps, with its fiercely proud tradition of excellence in combat, its hallowed rituals, and its unbending code of honor, is part of the fabric of American myth. No other group in America leaves so deep and permanent a mark on its members.

[Thomas Ricks, <u>Making The Corps</u>, 1997]

Introduction

Background: This project focuses on events that occurred many years ago during the summer of 1966. At that time the U.S. Marine Corps was battling North Vietnamese Army troops that had invaded South Vietnam.

> **SYNOPSIS:** On 6 August 1966 the Marine Corps "Groucho Marx" reconnaissance team left Dong Ha combat base in South Vietnam. Via helicopter, this clandestine four-man team was dropped into a valley in the rugged mountains 13 miles to the west.
>
> Two days later on 8 August 1966 after the team had seen many North Vietnamese soldiers, a reinforcement platoon was helicoptered into the valley. That afternoon after half of the platoon had been extracted, the enemy attacked in force. Marines set up a defensive perimeter atop a tiny knoll. Throughout the night of 8-9 August they battled soldiers of the 324-B North Vietnamese Army Division. Helicopters flew throughout the long night to resupply and reinforce surrounded Marines on the little hill. North Vietnamese troops withdrew at dawn on 9 August 1966.

Research Time-Line: Research that began in 1989 culminated with publication of the book *Bonnie-Sue* in 1996. One chapter of that book concerns events at issue herein. Research resumed three years later in 1999, continued into the year 2000, and was interrupted. Research began anew 14 years later in 2014 and continued into 2015.

In this project when statements from witnesses or participants are quoted, the date when such statements were made is noted. Such dates may fall into the (1) 1989-1996 time frame, the (2) 1999-2000 time frame, or the (3) 2014-2015 time frame. The reason for this wide range of time is explained above.

Battle Time-Line: In this project two chapters, "The Recon Patrol" and "The Groucho Marx Battle," relate events that occurred during a period of only four days. These events are presented chronologically in the interest of continuity.

Chronological presentation of diverse information from multiple sources is not a science. Content of military Command Chronologies, After Action Reports, Situation Reports, etc., often includes a time-of-day when specified events took place. Yet, in many instances the listed time-of-day is not the time an event *occurred*. Instead it is the time when information about the event was *received*. Further, many sources such as Casualty Cards and Unit Diary entries do not include any time-of-day information.

In view of the foregoing this project uses *consensus* time-of-day information for chronology purposes. Greatest weight is given to media or documents created at the time: tape recordings, logbook entries, etc. Significant weight is assigned to content of scholarly books and military records. Participant and witness recollections are used with caution (see below).

Personal Recollections: Memories obviously fade after the passage of a half-century. Most persons will have a dim memory, if any memory at all, of events they witnessed 50 years in the past. Most remember "bits and pieces" of different events all jumbled together. Further, two or more persons who express recollection of the same event often disagree. In fact, during research for this project multiple persons often expressed memory of the same event, but they offered totally conflicting information.

Only during life-changing circumstances would a normal person recall precise details of an event in which he was involved a half-century ago. Therefore, expressed personal recollections of persons involved as participants or witnesses are used in this project with extreme caution and reservation. Project chronology and details are based almost exclusively upon credible written documentation.

Source Documents: Few things on Earth are beyond dispute, but many come close. This project references altitudes, distances, radio frequencies, locations, etc. Such information comes from publications such as *Low Altitude Instrument Approach Procedures, Pacific and Southeast Asia* and the 1:50,000 scale military maps used by both ground and aviation forces, for example: "Quang Tri, Sheet 6442 IV, Series L-7014" map courtesy of U.S. Army Map Service.

Copies of old military documents reveal shackle codes, chains of command, radio call-signs, operational orders, artillery fire zones, map coordinates, troop rosters, etc. That information plus casualty records, maps, military manuals, logbooks, and personal documents enabled creation of a chronological outline.

Personal correspondence and diaries usually do not reflect a comprehensive "big picture" view. Yet, many such documents have been referenced in this project, for they offer unique insight into their originators' mindset.

Photograph captions often are subject to question. However, picture content speaks for itself, and photographs are displayed in this project for illustrative purposes.

Military Awards: Since time immemorial, individual achievement, bravery, leadership, and success in battle have been recognized by military commanders. Recognition frequently comes in the form of medals, citations, commendations, etc.

Military conduct referenced in this project resulted in several military awards. However, this project is not about such awards or medals. They are "another story." Readers seeking information about awards earned by Marines in Vietnam may choose to consult the technical publication: *Marines, Medals, and Vietnam*, by William L. Myers, ISBN 978-0-9674365-1-7.

National Strategy, Political Goals, and Economics: Exclusive of brief references in the chapters "Setting The Stage" and "The Rising Storm," this project does not address United States military strategy, political considerations, or economic issues related to the conflict in Vietnam. Significant issues indeed are involved. Yet, like military awards, these issues are "another story."

Quotations: This project uses *displayed* quotations in the interest of credibility and emphasis. Quotations are presented verbatim. However, routine errors in capitalization, punctuation, and spelling have been corrected without notice to the reader. Necessary interpolations are enclosed in brackets. Ellipses indicate intentional omissions. The source document or source person is identified by name.

Military Rank: Military rank usually changes with passing time.

A quoted person's military rank *when an oral or written account was made* is specified. However, when a quoted person spoke or wrote such an account after he left active duty (including military retirees), his former military rank is omitted.

Branch of Service: (1) When a quoted account was made by a person while he was on active duty in American armed forces, his branch of service will be specified and abbreviated as follows:

United States Air Force. . . . . . . USAF
United States Army. . . . . USA
Confederate States Army. . . . . . . CSA
United States Navy.. . . . . USN
United States Marine Corps.. . . . USMC

(2) When a quoted account was made by a person in the armed forces of a foreign country, his branch of service will be specified without abbreviations.

(3) When a quoted account was made by a person no longer on active duty (including retirees), no branch of service will be shown.

(4) Except for quotations from published books and articles, when a quoted account was made by a person holding high office or unique status (prime minister, military tactician, historian, etc.), that office or status will be specified.

Casualty Dates: The battle at issue began in the late afternoon of 8 August 1966 and continued through the afternoon and night until about 0620 Hours the next morning, 9 August 1966. Those who later initiated casualty documentation often adopted a "one size fits all" mode. For Marines WIA or KIA during the battle, 8 August is the specified date on most Casualty Cards. All Unit Diary entries specify 8 August as the casualty date. That date is not always correct.

Thirty-six Marines were either WIA or KIA during the battle. Some of them were WIA/KIA on 8 August. Others were WIA/KIA on the morning of 9 August. Also, many Marines sustained wounds on both days during the two-day battle. For many who were WIA or KIA during the long night, the date (either 8 August or 9 August) when they became a casualty is subject to question.

When Casualty Card or Unit Diary casualty data is displayed in this project and the date is subject to question, the explanatory note will read "8-9 August" (meaning, *either 8 August or 9 August*).

List of Marines and Corpsmen: There is no known military record or document – *per se* – that lists Marines or corpsmen who were on the knoll on 8-9 August 1966. There is no turnkey method for compiling such a list. However, archived records of the following military units confirm that they were involved:

    E Co., 2nd Bn., 4th Marines.. . . . (infantry company).

    2nd Bn., 4th Marines. . . . . (infantry battalion).

    4th Marines. . . . . (infantry regiment).

    1st Force Recon Co.. . . . . (reconnaissance company).

    3rd Bn., 12th Marines. . . . . (artillery battalion).

    VMO-2.. . . . . (Huey squadron).

    HMM-161. . . . . (H-34 squadron).

    HMM-263. . . . . (H-34 squadron).

    HMM-265. . . . . (H-46 squadron).

    MAG-16.. . . . . (helicopter command).

The following process was used to identify names of Marines and corpsmen who were involved.

(1) For each of the 10 military units listed above, a copy of the Unit Diary for August 1966 was obtained from Marine Corps archives. The typewritten Unit Diary includes the name, rank, service number, and MOS of each person attached to the unit that month.

(2) The name of each person listed, on each Unit Diary, was checked against the Marine Corps casualty index from the Vietnam era. When a match was found, a copy of the individual Casualty Card was obtained from Marine Corps archives. Among other things, a Casualty Card includes the casualty name, service number, military unit, date, place, and injury details. This identified many persons as having been on the knoll, or aboard helicopters that flew to the knoll.

(3) In each military unit, Unit Diary end-notes were checked to identify Marines WIA on 8-9 August, but whose minor wounds had not warranted a formal Casualty Card. This identified additional persons as having been on the knoll, or aboard helicopters that flew to the knoll.

(4) Command Chronologies (and After Action Reports, when available) were obtained for each military unit listed above. Some list no names. Others include lengthy combat narratives and names of Marines involved. Some contain separate casualty lists. These records identify additional persons as having been on the knoll, or

aboard helicopters that flew to the knoll.

(5) Military award citations identified some recipients as having been on the knoll, or having flown in support of those on the knoll.

(6) Supporting documentation for some military awards was available. Typed statements, signed by surviving witnesses within days of the battle, identified signatories as having been on the knoll.

(7) Various Marine Corps publications contain narratives about the struggle on the knoll. Most of them name many of the Marines involved.

(8) Some helicopter squadron records include flight schedules, aircraft assignments, mission numbers, and pilot names. These records confirm names of some Marines who flew to the knoll.

(9) Most helicopter pilots – even a half-century later – still have their cherished *Aviators Flight Logbook* (OPNAV 3760-31). Entries therein were made by squadron operations clerks (clerks, not the pilots, had custody of flight logbooks). For each flight, logbook entries include the date, Bureau Number, day or night hours, total hours, and flight code. The "remarks" column often includes the mission number, the location, and surname of the other pilot aboard. Logbook entries, combined with information from Item 8 above, confirm names of many Marines who flew to the knoll.

(10) From sources listed above and months of internet searches and personal contacts, the author compiled a list of Marines and a corpsman identified by documents as having been on the knoll. He also compiled a list of many (but not all) helicopter crewmen who flew to the knoll. He identified others who played key supporting rear echelon roles far from the battle site.

The author contacted all relevant involved parties that he could locate. However, civil and military records confirm that many other involved parties are now deceased.

Missing Information: This project is not all-inclusive. It does not attempt to detail *every* action, by *every* person, *every* day. It is a summary. Further, research results were not perfect. For example, four credible sources separately reported that three wounded infantrymen were shot while riding in helicopters *at* the knoll – not while actually *on* the knoll. Research identified the wounded Marines and the nature of their wounds. However, only one of them is confirmed to have sustained his wounds while riding in a helicopter.

Acknowledgment: Witnesses and participants who were contacted freely offered amplifying information, and many provided copies of documents that were of great assistance. Their generous cooperation is acknowledged and deeply appreciated.

Errata: This project is the work product of the author. Others could have researched, compiled, and presented the same information, and each such presentation would differ.

This project is neither perfect nor totally comprehensive, for no mortal endeavor can be. The reader may perceive omissions, errors, different opinions, overstatements, understatements, etc. Such actual or perceived shortcomings should be attributed to the author.

Combat leaves an indelible mark on those who are forced to endure it. The only redeeming factors were my comrades' incredible bravery and their devotion to each other. Marine Corps training taught us to kill effectively. But it also taught us loyalty to each other – and love.

[Eugene B. Sledge, With the Old Breed at Peleliu and Okinawa, 1981]

for

Abigail Elizabeth Rocheleau

and

The Corps

Close-Combat

There is no uglier spectacle than two men with clenched teeth and hellfire eyes, hacking at one another's flesh, converting precious living bodies, and priceless souls, into nameless putrescence.
[Thomas Carlyle, Past and Present, 1843]

There is no glory in close-combat. Those who claim otherwise have seen too many action-adventure movies, read too many fanciful novels, overdosed on video games, or believed contrived tales from *combat wannabes* who were far from the flak.

Modern warfare takes many forms. Many good men have served honorably in supporting roles: administration, maintenance, supply, supporting arms, motor transport, food service, intelligence, planning, logistics, etc. Such service and duties can be explained.

Close-combat is different. Those who have experienced it do not try to explain it to those who have not, for no mortal tongue can relate the searing emotions involved.   Oliver Wendell Holmes Jr., a U.S. Supreme Court justice, survived close-combat in his youth. In his later writings he termed it an "incommunicable experience."

Close-combat is a vile form of reality wherein a combatant can look into the eyes of men who are trying to kill him. There is no glory. The experience generates emotions that include terror, rage, horror, and madness. Yet, the greatest emotion is brotherly love for one's comrades-in-arms. This love transcends time. This undying love, this loyalty and bond, makes men willing to suffer, sacrifice, and die for each other. There is no greater love.

Greater love hath no man than this, that a man lay down his life for his friends.
[Jesus Christ, quoted in St. John 15:13, KJV]

This brotherly love, loyalty, and bond sustained a tiny band of U.S. Marines during a perilous night in August 1966.

If a man is fortunate he will, before he dies, gather up as much as he can of his civilized heritage and transmit it to his children.

[Will Durant, <u>The Lessons of History</u>, 1968]

Setting The Stage

When America uses force in the world, the cause must be just, the goal must be clear, and the victory must be over-whelming.
[George Bush, later U.S. President, 4 August 2000]

In the Beginning: South of China and east of India lies a mysterious land generally known as Indochina. According to legend the people of this huge storybook tropical peninsula were descended from the union of a dragon and a fairy. However, history tells us that Mongols from the north, and Thais and Indians from the west, migrated into this vast region of southeastern Asia during the First Millennium BC. They intermarried with local Indonesian natives and created a distinct new culture. These people named their country Viet Nam (Home of the Southern Viet People) and became known to the outside world as the Vietnamese. Their land extends 1,400 miles southward from China to the Gulf of Thailand.

In the Third Century BC the Chinese Han Dynasty army invaded and conquered Vietnam. Chinese emperors established colonial rule and imposed Confucian philosophy and the Chinese imperial system on the Vietnamese. Although the Vietnamese repeatedly tried to oust the invaders, they benefitted from ten centuries of foreign occupation. Chinese governors used Vietnamese labor to build roads, and they established an agricultural system of canals and dikes. Schools were founded to teach Chinese language, arts, and history.

The Chinese demanded labor from *[Vietnamese]* peasants and compelled them to serve in the provincial militia. . . . The agricultural wealth produced by the peasants' sweat was siphoned off by the Chinese.
[Edward Doyle et al, The Vietnam Experience, 1981]

Vietnamese Rebellions: The first major rebellion against Chinese occupation began in 39 AD. Over the next 800 years there were many such rebellions, and Vietnamese heroes and martyrs of legend are those who rose up against northern oppressors. The greatest martyr was Ly Bon, a Sino-Vietnamese noble who led a 20,000-man revolt in 544 AD. He enjoyed initial success but eventually was defeated and beheaded by the Chinese Army.

Despite such revolts Chinese rule remained firm until the fall of the great T'ang Dynasty. Taking advantage of Chinese instability, the Vietnamese rose up and drove out the despised northerners. The crucial battle at Bach Dang in 938 AD is as famous in Vietnamese history as the epic Battle of Yorktown in American history.

All warfare is based upon deception.
[Sun Tzu, The Art of War, circa 512 BC]

At Bach Dang the Vietnamese troops drove hundreds of iron-tipped pilings into the riverbed below water level. Then they lured the Chinese Navy into their trap. Chinese ships were heavily damaged, the Vietnamese routed the Chinese Army, and Vietnam became an independent nation at last.

Vietnam has been in continual social turmoil for the past 1,000 years. On various occasions, most notably in the Fifteenth Century, China again invaded Vietnam and was defeated only after inflicting great damage and loss of life. The two primary religious and political groups, Buddhists and Confucians, constantly bickered and vied for power. Montagnard mountain tribesmen often raided coastal villages of the more civilized Vietnamese farmers.

Life improved when Nguyen Anh became Emperor of Vietnam in 1802. He built the Great Mandarin Road from Saigon, in the south, about 900 miles northward to the rice-rich Red River Delta. From their regal Imperial Capital, the city of Hue (pronounced, *Whey*), later emperors began land reforms to benefit Vietnamese farmers. Still, regional strife lasted until the mid-1800s.

Western Colonization: European influence gradually had become a stabilizing factor. Marco Polo had come to Vietnam in 1280 AD. Over the next 500 years he had been followed by Portuguese, Dutch, and French traders who sought silk, cinnamon, spices, and tea. The nations of Europe had vied for control of Vietnam during the first half of the 1800s. In 1859 the French Army seized the military citadel in the southern city of Saigon, and by 1883 the French completed their military conquest of the entire country.

Within several years roughly 15,000 French colonialists ruled about 16 million Vietnamese. The colonial government imprisoned 20,000 opponents of French authority, and over 700 were guillotined without benefit of trial. In the countryside and in small villages, insurgents were labeled as "bandits." The French Army beheaded thousands of presumed bandits who were caught.

Emperor Tu Duc died in 1883 while cursing the despised French foreign invaders.
[Nguyen Nghi, Vietnamese historian, in a letter circa 1896]

By 1900 the French colony in Vietnam had become a market for European manufactured goods and a source of raw materials for French industry. The vast Red River Delta in the north, and the Mekong River Delta in the south, had become the rice bowls of southeastern Asia. French schools replaced Vietnamese schools. Nguyen emperors remained, but as figureheads only. During World War I approximately 86,000 Vietnamese troops fought in Europe under the French flag.

French became the second language of the Vietnamese. Farmers grew rice for shipment to Europe. Rubber tree plantations covered the highlands. Opium was sold to Chinese dealers for foreign export. Although the peasants' lot in life improved little, by the early 1900s major cities had adapted to French colonization. Saigon, often called the "Paris of the East" and the "Pearl of the Orient," evolved into a bustling commerce center. Citizens of historic Hue, straddling the Perfume River, could boast of the unparalleled beauty of the former Imperial Capital. Sacred tombs of the emperors and an Imperial Palace, modeled after the Chinese palace in Peking, were unique to all of southeastern Asia. Hanoi, the new French capital of Vietnam, became the cultural center of Indochina. With its wide avenues, university, and famed Temple of Literature, it was a showplace for the French Foreign Empire.

The American Alliance: During early years of World War II the potent Japanese war machine rolled south into Vietnam, and the

French Vichy government surrendered control of Indochina to the Imperial Japanese Army. The United States, by then at war with Japan, joined local Viet Minh communist guerrillas in an effort to defeat the Japanese occupation force. Japan capitulated in 1945. The president of the provisional government of the Democratic Republic of Vietnam, Ho Chi Minh, borrowed language from the United States Constitution and declared absolute Vietnamese independence.

Decisive Struggle at Dien Bien Phu: Vietnamese independence would be short-lived because the French Army again seized control of Vietnam. Financially aided by the United States, the French began an eight-year battle to defeat the now formidable Viet Minh army. Finally, deep in the mountains at remote Dien Bien Phu, 6,200 French paratroopers, indigenous soldiers, and mercenaries faced 48,800 Viet Minh troops under the command of Gen. Vo Nguyen Giap. His army was supported by 58,000 laborers and military engineers. Viet Minh troops surrounded Dien Bien Phu Valley with heavy artillery and began a siege on 13 March 1954. Outnumbered and surrounded, the French fought tenaciously, but without relief or resupply they were doomed. Viet Minh loudspeakers blared "Surrender or die!" in French, German, and Vietnamese.

Desperation gripped the bone-weary French by early May, but still they fought on. There was little food, not much sustenance other than coffee and cigarettes. Medical supplies had run out, and the French were almost out of ammunition. Resupply by air had become non-existent. Sixty-two French helicopters, fighters, and transport planes had been shot down by Viet Minh antiaircraft (AAA) batteries that ringed Dien Bien Phu Valley. Viet Minh artillery pounded the once proud French fortress into a muddy, bloody, and burning shambles. On 7 May 1954 the French commander, Gen. Christian de Castries, radioed Hanoi for the last time:

Au revoir, mon general. Au revoir, mes camarades.

Minutes later hundreds of Viet Minh soldiers swarmed over the French command bunker.

"C'est fini?"

"Oui, c'est fini."

The conference takes note of the agreements ending hostilities in Laos, Cambodia, and Vietnam . . . .
[from The Final Declarations of the Geneva Conference, 21 July 1955]

The French Army still occupied most of Vietnam, including all major cities. Yet, after the fall of Dien Bien Phu the French simply lost the *will* to continue the struggle. At the Geneva Conference it was agreed that (1) France would withdraw all of its combat troops, and (2) Vietnam would be divided at the 17th Parallel.

Vietnam Is Divided: The communist Viet Minh, led by Ho Chi Minh, would control the North. President Ngo Dinh Diem would remain in power in the South until nationwide elections could be held to unify all of Vietnam. Unfortunately it was not to be.

North Vietnamese Army (NVA) "political advisors" infiltrated into South Vietnam and organized sympathetic peasants into military units. These local Vietnamese guerrillas would become known as Viet Cong (slang for, *Vietnamese Communist*). They got Russian and Chinese weapons from their North Vietnamese supporters and began attacking troops of the new Army of the Republic of Vietnam (ARVN). When these attacks met with little initial success, NVA units marched southward across the 17th Parallel and orchestrated their own attacks on South Vietnamese military targets.

In the late 1950s the United States began sending military supplies and military advisors to assist the South Vietnamese. In 1959 the 301st NVA Division began constructing the famed Ho Chi Minh Trail, North Vietnam's supply line for its military forces in the South. Once again Vietnam was at war.

American Military Support: In South Vietnam, president Diem proclaimed that his republic would remain an independent nation. Diem was backed by the United States, which relied on a free and democratic South Vietnam to block further Russian and Chinese military expansion in Indochina. Dwight Eisenhower, President of the United States, was faced with communist military advances in Europe, Africa, and South America, so he challenged his military Joint Chiefs of Staff: "We must not lose Asia! We've got to look this thing right in the face!"

The United States inaugurated John Kennedy as president in January 1961. He cautioned the Soviets and Chinese:

> We shall pay any price, bear any burden, meet any hardship,
> support any friend, oppose any foe, in order to ensure the survival
> and success of liberty.
> *[John Kennedy, U.S. President, 20 January 1961]*

At that time there were less than 900 United States military advisors in South Vietnam. However, Kennedy and his successor, Lyndon Johnson, vowed to take all necessary steps to thwart the communist attacks in Vietnam.

U.S. Marines Arrive in Vietnam: On 15 April 1962, Palm Sunday, the ear-shattering growl of supercharged R-1820 Wright engines reverberated across the flight deck. Viewed from Pri-Fly high above, the *USS Princeton* (LPH-5) had become a kaleidoscope of whirling rotors and flashing anticollision lights. In cockpits of Sikorsky H-34 helicopters, U.S. Marine Corps pilots warmed their nine-cylinder radial engines at 2,000 RPM. Marines of squadron HMM-362 were headed for war in South Vietnam.

LtCol. Archie Clapp manned the right seat in the cockpit of the first helicopter. Below the metal firewall his engine hammered out 1,525 horsepower as his rotors bit into the morning air. The H-34 rose and then accelerated forward and upward, shuddering through translational lift. The helicopters clawed their way skyward and turned toward the Vietnamese coastline 16 miles to the west.

> The United States, as a leader of the free world, cannot afford
> further retreat in Asia.
> *[Richard Nixon, later U.S. President, April 1954]*

The helicopters flew over the mouth of the Mekong River on the aerial trip to their new home, the old World War II Japanese fighter airstrip at Soc Trang. There the Marines of HMM-362 landed 85 miles south of Saigon, the South Vietnamese capital city. The pilots and aircrewmen had come to South Vietnam to fly combat support missions for ARVN soldiers. Marines erected billeting and main-tenance tents and launched their first combat mission three days later on 18 April 1962.

U.S. Marines Relocate Northward: Five months later in September 1962 the Marines moved northward to Da Nang (formerly, *Tourane*) and operated from a compound at the huge airport west of the city. The task remained the same: fly combat support missions for ARVN soldiers. Initially the enemy consisted primarily of local insurgents and guerrillas. Marines used aerial-drop pamphlets to caution the farmers and fishermen:

> The Marines are here to help you. Do not run from them! If you run, they may mistake you for a Viet Cong and shoot you. Stand still and the Marines will not harm you. Tell this to your friends.
> *[English translation, text of an aerial-drop pamphlet]*

However, the war was changing. North Vietnam had 476,000 men in its armed forces, and four million of its male citizens were of draft age, 16 to 49. Only Russia, China, and the United States had more men in uniform. No longer content to supply guerrillas, North Vietnam began sending entire regiments of its own troops into the fighting in South Vietnam. Below the 17th Parallel they built fuel depots, barracks, workshops, and field hospitals. In response the United States poured in more military supplies to the embattled South Vietnamese. Yet, although America provided military advisors and combat aircrews, South Vietnam provided the infantrymen to fight communist invaders from the North.

By early 1965 the South Vietnamese government teetered on the brink of collapse. North Vietnam funneled munitions, troops, and all the tools of war into the fight. Without massive military intervention the outgunned South Vietnamese faced certain defeat.

U.S. Marine Infantry Battalions Arrive: On 8 March 1965 the first wave of the 3rd Battalion, 9th Marines, sloshed onto the beach north of Da Nang. Later that day another battalion flew down from Okinawa on C-130 aerial transports. With helicopters of HMM-162 for logistical support these Marines formed the 9th Marine Expeditionary Brigade. They had come to Vietnam to protect the city of Da Nang and its large airbase from NVA attacks.

> Our Country! In her intercourse with foreign nations, may she always be in the right. But, our Country! Right or wrong!
> *[Cmdr. Stephen Decatur, USN, in a banquet toast, 1816]*

Soon more infantrymen and more helicopter squadrons arrived. They set up an enclave at Phu Bai, south of Hue. Marines began aggressively patrolling the Vietnamese countryside. They aimed to destroy elusive North Vietnamese troops that had been wreaking havoc during their raids on southern cities.

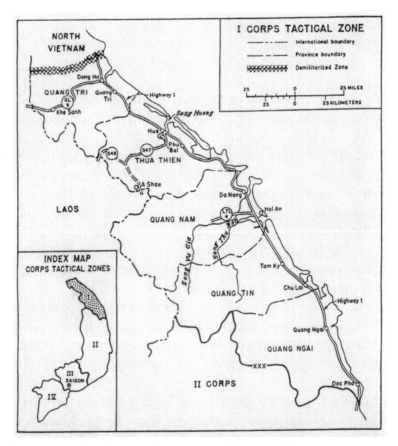

I-Corps military zone, the five northernmost provinces of South Vietnam assigned to U.S. Marines (map courtesy of U.S. Army).

Marines would be responsible for military matters in the five northernmost provinces of South Vietnam. This region included Vietnam's second and third largest cities, Da Nang and Hue. U.S. Army troops would assume a similar responsibility for the southern two-thirds of the country and its sprawling capital city, Saigon.

The Bloody Struggle Accelerates: In November 1965 deep in the mountainous central highlands, elements of the 1st and 7th Cavalry, U.S. Army, clashed with troops of the 304th NVA Division. In the brutal four-day Battle of Ia Drang Valley the American soldiers found NVA troops to be well trained, well equipped, highly disciplined, and professional.

> NVA units were equipped and armed with the most modern weapons and supplies Communist nations could provide. A war previously fought by improvising with whatever was available gave way by 1966 to a war fought with supply-line efficiency.
> *[Michael Lanning et al, Inside the VC and the NVA, 1992]*

Four months later in March 1966, U.S. Marines faced mechanized NVA units in the remote A-Shau Valley. In the inhospitable jungle of the Annamese Cordillera on the Laotian border far southwest of Hue, Marine helicopter gunships and transports flew to an ARVN outpost under attack by soldiers of the 95th Regiment, 325th NVA Division. Marines faced enemy infantry and also sophisticated AAA weaponry. During the struggle at A-Shau, 21 of the 24 helicopters in Marine squadron HMM-163 suffered "major damage," including those that were shot down and lost.

> HMM-163 and VMO-2 were directly instrumental in the rescue of 158 U.S. and Vietnamese *[troops]* from A-Shau.
> *[1st MAW, Command Chronology, 9-12 March 1966]*

Quang Tri Province, late Spring 1966: In 1966, Vietnam was the home of roughly 41,200,000 people. In Quang Tri Province, the northernmost province of South Vietnam, all had been relatively quiet. There was little reason for conflict there. On the fertile coastal plain, fishermen daily plied their trade, and rice farmers subsisted by cultivating the land as their fathers and forefathers had done. The rugged mountains and dense jungles to the west were almost totally uninhabited. There was a South Vietnamese military outpost in the provincial headquarters, the small city of Quang Tri. Also there were tiny outposts at Dong Ha and Khe Sanh below the Demilitarized Zone. The fertile coastal plain was the fabled "Street Without Joy" chronicled by the French historian and author, Dr. Bernard Fall.

From their combat base at Phu Bai, Marines often sent patrols northward into the sleepy rice paddies and hamlets of Quang Tri Province. They encountered only a few local Viet Cong insurgents. Mechanized warfare, siege warfare, 24-hour artillery duels, titanic battles reminiscent of the struggle for Stalingrad during World War II, attacks pitting thousands of Marines against the North Vietnamese Army, had not come to Quang Tri Province – not until that terrible and brutal summer of 1966.

None can realize the horrors of war, save those actually engaged. The dead lying all about, unburied to the last. My God! My God! What a scourge is war!
[Pvt. Samuel Johnson, Sixth Georgia, CSA, in a letter to his parents, 1864]

French Army soldiers in Vietnam during the late 1800s. During that era the right-of-conquest principle prevailed among Western World powers. Supported by the French Army, French colonialists and industrialists ruled Vietnam with an iron hand (this 1800s photo is now in the public domain due to copyright expiration).

French Army troops and indigenous allies attack Vietnamese troops who defended Saigon in 1859 (fanciful 19th Century etching).

In 1945 after World War II, a Japanese officer surrenders his sword in Saigon (photo courtesy of Imperial War Museum, London).

VIỆT-NAM DÂN CHỦ CỘNG HÒA

CHÍNH PHỦ LÂM THỜI

BỘ NGOẠI GIAO

*

TELEGRAM

YKB-3739-1

HANOI FEBRUARY 28 1946

MAR 11 RECD

PRESIDENT HOCHIMINH VIETNAM DEMOCRATIC REPUBLIC HANOI

TO THE PRESIDENT OF THE UNITED STATES OF AMERICA WASHINGTON D.C.

ON BEHALF OF VIETNAM GOVERNMENT AND PEOPLE I BEG TO INFORM YOU
THAT IN COURSE OF CONVERSATIONS BETWEEN VIETNAM GOVERNMENT AND FRENCH
REPRESENTATIVES THE LATTER REQUIRE THE SECESSION OF COCHINCHINA AND THE
RETURN OF FRENCH TROOPS IN HANOI STOP MEANWHILE FRENCH POPULATION AND
TROOPS ARE MAKING ACTIVE PREPARATIONS FOR A COUP DE MAIN IN HANOI AND
FOR MILLTARY AGGRESSION STOP I THEREFORE MOST EARNESTLY APPEAL TO YOU
PERSONALLY AND TO THE AMERICAN PEOPLE TO INTERFERE URGENTLY IN SUPPORT
OF OUR INDEPENDENCE AND HELP MAKING THE NEGOTIATIONS MORE IN KEEPING WITH
THE PRINCIPLES OF THE ATLANTIC AND SAN FRANCISCO CHARTERS

RESPECTFULLY

HOCHIMINH

*1946 telegram to Harry Truman, U.S. President, from Ho Chi Minh,
Vietnamese nationalist, asking President Truman to support Vietnamese independence (copy courtesy of U.S. National Archives).*

*After a seven-week siege at Dien Bien Phu, Viet Minh troops finally
overrun the French Army command bunker on 7 May 1954 (photo
courtesy of Vietnam Peoples' Army Museum).*

The Geneva Conference in late 1954. In part, the conference divided Vietnam at the 17th Parallel (photo courtesy of U.S. Army).

Viet Cong guerrilla fighters pose for the camera. Three in the front row have American-made radios (photo courtesy of U.S. Army).

Between Quang Tri and Dong Ha, Vietnamese farmers use water buffalo to prepare rice fields for planting (photo by the author).

An old French blockhouse and bunker stand along Colonial Route 1 atop Hai Van Pass between Da Nang and Hue (photo by the author).

Down from the North
(from an <u>Asian</u> Perspective)

It is not good for the Christian's health
     to hustle the Aryan brown,
For the Christian riles, and the Aryan smiles,
     and he weareth the Christian down;
At the end of the fight is a tombstone white,
     with the name of the late deceased;
And the epitaph drear: "A fool lies here,
     who tried to hustle the East."
*[Rudyard Kipling, <u>The Naulahka: A Story</u>
<u>of West and East</u>, 1892]*

Demilitarized Zone, 17 May 1966, 0045 Hours: Maj. Nguyen Van
halted his troops when they reached the northern bank of the Song
Ben Hai (aka, *Ben Hai River*) shortly after midnight on 17 May 1966.
He turned and looked at the 174 officers and men assigned to him.
In the moonlight their khaki twill uniforms and soft pith helmets
identified them as soldiers of the North Vietnamese Army (NVA).

Although they carried AK-47 assault rifles, they otherwise were
lightly armed. On this secret mission they had come not to fight, but
instead to reconnoiter defenses and military capability of *imperialist*
American Marines and their South Vietnamese *puppets*. Ahead lay
the meandering river in the Demilitarized Zone (DMZ) that separated
North Vietnam from South Vietnam.

Compatriots! Rise up! The hour for national salvation has struck!
We must sacrifice even our last drop of blood to safeguard our
country. Even if we have to endure hardships in the Resistance
War, with the determination to make sacrifices, victory will surely be
ours. Long live an independent and unified Vietnam! Long live the
victorious Resistance!
[Ho Chi Minh, Vietnamese nationalist, 20 December 1946]

On the northern riverbank the major rested his men and rechecked his field map. They had marched for four hours to reach this shallow point on the river where they could wade into South Vietnam. His comrades deserved this rest, Maj. Van reasoned. Their mission was crucial to the success of the coming invasion. Although dedicated to selfless principles of the Peoples' Army, the major was immensely proud that he had been chosen to lead this mission.

Of course, the major mused, he was indeed highly qualified. His father, the son of a prominent family in Vinh, had been martyred earlier in the revolution in an obscure skirmish against the French. After his father's death the major had vowed to continue the fight. He had excelled in school, studied at the university in Hanoi, received his commission in the army, and had been promoted three times. Yes, he thought somewhat narcissistically, he was the perfect choice for the assignment at hand. He and his 174 comrades had been training for this vital mission for many months. Finally the hour had arrived, and they were ready.

> The longer the struggle lasts, the more your enemy's position deteriorates, both diplomatically and psychologically. Time is on your side, not on the side of the imperialists.
> *[Mao Tse-tung, Chairman, Republic of China, 1964]*

Maj. Van watched as his troops rested and talked among themselves. Theirs would not be an easy task, he knew. They had to enter South Vietnam and remain undetected while gathering information on the positions, offensive capability, supplies, and defenses of the imperialist American Marines.

> *[The soldiers' thoughts]*, as some of them subsequently wrote in their diaries, were of their wives or girlfriends left behind in the North and of the dangerous mission that lay ahead.
> *[Robert Shaplen, The Road to War, 1970]*

These Americans were hard to figure out. The major knew from his studies in Hanoi and from his military training that the imperialist Marines, with their proud tradition, would be fierce fighters. On the other hand the Americans were foolish, maybe even a little crazy. They did not keep their military plans secret. Each week Hanoi got imperialist magazines like *Time* and *Newsweek*. These publications outlined plans of American military commanders. These capitalist magazines even offered a forum for American politicians to openly criticize the American war effort. How could they expect to wage war that way? Crazy! Foolish! It did not make sense. Privately, Maj. Van suspected that it all might be an elaborate imperialist plot designed to mislead the North Vietnamese Army.

Well, it now did not matter what politicians did, said, or thought. Now the issue would be decided on the battlefield, the major knew. The 10,850 troops of the 324-B North Vietnamese Army Division, backed up by about 23,000 more men from the 341st Division and 304th Division, were waiting. They were poised just north of the DMZ, ready to follow him southward and invade South Vietnam. First they would liberate Quang Tri Province, the northernmost province in South Vietnam and the home of 280,000 Vietnamese people. Then they would sweep southward into Thua Thien Province and capture the city of Hue, the old Vietnamese Imperial Capital.

South Vietnamese puppets would not pose a military problem for the potent North Vietnamese Army, but the imperialist American Marines would be different. The Marines would fight. However, the major was aware that he and his comrades could do much to negate the threat posed by American Marines.

Soldiers, be always on guard, for imperialist American Marines will fight like devils.
[Order 29, North Vietnamese High Command, April 1966]

Available intelligence indicated that the Marines had several infantry companies based at Phu Bai seven miles south of Hue. At Phu Bai the Marines also had a squadron of H-34 helicopters, about 20 to 24 of them. Perhaps the Marines had an infantry platoon or two at Quang Tri or Dong Ha. No one really knew for sure, but it was the major's job to find out. Did the Marines at Phu Bai have artillery support? Where were the bulk fuel tanks for their helicopters and ground vehicles? Where were their ammunition caches? Marines recently had begun using the old French airstrip at Dong Ha. What was afoot? From revolutionary sympathizers and spies it had been learned that more helicopters, about 80 to 90 of them, were based at

Marble Mountain far to the south. Did the imperialists have the troops, fuel, munitions, and logistic capability to relocate and sustain air and infantry operations at Quang Tri and Dong Ha?

Crucial questions! Maj. Van realized just how important a task he and his comrades faced. In large part, the success of the coming invasion hinged on his ability to document the military capability of American imperialists.

> What the bourgeoisie, therefore, produces, above all, is its own grave-diggers. Its fall and the victory of the proletariat are equally inevitable.
> *[Karl Marx et al, *The Communist Manifesto, 1848]*

The coming maelstrom would be a costly battle for both sides, Maj. Van knew. North Vietnamese forces would vastly outnumber the Marines. Yet, the Marines would not give up without a fight. They likely would try to use their helicopters to remain mobile in an attempt to compensate for their huge numerical disadvantage. It would be imperative for the North Vietnamese Army to move its 12.7mm, 23mm, and 37mm AAA guns onto the battlefield. The imperialist helicopters *must* be shot down or neutralized. Then the proud Peoples' Army would use its superior heavy artillery and overwhelming manpower advantage to bleed the Marines, wear them down, and destroy them.

In the long run his army could not lose, Maj. Van reasoned. North Vietnam had the fourth-largest standing army in the world, and American politicians dared not wage full scale war so far from home. The dedicated Peoples' Army was commanded by Gen. Vo Nguyen Giap, architect of the great victory over the French at Dien Bien Phu in 1954, only 12 years earlier. Many of the major's comrades would be martyred, but in the end their cause would prevail. The thick jungles and mountains would be their friend, their sanctuary.

> All of that terrain, all of that cover, ridge after ridge, murderous slides and gorges, all cloaked by thick monsoon mists. And whole divisions *[of NVA soldiers]* were out there in that.
> *[Michael Herr, *Dispatches, 1968]*

In the moonlight Maj. Van gathered his men around him for a final motivational briefing, an eve of battle pep talk. He had lived and trained with them, and now they were ready. He thought of his wife and children back in Vinh. He had been authorized to say only that he was embarking on a special mission, nothing more. The major knew the many dangers of his assignment, and he realized he might join his father in death as a hero of the Revolution.

From his studies at the university the major recalled how Julius Caesar had thrown down the gauntlet to his enemies by crossing the Rubicon River in 49 BC. Now he had his own Rubicon to cross. "How glorious!" he thought. With the North Vietnamese National Anthem, *Tien Quan Ca* (translation, *Forward, Soldiers*), on his lips he waded across the Song Ben Hai and led his loyal soldiers into South Vietnam.

I swear to learn to fight better and shape myself into a true revolutionary soldier, battling the invading American imperialists.
[Excerpt from NVA "Oath of Honor" circa 1965]

The North Vietnamese Army: North Vietnam had the fourth-largest standing army on Earth. All males between age 16 and age 49 were subject to a military draft. Since 1965 the military induction term had been specified as the "duration of the war." Deferments were granted to sole surviving sons, the sons of party officers, members of the Vanguard Youth civil labor battalions, and university students.

Ho Chi Minh was the beloved and highly visible national leader. Yet, all genuine control, both military and political, was vested in the Central Committee of the Lao Dong Party. The Committee directed the NVA High Command, which planned military field operations and training. The Committee also directed activities of the National Liberation Front, which had been established to organize and equip civil insurgency groups in South Vietnam.

Army inductees got basic training in "School of the Soldier," the North Vietnamese version of *boot camp*. In addition to rigorous physical conditioning the three-month school taught close-order drill, military customs and courtesy, military discipline, infantry tactics, assault strategy, air defense tactics, marksmanship, and camouflage techniques. After completing School of the Soldier, inductees spent two weeks in a classroom for political indoctrination. Those who excelled received specialized training to become radiomen, sappers, EOD experts, etc.

Radiomen learned Morse Code and received unique training. Many had been selected for their fluency in English. Each battalion had Type 71-B Chinese radios (later, *Type 63*) for voice contact with its regiment. English speaking radiomen would be able to monitor American voice communications.

Annex D, Communications: The enemy is capable of interception, jamming, and imitative communications.
[Task Force Charlie, Operational Order 1-66, 23 June 1966]

Each NVA infantry battalion consisted of (1) a command staff, (2) three infantry companies, (3) a combat support company, and (4) three independent platoons: signal platoon, reconnaissance platoon, and sapper platoon. In rear areas and staging positions the signal platoon radiomen would lay wire to connect each company to its battalion, and each battalion to its regiment. Runners and couriers supplemented these land-lines. Men of the reconnaissance platoon were viewed as the battalion elite. Their military intelligence duties included enemy surveillance, route selection, and identification of drinking water sources. Those in the sapper platoon had gotten technical training at Son Tay, and their perilous assignment afforded them great honor.

Within each NVA platoon were two to four squads. Each squad consisted of three or four cells. Four soldiers constituted a cell, the smallest fighting unit. These four men were battle-buddies. They trained together, marched together, ate together, and fought together.

A typical NVA infantry division . . . had a field hospital that could treat approximately 150 patients at one time. Each of the division's regiments had a medical company of 50 to 120 men each.
[Michael Lanning et al, Inside the VC and the NVA, 1992]

In each battalion a combat support company fielded the heavy weapons: mortars, recoilless rifles, and 12.7mm AAA machineguns. Heavier weapons were maintained at regiment and division level, and each division political officer had a staff of 32 to 40 men.

The North Vietnamese Soldier: Each new NVA soldier had been trained in conventional warfare tactics and weapons. Most would be sent southward to fight the Americans. Morale initially was high. Many soldiers bore the macho and popular tattoo: "Born in the North to Die in the South." At the outset most were eager to sacrifice and endure hardships to achieve the goal of Vietnamese reunification. Toward that end the ever-present political officers warned soldiers that Americans were cannibals who ate small children. Barbarians like the Americans should be exterminated without mercy, political officers admonished their troops.

After an NVA soldier left North Vietnam and headed southward his family would receive the monetary equivalent of twelve United States dollars each month. An NVA private earned half of that amount. When the soldier reached his unit in South Vietnam he found that the military postal system mirrored the system in use in North Vietnam. Yet, delivery was unreliable. Letters from a soldier to his family went from company, to battalion, to regiment, to division. NVA couriers carried division mail to supply depots in Laos and Cambodia. From these sanctuaries, trucks shuttled mail and military supplies to and from North Vietnam. Of course, this system was designed to support the war effort, so only a very limited number of personal letters was allowed. The average soldier could dispatch a letter to his family only twice each year.

> Mail *[from soldiers]* should be censored by the command staff.
> *[Excerpt from NVA "Rules of Secrecy" circa 1964]*

Most soldiers had come from homes on farms or in cities. Only a handful had ever seen a tropical jungle. However, in the South, jungle cover overhead was necessary to conceal NVA troops from American aerial surveillance. Life in the jungle was harsh. Humidity level over the treetops might be only 50 percent, but at ground level it remained at 95 percent. Wet clothing could not be dried, and it literally rotted off of a soldier's body. An assortment of scorpions, snakes, centipedes, leeches, and stinging insects made life miserable. Mosquitoes carried malaria. Dysentery and intestinal parasites were common, and both affected morale and combat readiness.

> If a man had told me 12 months ago that men could stand such hardships, I would have called him a fool.
> *[Lt. James Langhorne, CSA, in a letter, 8 January 1862]*

However, from a military standpoint the NVA soldier in South Vietnam was well equipped. He wore a green or tan khaki uniform and hard-sole canvass boots made in China. He had a cloth-covered sun helmet, often called a pith helmet. His 7.62mm AK-47 assault rifle had been manufactured in either China or Russia. Most soldiers wore a canvass Chicom vest. Its large center pouch held a 31-round rifle magazine. Two smaller pouches contained a rifle cleaning kit, cotton patches, solvent, and oil. More ammunition, grenades, and a first aid kit were carried on a web belt at waist level. Other combat supplies fit inside a backpack. A small short-handled shovel was strapped to the pack, for *digging* would become a way of life when combating the Americans.

> The greatest happiness is to vanquish your enemies.
> *[Genghis Kahn, Mongol conqueror, circa 1224]*

A separate canvas bag held the soldier's other essentials: spare uniform, rubber sandals, raincoat, blanket, and mosquito net. Each soldier had a small one-man tent that he could use as a hammock, weather permitting. He had been issued water purification tablets, quinine tablets, and vitamin pills. Unless NVA supply lines were interrupted by enemy action, his battalion would keep him supplied with a kilogram of salt and seven kilograms of rice. Fish, rats, monkeys, snakes, birds, and whatever a soldier could catch or kill would supplement his diet. In bivouac areas he would be given cigarettes, beer, and occasional candy. Thus equipped and supplied, NVA soldiers were ready to fight.

> Blood is the price of victory.
> *[Carl von Clausewitz, On War, 1832]*

North Vietnamese Army soldiers gather for a briefing; location and date not documented (photo courtesy of U.S. National Archives).

One of many versions of the AK-47 assault rifle used by North Vietnamese soldiers. This 7.62mm rifle had been developed in the Soviet Union in 1946. After six decades the AK-47 would remain the most popular and most used miliary rifle in the world because of its low production cost and legendary reliability.

Flags used by North Vietnamese Army troops. Initially a yellow star was superimposed on a red background. Later "quyet thang" was added. Loosely translated, it means "Determined to Win."

At Dong Ha combat base on 3 September 1967, U.S. Marine Corps JP-4 fuel (essentially kerosene) bladders burn after a barrage of North Vietnamese 122mm rockets whistled down onto the combat base (photo courtesy of U.S. Marine Corps).

Supersonic MIG-21, NATO code-name "Fishbed," jet fighter flown by the North Vietnamese Air Force (formally, Peoples' Liberation Army Air Force). Later MIG-21 variants are considered to be third-generation jet fighters. The MIG-21 had the longest production run (1959 to 1985) of any fighter aircraft in the world (photo courtesy of National Museum of the U.S. Air Force).

Modern-day Vietnamese Army soldiers pass-in-review on one of the many disputed Spratly Islands near the Vietnamese coast (photo courtesy of Ha Petit).

A Vietnamese soldier stands guard during a POW exchange on 12 February 1973 (photo courtesy of U.S. Department of Defense).

Insignia of the Peoples' Army of Vietnam.

The Rising Storm

God of our fathers, known of old,
Lord of our far-flung battle line,
Beneath whose awful hand we hold
Dominion over palm and pine.
Lord God of Hosts, be with us yet,
Lest we forget – lest we forget!
[Rudyard Kipling, Recessional, 1897]

Demilitarized Zone, 28 May 1966: The 324-B North Vietnamese Army Division, commanded by SrCol. Nam Long, began moving southward through the DMZ and into South Vietnam. The division consisted of three infantry regiments: the 90th, 812th, and 803rd. In addition to infantry battalions each regiment had a weapons battalion equipped with heavy mortars, AAA batteries, and antitank rockets.

There have been many reports of enemy units moving south through the Cam Lo district of Quang Tri Province.
[Task Unit Charlie, Operational Order 1-66, 23 June 1966]

Soon the 341st NVA Division began moving southward to join 324-B. Logistics were crucial. Food stockpiles and munitions had to be stored in the mountains of northwestern Quang Tri Province and hidden under the jungle canopy. Two NVA battalions were pressed into service transporting rice. One soldier, later to be captured, had a diary which included the following *translated* entries:

19 June 66: We were in woods near the DMZ. This afternoon we were ordered to move husked rice to the other side of the Ben Hai River. We waited until nightfall, but the rice had not arrived.

20 June 66: Early in the morning we were ordered to take our empty rucksacks and rush to the woods to pick up rice. . . . We received rice at 0800 and moved southward immediately. Arrived at the northern riverbank at 1200. *[Here]* the river is about twenty meters wide and the current flows swiftly through a gorge. Heavy foliage

covered both sides of the river. We waded knee-deep across, and at 1210 we set foot on South Vietnamese soil. We quietly walked through mountains and heavily forested areas while *[American]* aircraft buzzed crazily overhead. It was quite a rough route, going up and down. There weren't any level sections of more than 100 meters. At 1400 we arrived at the rice depot and turned in the rice. We then began a return trip *[to get more rice]* . . . .

Dong Ha, 23 June 1966: Marine Corps aerial reconnaissance had spotted NVA troop columns south of the DMZ and in the mountains northwest of Cam Lo. This discovery corroborated information from a disgruntled NVA soldier who had deserted the previous month on 19 May. In response the Marines activated Task Unit Charlie at Dong Ha on 23 June 1966. The unit initially consisted of:
– An infantry company from 2nd Battalion, 1st Marines.
– 2nd Platoon, 1st Force Reconnaissance Company.
– 1st Platoon, 3rd Reconnaissance Battalion.
– Battery H, 3rd Battalion, 12th Marines (artillery).
Reconnaissance (spoken, *Recon*) teams began slipping into the mountains. Their covert mission called for documenting positions and capabilities of North Vietnamese troops in jungles and rugged terrain west of Dong Ha.

Reconnaissance *[teams]* will determine type, size, location, and activity of enemy forces. *[They will]* engage *[the enemy]* with supporting arms *[mainly, air-strikes and artillery]* when *[the]* situation permits.
[Task Unit Charlie, Operational Order 1-66, 23 June 1966]

There were no medical facilities at Dong Ha exclusive of U.S. Navy corpsmen attached to the Recon, infantry, and artillery units. If wounds required more expertise than corpsmen could provide the wounded Marine could be driven 13 miles southward to an aid station at Quang Tri, the small provincial capital. Those with serious wounds could be flown 39 miles southward to the Alpha-Med field hospital at Phu Bai, headquarters of the Fourth Marine Regiment, or farther southward to Charlie-Med at Da Nang.

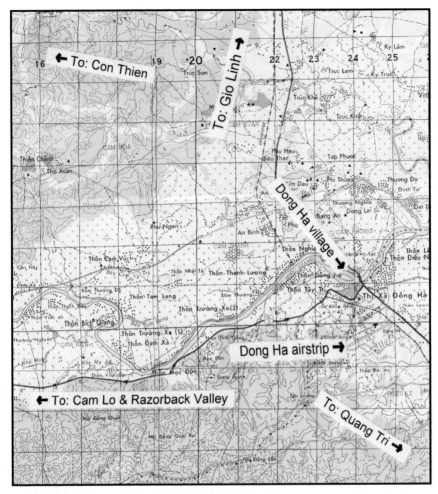

A part of the Series L-7014, Sheet 6442-IV, scale 1:50,000 "Quang Tri" map. It depicts the Dong Ha dirt airstrip (lower right) built by the French in the mid-1900s. The Marine Corps established a combat base around this airstrip in June 1966. North of the airstrip lies Dong Ha Village (right center) on the southern bank of the Mieu Giang River. Site names have been added to orient the reader.

Dong Ha was on the western fringe of the coastal plain. The South China Sea lay to the east, and the mountains and dense jungles lay to the west. Nearby in rolling hills near Dong Ha, Marines would establish artillery outposts at (1) Con Thien to the northwest, at (2) Gio Linh to the north, and at (3) Cam Lo to the west (map courtesy of U.S. Army Topographic Command).

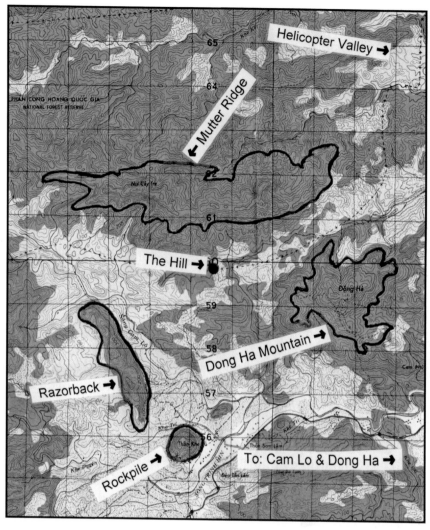

Part of the Series L-7014, Sheet 6342-I, scale 1:50,000 "Cam Lo" map that depicts "The Hill" (map coordinates XD-986599) area in Razorback Valley where the battle was fought on 8-9 August 1966. Prominent terrain features have been <u>bold-outlined</u>. Site names have been added to orient the reader.

With steep and almost vertical sides, the 700-foot-high Rockpile (lower center) offered an almost impregnable observation post. The peak could be accessed and resupplied only by helicopter. The nearby Razorback Ridge, with peaks over 1,000 feet high, was honeycombed with caves. Some were natural caverns, and others were manmade. Nui Cay Tre Ridge, aka "Mutter Ridge" (upper *center), would be a North Vietnamese fortress in the autumn months of 1966. Struggles for control of this jungled ridge would be among the most brutal of the entire war. The remote Song Ngan Valley, aka "Helicopter Valley" (upper right), is the site of the initial Marine Corps assault on North Vietnamese Army troops in July 1966 (map courtesy of U.S. Army Topographic Command).*

Razorback Valley and Ngan River Valley, July 1966: Thirteen nautical miles (16 statute miles) west of Dong Ha two rocky promontories dominate the western end of a vast valley. At map coordinates XD-979558 near the riverbank of the Cam Lo River, a gnarled granite mass juts over 700 feet straight up into the sky. This craggy peak had a name, Thon Khe Tri, but Marines came up with a more descriptive moniker, the "Rockpile." If one could get to its top, the lofty Rockpile would offer an unparalleled observation post. It commanded the valley and was almost inaccessible from the ground because of its steep sides. Helicopters would be the only practical way to reach the summit.

> A seven-hundred-foot hill known as the Rockpile, a sort of toothpick type mountain, stuck out in the middle of an open area *[with]* sheer cliffs straight up and down.
> *[Bruce Norton, Stingray, 2000]*

Centered at map coordinates XD-964577 and beginning a mile northwest of the Rockpile stands a two-mile-long ridge of solid rock with peaks over 1,000 feet high. Sides of the jagged ridge run almost vertically to the valley floor, and consequently they are not covered with vegetation. The ridge looks like the exposed backbone of an enormous subterranean monster. Marines gave the ridge a descriptive name, the "Razorback," and the huge valley east of the Razorback became known as "Razorback Valley."

> 2 UH-1E slicks and 1 UH-1E gunship *[are]* to be located at Dong Ha for deployment whenever *[Recon]* patrols are in the field.
> *[Task Unit Charlie, Operational Order 1-66, 23 June 1966]*

Between Razorback Valley and Con Thien the small Song Ngan (aka, *Ngan River*) flows through another valley. Five-to-eight man

Marine Recon teams slipped into the mountains surrounding the Ngan River Valley and Razorback Valley. Recons formed the eyes and ears of the Third Marine Division. They did not intend to fight. Their mission called for probing the jungle and reporting enemy troop presence and movement via their PRC-10 and PRC-25 radios.

> During the period 1-15 July a total of 18 reconnaissance patrols were conducted, 14 of which had to be withdrawn early due to significant enemy contact.
> *[Task Force Delta, After Action Report, Operation Hastings]*

Recon teams had plenty to report. The NVA was there, almost everywhere. Recons found camouflaged field hospitals, stockpiles of rice and ammunition, troop concentrations, mortar pits, trench lines, and bunkers. Fourteen Recon teams radioed for a quick emergency extraction because of impending contact with enemy troops.

> The intelligence was fascinating. The 324th Division of the North Vietnamese Army had crossed the border, it said, and had massed in Quang Tri Province next to the 17th Parallel's demilitarized zone.
> *[Time Magazine, 29 July 1966]*

Razorback Valley, 6 July 1966: An NVA soldier captured near the Rockpile told interrogators that he had been a member of the 5th Battalion, 812th Regiment, 324-B Division. He confirmed that all three regiments of his division were inside South Vietnam.

> *[The captive]* stated it was the intention of the 324-B Div*[ision]* to infiltrate across the DMZ and take over Quang Tri Province. ....
> Two more NVA soldiers were captured, who corroborated the intentions of the 324-B Division.
> *[U.S. Marine Corps, AARUGHA, 1989]*

Ngan River Valley, 9 July 1966: A Marine patrol chanced to capture a lieutenant from the 812th NVA Regiment. He reported that another NVA Division was poised to sweep in from Laos along old Colonial Route 9. According to the lieutenant, the three NVA Divisions had a twofold mission: (1) liberate Quang Tri Province, and then (2) push southward to capture the former Imperial Capital, the city of Hue.

Recommend lifting of restrictions on Arc Light *[B-52]* targets in Laos . . . between Tchepone and the border. . . . A large North Vietnamese force, reported as 15,000 troops, is between Tchepone and Quang Tri Province, prepared to reinforce the 324-B Division. Also an unidentified NVA division is in the southern provinces of North Vietnam, prepared *[for]* movement across the DMZ. . . . In summary *[because of these three NVA Divisions]* I believe the enemy . . . will "go for broke" in northern I-Corps.
["Eyes only" secret message from CG-MACV to Gen. Earle Wheeler, Chairman of the Joint Chiefs of Staff, July 1966]

A fortified enemy command post had been spotted 11 miles west-northwest of Dong Ha on top of Hill 208. This enemy headquarters was *inside* South Vietnam. The 90th NVA Regiment was entrenched and waiting in the rugged Ngan River Valley. Roughly three miles to the southwest the 812th and 803rd NVA Regiments were encamped near the Rockpile in Razorback Valley. Other battalions were strung out below the DMZ, from the mountains eastward to the coastal plain. Worse yet, the 341st NVA Division was moving southward to join 324-B, and the division in Laos was poised to attack from the west.

The North Vietnamese were constructing . . . deep and well-covered bunkers, heavy trenches with bays for automatic weapons, foot-bridges and cables across rivers and streams, supply storage areas, and thousands of foxholes.
[Robert Shaplen, The Road to War, 1970]

Dong Ha, 11 July 1966: The military and political implications of loss of the city of Hue were unthinkable. Hue could not be allowed to fall to the North Vietnamese. Far to the south in Saigon the Military Assistance Command Vietnam (MACV) acknowledged the looming threat. Gen. William Westmoreland, of the U.S. Army, was the MACV commander. His earlier request was still being "studied," so he flashed another urgent message to Washington.

Sizeable enemy forces have recently moved into areas in Laos north and south of Highway 9 . . . . Some of these forces have already crossed the border into South Vietnam and *[have]* moved

to the east. I urgently request authority to extend *[B-52 bomber]* operations into *[Laos]* west of Khe Sanh.
["Eyes only" secret message from CG-MACV to Gen. Earle Wheeler, Chairman of the Joint Chiefs of Staff, July 1966]

Marines did not have the manpower to form a defensive line and stop the potent and mechanized North Vietnamese Army. Further, Marine artillery was no match for long-range NVA batteries. There was only one viable option remaining. Before the NVA could begin their offensive the Marines must strike first.

We are so outnumbered there is only one thing to do – attack!
[Adm. Andrew Cunningham, British Royal Navy, at Taranto, 11 November 1940]

Marines replaced small Task Unit Charlie, formed much larger Task Force Delta, and headquartered it at Dong Ha. They would begin with a two-battalion offensive into the Ngan River Valley. The coming assault was given a name, "Operation Hastings," named for the famous Battle of Hastings in England exactly 900 years earlier in the year 1066.

The coming battle below the DMZ in Vietnam would involve the latest technology in weaponry. Messengers of death would be riflemen, not archers. The shield, battleaxe, and lance would be replaced by mines, mortars, and artillery. This time the struggle would last not merely one day. It would rage for over two years.

Dong Ha, 15 July 1966, 0710 Hours: After four days of planning and logistic buildups the Marines were ready. All around the Dong Ha airstrip, Marines and helicopters covered the terrain. From the two H-46 squadrons then in Vietnam, HMM-164 and HMM-265, 27 helicopters had arrived and refueled. Huey gunships of VMO-2 were already there, armed to the teeth. Nearby, rows of older H-34s had landed, ready for duty. TAFDS (temporary airfield fuel dispensing system) bulbous fuel bladders held 29,000 gallons of 115/145 aviation gasoline and JP-4 jet fuel. Two weeks later one of the H-46 pilots would recall the spectacle.

We could almost hear the bugles blowing!
[1stLt. Huey Walsh, USMC, oral account, 27 July 1966]

The transport helicopters, H-34s and H-46s, had flown up from Marble Mountain before dawn. One by one, pilots shut down their engines and crawled out to stretch their legs and wait. Yet, Marine crew chiefs stayed busy. They labored as a mechanic and loadmaster on the ground, and as a door gunner when in the air. Now they all carefully checked their helicopters: fluid levels OK, hydraulics OK, engines OK, and avionics OK. With these tasks completed they congregated with their gunners for conversation and a cigarette.

Pilots, crew chiefs, and gunners all appeared hip to their role, professionally insouciant. Over fire resistant nomex flight suits they wore auto-pistols or revolvers on low slung belts with plenty of ammunition. Many irreverently wandered over to what grandiosely was known as Air Operations North (verbally, *Op's North*). Only three short days before it had been a simple tarpaulin stretched over poles. Now Op's North was housed in a full General Purpose (GP) tent complete with status boards and radio wizardry.

Marine infantrymen (aka, *Grunts*) in their battle regalia lined up behind their assigned helicopters. They dropped their gear and eased down onto the grass to wait. Each seemed mentally lost in the gray land between imagination and reality. Most were 18 to 20 years of age, a year or two removed from shooting hoops in high school, too young to buy a beer in the world they had left behind. A disproportionate percentage of them came from rural bible-belt southern states.

Before becoming a Marine many infantrymen had lived on the fringe of mainstream Americana. Some had come from coal mining towns, hard scrabble farms, or urban ghettos. A judge had given a few a choice: go to jail, or join the armed forces. Others had come from the middle class, and a few were college graduates attracted by the mystical lore of the Corps. Yet, regardless of their background they all wore the iconic eagle, globe, and anchor emblem of the U.S. Marine Corps. They had become professional killers, modern-day swashbucklers in the U.S. Armed Forces. Mother Green!

The deadliest weapon in the world – a Marine and his rifle.
[Words on a sign at MCRD, Parris Island, South Carolina]

Each infantryman carried an M-14 rifle. Some had taped pairs of M-14 magazines together, end to end, allowing them to fire two magazines with only a flick of their experienced wrists. Seven grenades hung from each belt, two smoke grenades and five M-26 "baseballs" with a killing radius of 15 to 20 meters. More ammunition, three canteens of water, an entrenching tool (a small shovel), machete, first aid kit, flak jacket, steel helmet, and field pack completed their gear, over 80 pounds per man.

Marine infantrymen knew what lay in store for them. The coming battle would be fought on terrain that is maddening. The mountains west of Dong Ha are cloaked by 60- to 100-foot-high jungle canopy. Beneath that dense foliage lies a tangled and nearly impenetrable mass of vines and undergrowth so thick that machetes would be needed to hack through it. Forward visibility would range from five to fifteen feet. The thick jungle cover overhead is so dense that at midday it would appear almost as dark as at midnight. In addition to NVA soldiers, the jungle and the terrain would be a fearsome enemy.

The old Puritan belief that Satan dwelt in Nature could have been born here.
[Michael Herr, Dispatches, 1968]

There would be no breeze to ease the stifling suffocating heat. There would be no relief from swarms of stinging insects that would make days and nights miserable. The jagged jungled Cordillera is a wild uninhabited wilderness. It is spooky beyond mortal belief, a wild foreign land, a tropical version of mythical Shangri-La where demons, trolls, and evil spirits might live and roam the Earth.

It is terrible terrain for fighting.
[Newsweek Magazine, the next month on 8 August 1966]

Marine infantrymen knew this. They also knew that lurking in that murky and foreboding jungle, dug-in, camouflaged, concealed, well armed and trained, were Gen. Giap's legions, 10,850 soldiers of the 324-B North Vietnamese Army Division. Backing-up those troops would be men of the 341st NVA Division. North Vietnamese soldiers were not mere gooks or slopes, not insurgents or guerrillas, not the local Viet Cong. They were *Mister Charles*, the most professional fighting men Asia had produced.

The NVA would be ready. From vantage points high in the mountains, NVA spotters doubtless had watched the Marine build-up at Dong Ha and Cam Lo over the past few days. They were not blind to clouds of red laterite dust that billowed skyward as Marine C-130 turboprop transports shuttled in and out of the Dong Ha dirt airstrip. NVA spotters could see Marine six-by convoys rolling into Cam Lo along Colonial Route 9, a one-lane-wide dirt road. The NVA had a grandstand seat. Without question the NVA knew of the Marine build-up, and NVA commanders knew the Marines had come to fight. The waiting game was over.

Dong Ha, 15 July 1966, 0745 Hours: Twenty H-46 helicopters loaded with Marines from the 3rd Battalion, 4th Marines, took off from Dong Ha and headed westward. Huey gunships from VMO-2 led the aerial armada toward the Ngan River Valley. The rest of the 3rd Battalion plus the 2nd Battalion, 4th Marines, waited at Dong Ha for their turn to fly westward.

> *[Operation]* Hastings kicked off with 20 H-46s, 4 H-37s, and 10 H-34s lifting 1,200 troops into two separate LZs, with A-4 *[ground attack jets]* conducting LZ preps in each LZ.
> *[3rd Marine Division, Command Chronology, July 1966]*

VMO-2 gunships (call-sign, *Deadlock*) coordinated an air-strike around LZ Crow, the intended landing area at map coordinates YD-038649. Ground-attack A-4 Skyhawk jets (call-sign, *Oxwood*) from Chu Lai, and F-8 Crusader jets (call-sign, *Condole*) from Da Nang, blasted the surrounding jungle with 500-pound bombs and napalm. Then Marine howitzers at Cam Lo sent dozens of high-explosive 105mm and 155mm shells whistling down into the landing area.

Ngan River Valley, 15 July 1966, 0755 Hours: The flight of Huey and H-46 helicopters swept westward toward the Rockpile and then turned to the north. Below lay the jungle, an unbroken sea of green, a vast and foreboding emerald rain forest. To the west the eastern stone wall of the massive Razorback glistened like a mirror in the early morning sunlight.

Into the valley of Death
Rode the six-hundred.
[Alfred Tennyson, The Charge of the Light Brigade, 1854]

The flight turned eastward and roared down into LZ Crow, the only clear area in the valley. The helicopters landed. Infantrymen charged out and dove for cover as enemy fire began whipping across the LZ. Nonetheless, more Marines from the 3rd Battalion rotored in to join their comrades. Before the troop lift was finished three H-46s were downed in LZ Crow. They would never fly again.

Two miles northeast of LZ Crow the Marine assault continued as troops from the 2nd Battalion, 4th Marines, rotored into LZ Dove. More Recon teams were dropped into the mountains to report enemy troop movement. The NVA seemed to be almost everywhere. Two Huey gunships escorted an H-34 that inserted a Recon team, and the result was typical.

Two UH1Es . . . escorted Barrelhouse 2-1 *[an H-34]* on a Recon insertion at YD-049610. The *[radio]* call for extraction came almost immediately as the Recon team made contact with the enemy. The Hueys covered the extraction, firing suppressive fire into and around the LZ . . . .
[VMO-2, After Action Report, 15 July 1966]

The sun gradually dipped down toward mountaintops west of Dong Ha. Marine infantrymen needed more ammunition, but they needed water even more. All day they had struggled against NVA soldiers in stifling heat and suffocating humidity under a merciless sun. The heat, the terrain, and their exertion had taken the expected toll. It had sapped their strength. Water, precious water, was their most critical need.

The heat with no breeze and unlimited humidity was devastating.
[Capt. Robert Modrzejewski, USMC, 15 July 1966]

Ngan River Valley, 15 July 1966, 1815 Hours: All afternoon the helicopters zipped in and out of LZ Crow and LZ Dove, bringing in supplies and hauling out wounded Marines. However, the NVA had anticipated the flights and had placed 12.7mm (equivalent to the American .50 caliber) ground-to-air machineguns at strategic spots near potential landing areas. Late in the afternoon a flight of eight H-46 helicopters from HMM-265 (call-sign, *Bonnie-Sue*) headed for LZ Crow with supplies and reinforcements. Pilots planned to drop off the troops, pick up casualties, and fly back to the Delta-Med aid station at Dong Ha. It was not to be. NVA 12.7mm fire swatted one of the helicopters down from the sky.

> 1815 Hours: A CH46-A of HMM-265 was hit at 1,500 feet and commenced burning. The aircraft exploded after hitting the ground and the fate of the crew and 12 troops aboard is unknown . . . .
> *[MAG-16, SITREP, 15 July 1966]*

Marines lost five big H-46s in the Ngan River Valley on 15 July. In the Vietnamese language, *song* means *river*, and the Song Ngan did flow through the valley. Yet, the valley got a new name after that first day of combat. The new name was descriptive and would become a part of Marine Corps lore. That bloody day the Ngan River Valley became "Helicopter Valley" to the Marines.

> Any unit that occupies a position for more than 24 hours can expect to be mortared. . . . Most mortar attacks are experienced at resupply time when the arrival and departure of helicopters give away the unit location.
> *[Task Force Delta, After Action Report, July 1966]*

When Marines charged into Helicopter Valley their world was changed forever. For helicopter crews, days became a nonstop ballet of troop lifts, Recon inserts, resupply missions, and medevac flights to recover the dead and wounded. For infantrymen who battled the NVA the world ceased to exist beyond I-Corps (pronounced, *eye-core*), the northernmost military region in South Vietnam.

Helicopter Valley, 15 July 1966, 1930 Hours: Twilight, followed by darkness, settled over the jungle in Helicopter Valley. The curtain of nightfall slowly was drawn shut. Men of the 3rd Battalion, 4th Marines, had dug fighting holes and had set up a defensive perimeter. In the darkness NVA troops began working their way around the

Marine battalion.

No moonlight filtered down through the thick foliage. Out of the misty night the NVA came. Their mortar barrages were followed by ground assaults. Firefights raged around LZ Crow. The combatants, invisible in the impenetrable dark, fired at muzzle flashes. Tracers, green for the NVA soldiers and red for Marine infantrymen, sliced through the ebony night.

3/4 reported they were completely surrounded and receiving fire.
[Task Force Delta, After Action Report, 15 July 1966]

After a brief respite the NVA swarmed forward in force, and they charged through the Marine perimeter. In hand-to-hand fighting the Marine infantrymen threw themselves at onrushing enemy soldiers. In tangled undergrowth the sharp crackle of M-14 and AK-47 rifle fire was broken by dull thuds of fists and rifle butts striking human flesh. Screams and moans of the dying pierced the dark night as combatants drove their bayonets home.

Get the blade into the enemy. This is the main principle in bayonet fighting. It is the blade that kills.
[Marine Corps Association, Guidebook for Marines, 1962]

Sgt. Gary Lucus, horribly burned but still conscious, had been the gunner on the H-46 that had been shot down at 1815 Hours. During a lull in the fighting the battalion chaplain crawled to the spot where Lucus lay concealed between two logs. Years later Lucus would remember the chaplain's whispered promise to him: "Son, I won't leave you."

Again the NVA swarmed forward out of the night. Again and again they hammered the perimeter, but Marines threw them back each time. Sgt. Lucus and the chaplain watched the NVA repeatedly charge and then fall back, jumping over logs that formed their hiding place. Finally the chaplain unholstered his .45 caliber pistol and prayed aloud. He asked his God to forgive him for "shooting other human beings." He kept his promise. He never left Lucus, and the Marines held throughout the night.

USS Princeton, 16 July 1966, 0645 Hours: Dawn revealed 16 drab green H-34 helicopters spotted on the flight deck of the helicopter carrier *USS Princeton* (LPH-5). The ship slowly cruised parallel to the Vietnamese shoreline roughly 12 miles from the beach. Below decks the last elements of the Battalion Landing Team (BLT) were saddling up. A company of Marines would fly ashore by helicopter, and two more companies were packed into amphibious landing craft ready to storm the beach.

At 0730 Hours the armored amphibians churned ashore two miles north of the mouth of the Cua Viet River. India and Kilo Companies, 3rd Battalion, 5th Marines, slogged inland near the hamlet of Giem Ha Trung. Simultaneously, infantrymen from Lima Company flew toward the shore in H-34s. Eight minutes after takeoff from the *Princeton* the flight leader radioed: "Feet dry" (meaning, *over land*). The helicopters pressed on westward past Marines on the ground. As usual, infantrymen in helicopter cabins silently endured the ride, for conversation above the deafening roar of the pounding Wright radial engine was impossible. H-34 gunners hunched over their M-60s and intently scanned the terrain below.

Discovery of two 37mm shell casings in northern Quang Tri Province provided the first firm evidence of this weapon. Aircrews had previously reported possible 37mm AAA fire in the same area.
[3rd MAW, Command Chronology, August 1966]

Over the LZ the H-34s spiraled earthward. One group landed at YD-261710, a series of flooded rice paddies on the eastern bank of a small stream. Another contingent landed two miles to the southeast on the coastal plain. As the morning progressed additional units of the 3rd Battalion flew ashore, and by midday the entire BLT would be on the beach. Their mission called for blocking the coastal plain to keep the NVA in the eastern DMZ from continuing southward.

Dong Ha, 16 July 1966, 0800 Hours: As the sun inched higher above the eastern horizon, Dong Ha bustled with activity. Four squadrons of helicopters would carry the 2nd Battalion, 1st Marines, to YD-073664. Code-named LZ Robin, the landing area lay a mile northwest of LZ Dove. The terrain at LZ Robin featured rolling hills covered with chest-high elephant grass. The assault would be led by H-34s from HMM-163 (call-sign, *Superchief*). The helicopters would be escorted by gunships from VMO-6 (call-sign, *Klondike*). One by one, Hueys and H-34s lifted and spawned blinding clouds of red laterite dust. They flew to the northwest and were followed by larger H-46s. The HMM-163 Command Chronology later would contain a Special Operations Narrative:

> A multi-squadron flight made up of *[helicopters]* from *[HMM-163]*, HMM-161, HMM-164, and HMM-165 *[would]* lift the Second Battalion, First Marines. Gunship support was provided by Klondike *[helicopters]* from VMO-6 . . . . Due to the abundance of plotted *[12.7mm AAA]* positions located throughout the operating area, a specific approach and retirement route was plotted. . . . The LZ consisted of a large flat area of burned-off grass. One area was completely free of obstacles while another smaller area to the south was littered with burned trees. . . . The Superchief aircraft landed, successfully evading the obstacles. . . . A stiff west wind combined with *[an]* early morning H-hour allowed for a straight-in approach with the sun to our back. Two complete waves of aircraft, plus a third wave of . . . Superchief aircraft, completed the lift.

Marine battalions west of Dong Ha and Cam Lo depended upon helicopters for resupply. Helicopters were their lifeline. There were no roads or trails leading to troops in the field. Food, water, ammunition, and all the tools of war were flown to Marine infantrymen in the field via helicopters.

> The helicopters of MAG-16 flew around-the-clock in support of Operation Hastings.
> *[1st MAW, Command Chronology, July 1966]*

The Rockpile, 16 July 1966, 1430 Hours: A Recon team flew to the Rockpile via helicopter. The H-46 hovered with only one wheel on the craggy peak, and the Recons jumped out. From their perch over 700 feet above the valley floor they had a commanding view. NVA in the valley below posed no threat to men atop the Rockpile. Yet, from time to time playful rock-apes, miniature gorillas, threw sticks and stones at Recons who had invaded their lofty domain.

Recons on the Rockpile saw numerous NVA troop columns and radioed enemy positions to artillerymen of Hotel Company, 3rd

Battalion, 12th Marines (call-sign, *Polish Hotel*) at Cam Lo. Within minutes, 155mm high-explosive shells rained down onto the North Vietnamese. That night the Recons would spot NVA lanterns and campfires and would direct artillery fire onto them also.

Helicopter Valley, 16 July 1966, 1800 Hours: By late afternoon on the second day of Operation Hastings the 2nd Battalion, 4th Marines, had pushed westward to LZ Crow. There they linked-up with the 3rd Battalion, 4th Marines. Although there had been scores of firefights, the larger NVA units had not yet been committed to battle.

North Vietnamese troops were in the valley in great strength, no doubt about it. Marine infantry overran an NVA field hospital with 200 beds, all perfectly concealed beneath the dense jungle canopy. They shot the NVA guards and destroyed the hospital and its huge cache of antitank mines and antiaircraft ammunition.

Also discovered was a cache of approximately 250,000 rounds of 7.62 ammunition, 183 82mm mortar rounds, 1,200 pounds of medical supplies, 3 ChiCom service rifles, 31 grenades, and numerous documents.
[Task Force Delta, After Action Report, 16 July 1966]

Where were the main force NVA units? The Marine Command did not know for sure, but all signs indicated that the NVA command post was still atop Hill 208. Reconnaissance by air confirmed that it was heavily fortified.

Commanded by Capt. Robert Modrzejewski, Kilo Company from the 3rd Battalion, 4th Marines, had pushed southward to cross the Ngan River. Kilo Company had planned to probe NVA defenses on Hill 208 after crossing the river. However, thus far the entrenched NVA on the southern riverbank had repulsed Marines each time they tried to cross. Kilo Company began digging-in for the night.

At 1900 Hours the North Vietnamese stormed all sides of the Kilo perimeter. First, NVA mortars rained down from the sky. Then the NVA infantrymen charged forward out of the dark night. Most Marine casualties came from grenades. The battle raged until just before midnight, when NVA troops withdrew toward Hill 208. One Marine later would explain:

We could hear bodies being dragged through the jungle for hours after the shooting stopped.

Daylight the following morning revealed 79 more NVA bodies that had not been dragged away. Many of them lay within ten feet of Marine fighting holes.

Helicopter Valley, 17 July 1966, 0900 Hours: More Marines helicoptered into the jungle southwest of Helicopter Valley. The Recon team high atop the Rockpile radioed more reports of NVA troop movements, so another swarm of MAG-16 helicopters roared into the valley to the east. They carried the 2nd Battalion, 1st Marines. The hunt for main force NVA units was shifting into high gear.

> 1/1 remained in *[the]* Task Force Delta reserve, and 1/3 continued to provide security for *[the]* Task Force Delta command post *[at Dong Ha]* and 3/12 *[artillery]* units *[at Cam Lo]*.
> *[Task Force Delta, After Action Report, 17 July 1966]*

By nightfall on 17 July a major confrontation was brewing. Thus far the NVA had tenaciously resisted all Marine efforts to cross to the southern side of the Ngan River. The NVA had dug-in, fortified their positions, and defended likely avenues of attack on their fortress atop Hill 208. Both adversaries lobbed mortars onto their opponents. North Vietnamese soldiers and Marine infantrymen obviously knew that a major battle was inevitable.

Helicopter Valley, 18 July 1966, 1400 Hours: The 3rd Battalion, 4th Marines, was helicoptered into LZ Crow to help. Most of the battalion pushed to the northeast according to plan. Kilo Company, commanded by Capt. Modrzejewski, remained behind to destroy captured ammunition, and demolitions specialists planned to destroy three downed H-46s that were still in LZ Crow.

> As K/3/4 moved out, bringing up the rear of the column, they started receiving mortar fire. . . . Columns also began receiving small arms and automatic *[weapons]* fire from an estimated 1,000 NVA.
> *[Task Force Delta, After Action Report, 18 July 1966]*

At 1740 Hours enemy troops stormed out of the surrounding jungle and charged the men of Kilo Company. The company faced two NVA battalions. The battle would rage for hours on level terrain covered by elephant grass.

> They were blowing bugles and we could see them waving flags . . . . We were being attacked by a thousand men. We just couldn't kill them fast enough.
> *[John McGinty, quoted in U.S. Marines in Vietnam: An Expanding War, 1966, 1982]*

Hardest hit was the 32-man First Platoon led by SSgt. John McGinty. The NVA relentlessly charged forward. There were too many of them. Fighting against overwhelming odds, First Platoon was being ripped to pieces. NVA soldiers rammed their way between platoons, then between squads. The overwhelming sensation was deafening bedlam. No one could hear individual weapons firing, the shouts, and the screams.

> The NVA attacked the 3rd Bn., 4th Marines, in column and separated the column in several places. . . . Approximately 1,000 NVA attacked two platoons in the rear of the column . . . and heavy close-in fighting ensued.
> *[3rd MarDiv, Command Chronology, 18 July 1966]*

Sgt. McGinty was hit, then hit again. Yet, he stayed on his feet and shouted encouragement to his men. Desperation gripped the surviving Marines of First Platoon. Their only corpsman was dead, ammunition was running out, and the NVA swarmed toward them in waves. Marines who were still alive were wounded.

> There is many a boy here today who looks on war as all glory. But boys, war is Hell!
> *[William Sherman, former USA general, 12 August 1880]*

Bleeding and on his knees, McGinty crawled from man to man, helping the wounded reload their weapons, yelling encouragement, directing rifle fire from what was left of his platoon. Modrzejewski, wounded the night before, had refused evacuation so that he could stay with his men. Now he manned the radio and called for air-strikes and artillery. Dropping his radio, the captain grabbed ammunition boxes and ran from platoon to platoon, squad to squad, to resupply his men. Running upright in the chest-high grass he presented the NVA with a perfect target, but he seemed to have a charmed life.

Helicopter Valley, 18 July 1966, 1800 Hours: Deadlock gunships from VMO-2 were on the way to join the fight. Target coordinates lay on the eastern edge of LZ Crow. The deafening bedlam of battle punctuated radio transmissions. Kilo Company was cut off. The enemy was attacking from the north, west, and south, Modrzejewski radioed above the din. He wanted to conduct a fighting withdrawal to the east, but one platoon was isolated and being ripped apart. He would not abandon those Marine brothers.

Gunships arced down for strafing runs. NVA infantry was there, clearly visible, almost everywhere. North Vietnamese were fighting their way across what had been the 3rd Battalion command post.

"Deadlock's rolling in hot."

Firing both guns and rockets, the gunships made pass after pass. The North Vietnamese could crouch down in chest-high elephant grass or take cover under trees along the river. After gunships passed over them they could stand up to fire. However, some NVA soldiers elected to stay in the open where they stood, fought, and openly challenged the gunships.

Helicopters are not tanks. Those windshields are not jet-age plastic that bullets bounce off of.
[Capt. J.W. Rider, USMC, quoted in Marine Corps Gazette, October 1967]

The combination of aerial firepower and the grit of Kilo Company slowly blunted the NVA assault. The tide of battle gradually turned. Sgt. McGinty, bleeding and battered but still alive, and his remaining men linked-up with the main body of Kilo Company. Survivors withdrew while still under intense small arms and automatic weapons fire. They left no wounded men on the battlefield, but they had to leave their dead. There were not enough walking-wounded men to carry those who had been killed.

By 1900 Hours, resupply H-46s and H-34s from Dong Ha had

arrived over the valley. Ammunition and water were the most urgent needs, but there were scores of wounded men to be evacuated. The transport helicopters hovered over the treetops, using their hoists to reach the Marines below. Gunships swooped and darted overhead, trying to pinpoint NVA soldiers concealed under the vegetation.

All aircraft took fire.
[HMM-161, After Action Report, 18 July 1966]

The tactical situation on the ground was mass confusion. Marines were spread out in various locations and concealed from aerial view by the jungle canopy. Firefights raged up and down the valley floor. Three helicopter squadrons pitched in to help, but HMM-161 alone hauled 120 medevacs back to Delta-Med at Dong Ha.

Helicopter Valley, 18 July 1966, 1945 Hours: Night finally settled over the battleground. Marines of Kilo Company had opposed most of an NVA regiment. Withdrawing toward the northeast, what was left of the company straggled to a point a mile from LZ Crow, and there they dug-in for the night. Resupply and medevac helicopters had no place to land. In the dark they used their hoist cables to lower supplies down through the trees to the valley floor. Wounded men were hoisted up into hovering helicopters in the same manner. Post-battle words written 104 years earlier seemed to express the thoughts of most Marines.

That terrible autumn day had been a long one, but the late afternoon *[had]* seemed even longer. The sun *[had]* seemed almost to go backwards in the sky. I thought that night would never come.
[Lt. James Graham, CSA, at Antietam, 17 September 1862]

Night enveloped man and machine, but it did nothing to slow the pace of helicopter missions. Marine aircrews still made flight after flight to support their warrior brothers in Helicopter Valley. Trying to find infantrymen in the dark, one pilot recalled a gallows humor cliche often voiced by pilots:

Flying at night is just like flying in the daytime – except that you can't see where you're going.

Under enemy fire, flying into small landing zones surrounded by tall trees is difficult enough during the day. At night such flying demands all the skills a helicopter crew can bring to bear. The hardest task is *finding* troops on the ground. In the dark, smoke grenades are useless. At night, infantrymen signal helicopters with a flashlight, a mere pinpoint of light far below – hopefully not from the NVA. A cautious power-on approach is the only way to descend. With no depth perception at night, pilots have to almost *feel* their way down, and they never know if a potential landing area will be suitable until they get down to it. To avoid giving the NVA a visible target they keep their anticollision lights and running lights turned off. Hover lights are not used for the same reason, and only an idiot would turn on the searchlight, for it would become a bull's-eye. The tension becomes alive, tangible, almost sexual.

LtCol. Arnold Bench was in the valley with his command, the 2nd Battalion, 4th Marines, that deadly July night. He watched as the helicopters swooped down out of the black sky, and he marveled at the elan of MAG-16 helicopter crews. Writing about them years later, he would note:

> On a pitch-black night they descended into an unlighted gorge, talked in by their exhaust glow, to have a flare popped when they were only a few feet off the landing zone.

The NVA paid a high price for their human wave assaults. After that bloody day they abandoned mass formation assault tactics in favor of hit-and-run ambushes. They would fight in strength only when defending well fortified positions.

Helicopter Valley, 19 July 1966, 1120 Hours: Marine infantrymen also had paid a terrible price. There had been 32 young Marines in McGinty's understrength First Platoon. Twenty-six of them were either dead, or grievously wounded and incapacitated. Only six men, all of them wounded, were still able to defend their perimeter. Kilo Company – an entire company – had been decimated down to only 73 breathing survivors, and many of those were badly wounded. When asked about his Marines, Capt. Modrzejewski would recall:

> I had kids who were hit in five or six places.

The bitter fighting on 18 July had been the most brutal thus far in the campaign. Kilo Company had been ravaged and was no longer an effective fighting unit. Helicopters pulled survivors out of the jungle and carried them to Dong Ha. Later that day C-130 transports would fly them southward to Phu Bai to regroup.

> At 1120 Hours K/3/4 was lifted to Dong Ha. At 1315 Hours K/3/4 was lifted via fixed-wing to Phu Bai *[39 miles to the south]*.
> *[Task Force Delta, After Action Report, 19 July 1966]*

Helicopter Valley, 20 July to 3 August 1966: The fighting resumed after a day of regrouping for both adversaries. Day after day the Marines and NVA dueled around the Rockpile, the Razorback, Cam Lo, Con Thien, Ca Lu, and in Helicopter Valley. The region evolved into a meat grinder, a killing ground.

> A Shock and Resuscitation unit *[called Delta-Med had been]* established at Dong Ha. . . . Casualties were evacuated to Alpha-Med *[at Phu Bai]*, and the more serious ones were evacuated to Charlie-Med *[at Da Nang]* . . . . Facilities aboard the USS Princeton as well as the USS Repose *[also]* were utilized.
> *[Task Force Delta, After Action Report, Operation Hastings]*

By the end of July, Marine intelligence discovered that some battalions of the 324-B NVA Division were moving westward into dense and impenetrable jungle areas. Task Force Delta concentrated on locating and eliminating North Vietnamese troops remaining in Helicopter Valley and in Razorback Valley. On paper, Operation Hastings ended at 1200 Hours on 3 August 1966.

> The enemy fought tenaciously *[and had]* stockpiles of supplies pre-positioned in and north of the DMZ in the heavy jungle, but in areas that could be supported by *[NVA]* truck transportation. . . . Reconnaissance teams have been introduced into Laos . . . and have discovered a major infiltration route through a valley that crosses the border . . . and a logistic complex approximately 7 kilometers south of Highway 9.
> *["Eyes only" secret message from CG-MACV to Gen. Earle Wheeler, Chairman of the Joint Chiefs of Staff, July 1966]*

Ominous intelligence revealed that two more NVA Divisions, the 304th and the 341st, were massing on the edge of the DMZ. An unidentified enemy division was staged west of Khe Sanh along the Laotian border. Consequently, on 3 August 1966 when Operation Hastings ended, Task Force Delta kicked off a search-and-destroy plan, "Operation Prairie," for the region. In reality, little had changed except the name.

The Grunts themselves knew, the madness, bitterness, the horror and doom of it. . . . The belief that one Marine was better than ten Slopes saw Marine squads fed in against known NVA platoons, platoons against companies, and on and on, until whole battalions found themselves pinned down and cut off. That belief was undying, but the Grunt was not.

[Michael Herr, Dispatches, 1968]

An H-34 from HMM-163 waits in the grass near the dirt airstrip at Dong Ha in June 1966. HMM-163 helicopters were recognized by huge non-regulation, non-standard, non-official "evil eyes" painted on the nose of each helicopter in the squadron.

This paint scheme was born in late 1965. The squadron commanding officer and his staff searched for a unique and unifying theme for their Marines. One of the pilots who had flown for Air America in Laos, Thailand, and Cambodia suggested a pair of "evil eyes." He was well versed in oriental culture, and he explained that Vietnamese are traditionally afraid of two things: (1) evil spirits, and (2) being watched. Further, the bulbous nose of an H-34 would be the perfect place for a pair of ominous and watchful eyes.

Various designs were evaluated, and the squadron settled on wicked-looking "evil eyes" (this theme would last over 50 years). Huge white eyes with black eyeballs were painted on the engine clamshell doors on the front of each H-34. The "evil eyes" became famous throughout Vietnam. During later eras the "evil eyes" would be painted on HMM-163 H-46s, and still later on squadron V-22 Ospreys that would deploy to the Middle East (photo by the author).

A 105mm howitzer at Con Thien fires at NVA positions in the DMZ three miles to the north (photo courtesy of U.S. Marine Corps).

Men from the 4th Marine Regiment patrol below the DMZ during Operation Hastings. In dense jungles, streams often were the most practical route of travel (photo courtesy of U.S. Marine Corps).

Vietnamese boys ask Marines to give them cigarettes at Dong Ha in early July 1966. For military security reasons the boys soon were banned from the expeditionary combat base (photo by the author).

These GP tents were the living quarters for Marine infantrymen of E/2/4 at Dong Ha in July 1966 (photo by the author).

In early July 1966 this sandbagged bunker was positioned on the southern side of the Dong Ha dirt airstrip (photo by the author).

Marines charge uphill toward NVA trenches after artillery and air-strikes have denuded the hill (photo courtesy of U.S. Marine Corps).

A Marine from M/3/4 carries ordnance and charges uphill during Operation Prairie (photo courtesy of U.S. Marine Corps).

A Marine M-60 machinegun team fires at NVA soldiers on Nui Cay Tre Ridge in October 1966 (photo courtesy of U.S. Marine Corps).

Marines climb up a steep and rough jungle slope near the massive Razorback (photo courtesy of U.S. Marine Corps).

A "super-gaggle" of H-46 helicopters flies ammunition and supplies to an outpost on Hill 881 (photo courtesy of U.S. Marine Corps).

A Marine rifle company prepares for another night in the field a mile below the DMZ (photo courtesy of U.S. Marine Corps).

A Huey brings supplies to a Marine artillery outpost that has been hacked out of the jungle (photo courtesy of U.S. Marine Corps).

This H-46 has flown SLF Marines to the sandy coastal plain below the DMZ (photo courtesy of U.S. Marine Corps).

In the fertile rice basin south of Da Nang, a Sparrow Hawk quick reaction force flies down to land in rice paddies adjacent to a small village under the trees (photo by the author).

An M-14 rifle used by Marines in 1966. The M-14 is based upon the M-1 Garand rifle in use by the U.S. Armed Forces during World War II. Primary changes included replacing the eight-round clip with a twenty-round magazine and adding an option for full automatic fire. The Marine Corps had begun replacing the reliable old M-1 with the new M-14 in the early 1960s. The 7.62mm M-14 would be the last American "battle rifle" that fires full power rifle ammunition.

Marine infantrymen at Dong Ha leave their GP tents and prepare for a helicopter ride to Razorback Valley (photo by the author).

Loaded with ordnance, two Marine F-4 Phantoms head northward from Da Nang (photo courtesy of U.S. Marine Corps).

A helicopter pilot snaps a photograph as his H-46 prepares to land near a small village on the coastal plain (photo by the author).

Marines load wounded comrades into a Huey near Nui Cay Tre Ridge, aka "Mutter Ridge" (photo courtesy of U.S. Marine Corps).

An H-46 lands in rough terrain in the Que Son Mountains to pick up wounded Marines (photo courtesy of U.S. Marine Corps).

Construction of the massive command bunker at Khe Sanh combat base during the late months of 1966 (photo by the author).

Marine infantrymen at Dong Ha wait behind their helicopter for a ride to Razorback Valley (photo by the author).

Primitive living conditions at Dong Ha (photo by the author).

Infantry billeting tents on Hill 55. The hill offered a commanding view of the vast rice basin south of Da Nang (photo by the author).

Remains of an H-46 helicopter that crashed and burned at Khe Sanh in heavy fog at night on 27 January 1967. The H-46 crew had been trying to resupply a surrounded Recon team in Laos, where two helicopters already had been downed (photo by the author).

In early July 1966, before the battles in the mountains to the west, helicopter crew chiefs and gunners gather for conversation between Recon insert missions at Dong Ha. The small building, right background, was the old French airport terminal (photo by the author).

The Recon Patrol

Vietnam is a nasty place to fight. But there are no neat and tidy battlefields in the struggle for freedom. There is no good place to die.
[Hanson Baldwin, in The New York Magazine, *21 February 1965]*

Northern Quang Tri Province, 3-6 August 1966: The offensive known as Operation Hastings had ended on 3 August 1966. Yet, the North Vietnamese Army continued to funnel troops into the DMZ and into mountains and jungles of northern Quang Tri Province. The Marine Corps now elected to stand back and use artillery and airpower to whittle away at the invaders from the North, a less costly tactic than frontal assaults by Marine infantrymen. However, mobile NVA battalions were concealed by dense jungle vegetation.

A captured North Vietnamese Army soldier said he was a member of a reinforced company entrenched in well-fortified caves north of *[what he called]* "the Rock Pile" .... This company is part of a battalion whose mission was to secure "the Rock Pile" and sweep east and capture *[the Marine artillery batteries at]* Cam Lo. The captive stated that the unit has Chinese advisors.
[3rd Bn., 12th Marines, Command Chronology, August 1966]

Marines had reduced the size of their task force at Dong Ha. Four infantry companies from the 2nd Battalion, 4th Marines (known by their slang moniker, *Magnificent Bastards*), formed the heart of the fighting force. For intelligence gathering purposes the four infantry companies were supported by the fabled 1st Force Reconnaissance Company (spoken, *First Force Recon* or simply *First Force*). MAG-16 Forward provided a rotating detachment of helicopters at Dong Ha, with more helicopters less than an hour away at Marble Mountain and Phu Bai. Available fixed-wing close air support was based at Da Nang and Chu Lai.

We want to kill the enemy with our supporting arms – not with rifles, grenades, and bayonets.
[Task Force Delta, After Action Report, Operation Hastings]

Artillery fire would be provided by Hotel Battery, 3rd Battalion, 12th Marines (call-sign, *Polish Hotel*), reinforced with 155mm howitzers. Cruising several miles offshore the destroyers *USS Beale* (DD-471) and *USS Mullinnix* (DD-944) could provide 5-inch gun support for coastal areas within range. Also available were platoons from the 3rd Tank Battalion, the 3rd Antitank Battalion, and the 3rd Engineer Battalion. The artillery and tanks were staged at Cam Lo, map coordinates YD-108573, six miles west of Dong Ha. Security there was provided by two infantry companies, for the mountains to the west were enemy territory. There was almost no contact between Marines and Vietnamese civilians in Dong Ha village, but a few conflicts did arise.

At 1330 Hours, Corporal *[name redacted]*, 2d Plt., Company H, shot and killed a civilian child, Troung Duc Chau, 12 years old, who was aggravating *[the]* sentry on post. Condolence payment was made to *[his]* mother, Nguyen Tri Luong, of 3,000$ NV.
[2nd Bn., 4th Marines, Command Chronology, August 1966]

Recon Teams: Marines had airpower and ground firepower. But to locate North Vietnamese troops in the mountains and jungles to the west, Marines would use their "eyes and ears." Reconnaissance Marines (spoken, *Recons*) were commandos of the Corps. They were lethal gunfighters and skilled manhunters. In addition to standard Marine training, each Recon had survived a unique training and qualification regimen that would have broken most mortals. The elite Recons were pathfinders for Marine infantry battalions.

Recon teams, four or five men per team, were routinely inserted by helicopter into enemy territory. These so-called "Stingray" teams would fight only as a last resort. Their mission called for clandestine observation to pinpoint enemy troops, fortifications, and staging areas. Reporting by battery powered radios, they would direct the fire of Marine artillery and call for air-strikes.

MISSION: Observe and maintain surveillance of main valley running east-west through area of operation, capture one prisoner, be prepared to call supporting arms *[meaning, air or artillery]* on enemy targets of opportunity.
[Written mission for Groucho Marx Patrol, Team 61, 6th Platoon, 1st Force Recon, 6 August 1966]

There was another kind of team at Dong Ha: Nungs. They were Chinese mercenaries, soldiers of fortune paid by the Central Intelligence Agency (CIA). Marine helicopters would load-up with Nungs at Dong Ha (later, *Khe Sanh*), fly them westward, and drop them off in Laos 35 to 45 miles to the west.

In Laos the Nungs would ambush NVA troops at night. As proof of their kills they would save the right ear of each victim (on 13 October 1967 the MACV commander, Gen. William Westmoreland, USA, would ban cutting ears off of dead enemy soldiers, but his order did not apply to civilians, foreign nationals, or the CIA). If Nungs returned alive from a cross-border mission the CIA would pay each of them "by the ear." Led by an Australian mercenary who could speak English, Nungs were barbarians, savage assassins in a savage land. They fought for the highest bidder. Fortunately, at the time the CIA was willing to pay them more money than anyone else.

Another good thing we've done is insert mercenaries into Laos. There are some weird things going on over here. The poor folks back home have no idea.
[Capt. Joseph Snyder, USMC, in a letter, March 1969]

The Covert CIA War: In the mid-1960s the United States military commander in Vietnam, Gen. Westmoreland, did not have authority to send United States infantrymen beyond the territorial borders of South Vietnam. Consequently an unconventional warfare task force, the "Studies and Observation Group" (SOG), had been created by the U.S. Joint Chiefs of Staff on 24 January 1964. In this black-ops program, North Vietnam was called *New York*, and Cambodia was known as *Arizona*. Highly classified covert SOG operations were controlled by a "Counterinsurgency and Special Activities" staff at The Pentagon in Washington, DC.

Execute an intensified program of harassment, diversion, political pressure, capture of prisoners, physical destruction, acquisition of intelligence, generation of propaganda, and diversion of resources against *[North]* Vietnam.
[Mission statement, Studies and Observation Group]

SOG spawned tangential operations. "Leaping Lena" had been born on 15 May 1964, and it had trained U.S. Special Forces and local mercenaries for combat missions in Laos. Leaping Lena had morphed into the larger "Project Delta" by October 1964. Another child of SOG, "Shining Brass," had been established in September 1965. Shining Brass teams had flown into Laos to control air-strikes and conduct hit-and-run attacks on North Vietnamese troops. Yet, by the mid-1960s most Marines in Vietnam collectively referred to all CIA programs as Project Delta.

By the summer of 1966 many Project Delta hunter-killer teams were staged from Khe Sanh, west of Dong Ha and only six miles from the Laotian border. The SOG command dispatched Marine helicopters on the clandestine Project Delta flights. On these cross-border missions each helicopter crewman carried a "blood chit" for use if he was shot down in Laos. A blood chit might help a downed helicopter survivor – and it might not. It was a large silk banner folded inside a packet. This colorful banner displayed the American flag and a notice printed in 14 languages.

I am an American. I do not speak your language. Misfortune forces me to seek your assistance in obtaining food, shelter, and protection. Please take me to someone who will provide for my safety and see that I am returned to my people. I will do my best to see that no harm comes to you. My government will reward you.
[Notice printed in 14 languages on each Blood Chit]

Dong Ha, 6 August 1966, 1900 Hours: In the late afternoon as the sun sank toward the western horizon, four Recons prepared to leave Dong Ha for a helicopter ride 13 miles to the west. The small team was known as "Groucho Marx," their radio call-sign. The team had adopted the stage name of the vaudeville and television comedian, Groucho Marx (1890-1977). The call-sign was unique. Most Recon call-signs embodied a lethal or macho image: Killer Kane, Hateful, Petrify, Grim Reaper, Striker, Breaker, Texas Pete, etc.

The men of Groucho Marx carried two radios, a PRC-25 and a PRC-10, in addition to their weapons and supplies. Their only other special equipment was a set of vital 7 x 50 power binoculars. Each Recon was heavily laden, for they were scheduled to spend three days in the bush. Each man wore what was called an "ARVN pack," much larger than the standard Marine Corps pack, and bought on the black market from local Vietnamese. Also each Recon wore a small fanny-pack hooked onto his web belt and suspender straps. Crammed into these two packs was everything a Recon might need.

> Each patrol was a self sustaining unit, carrying all of its needs for the expected period of operation . . . . There was no resupply of *[Recon]* units in the field.
> *[1st Force Recon, After Action Report, Aug.-Nov. 1966]*

Each Recon carried two or three C-Ration meals for each day. They had taken each meal out of its cardboard box in the interest of space conservation. The C-Ration pack of four cigarettes would be left behind. Each can had been opened with the standard P-38 tool and then resealed with wide adhesive tape in the interest of noise discipline in the bush. Each man carried three canteens of water for each day, for they would operate on high ground where no fresh water would be available. Recons carried two canteens hooked onto their web belts, and the others were put inside their ARVN packs. Each canteen was made of plastic for noise discipline purposes.

Groucho Marx was led by SSgt. Billy Donaldson. The Oklahoma native was highly qualified, beginning with completion of airborne school in 1960. On this patrol his assistant patrol leader was Cpl. Tom Bachta, a veteran of many earlier patrols in the mountains west of Dong Ha. With them were two men who were new to the team, LCpl. James Hager and PFC (name unknown). The PFC had arrived in Vietnam the previous month.

Donaldson and Bachta were accustomed to contact with the NVA. Only three days earlier on 3 August they had directed artillery fire onto a nearby NVA troop column.

Artillery was credited with 15 KIA by the Groucho Marx recon team.
[2nd Bn., 4th Marines, Command Chronology, 3 Aug. 1966]

An hour later the Groucho Marx team had been extracted by a Huey from VMO-2 (call-sign, *Deadlock*) while under heavy NVA fire. The Huey pilot, 1stLt. Richard Drury, almost got his arm blown off by an NVA heavy caliber round during the extraction.

On a retraction of a Recon team code-named "Groucho Marx" . . .
Lt. Drury's aircraft sustained hits from a .50 caliber machinegun, wounding him severely in the right hand, arm, and leg.
[VMO-2, Command Chronology, 3 August 1966]

Although critically wounded, the pilot would survive. Now, just 72 hours later Groucho Marx was headed back into the bush. With enough C-Rations, water, and radio batteries to last three days the four men crawled into a Huey near the Dong Ha airstrip.

Four Hueys took off from Dong Ha and headed toward the hills, mountains, and jungles to the west. The helicopter carrying the four Recons was a "slick," a passenger and cargo hauler not equipped with guns or rockets. Another Huey slick was the Search & Rescue (SAR) helicopter. If the first slick got shot down the SAR Huey would try to swoop down and rescue any survivors. Trailing behind the two slicks, two Huey gunships could provide machinegun and rocket support if necessary.

The Huey, in its many varied missions – Recon inserts and retractions, attack, armed escort, TAC(A), medevac, observation, and VIP transport – continues to show a multiplicity of capabilities.
[VMO-2, Command Chronology, August 1966]

Razorback Valley, 6 August 1966, 1910 Hours: The Huey spiraled down and dropped off the Recons in a small bombed-out area in a lush subtropical valley 13 miles west of Dong Ha. Had the Recons been geologists or botanists they would have been awed by the sheer beauty and ruggedness of the land. To the west lay gnarled black stone cliffs that formed the long eastern wall of 1,000-foot-high Razorback Ridge, centered at map coordinates XD-964577. To the south two miles away the massive Rockpile, map coordinates XD-979558, jutted over 700 feet straight up into the sky. To the east lay Dong Ha Mountain, Hill 549 at YD-019593 on their maps. The jungled Nui Cay Tre Ridge (later called, *Mutter Ridge*), centered at XD-980613, walled in the valley on the north. The steep terrain and thick vegetation were maddening.

> The terrain in the objective area was found to be thick secondary undergrowth intermingled with vines and thorns. . . . The canopy averaged 20-30 feet *[high]*, and it was very mountainous in this area, with slopes up to 50 *[degrees]*. Movement was very difficult; average distance covered was 150 meters an hour.
> *[1st Force Recon, Command Chronology, August 1966]*

However, the Recons were not interested in scenery. They had come into Razorback Valley to hunt men. After the Huey had dropped them off, the pilots had pulled in collective pitch and headed skyward. However, at half-mile intervals they had made three more *feint landings* to hopefully confuse NVA spotters. Then they flew several miles to the south and orbited, boring lazy holes in the sky over the Cam Lo River, waiting for Groucho Marx to radio that the patrol had not been detected by North Vietnamese troops. Protocol mandated strict radio contacts.

> (1) All patrols will check-in immediately upon insertion.
> (2) Patrols will call-in situation reports every hour . . . .
> (3) Patrols out of *[radio]* contact with *[Dong Ha]* for a period in excess of two hours will move to the last position where communication was obtained. If there is no contact for three hours the patrol will abort its mission . . . .
> *[Task Unit Charlie, Operational Order 1-66, 23 June 1966]*

Of course the four Recons could not stay on the valley floor, and it was getting dark. They crept eastward and up-slope through chest-high elephant grass to a remote and thickly vegetated spot at XD-998597, where they planned to spend the night. This would be their "harbor site." SSgt. Donaldson selected a dense thicket of elephant grass and tall bamboo. In reaching this site they had avoided ridges and valley streambeds, for those likely would be traversed by the

NVA. At the selected harbor site the ground was covered by large dead bamboo leaves that would crackle underfoot. Anyone creeping toward the site would be heard 200 feet away. Silence was critical, and one Recon explained:

I could hear a snake if it crawled across those brittle dead leaves.

Each Recon scraped the ground bare where he would lie during the night. That way, inadvertent body movement while asleep would not rustle the leaves and aurally compromise their position. Two Recons would sleep while the other two, sitting motionless and silent back-to-back, would stand watch. Every two hours they would rotate the watch. Here they spent the night, motionless and silent. A cold, a cough, or sneezing would have excluded a Recon from the patrol. Noise discipline and stealth were crucial.

Each hour Groucho Marx would provide a SITREP (meaning, *situation report*) to Dong Ha via their newly issued PRC-25 battery powered radio on frequency 49.6. They also had a backup PRC-10, but it was considered to be little better than two cans and a string.

New Developments: Introduction of the PRC-25 radio into the communications system. Battalion now has 67 PRC-25s . . . . The battalion will now turn in . . . all but eight *[old]* PRC-10 radios.
[2nd Bn., 4th Marines, Command Chronology, August 1966]

The team did not have to radio Dong Ha, for a 1st Force Recon radioman there (call-sign, *Primness*) was in a hardback GP tent north of the dirt runway. He would initiate contact on the hour. The team would reply and pass along pertinent information. If NVA soldiers were near or when noise discipline was paramount, the Groucho Marx radioman would not have to speak. If he did not answer two radio queries, the Primness radioman would ask if the team was all secure. Two clicks of the mike was a sufficient response.

It was all done by keying the handset. Every hour *[headquarters]* would ask if they were Alpha Sierra *[meaning, all secure]*.
[Michael Lanning et al, Inside Force Recon, 1989]

Razorback Valley, 6 August 1966, 2300 Hours: An hour before midnight the two Recons standing watch heard Vietnamese voices talking and laughing as NVA soldiers walked through undergrowth near a streambed in the valley below. The sounds continued for about an hour and then died out. All was quiet for the rest of the night, exclusive of Harassment & Interdiction (H&I) fire from artillerymen at Cam Lo.

> 062300H / XD-998597: The patrol heard voices and sounds of walking. This was down in the valley below them 300 to 400 meters from the patrol's position. *[This]* movement was heard at XD-980605 and was not heard after 2400 *[Hours]* that night.
> *[Groucho Marx Patrol Report, Team 61, 6th Platoon, 1st Force Recon, 7 August 1966]*

Razorback Valley, 7 August 1966, 0650 Hours: Daylight slowly illuminated Razorback Valley, and men of Groucho Marx crept to the edge of the bamboo thicket. From this vantage point they had a clear view of the valley floor to the north and west of them. Groucho Marx was supposed to observe and report. They were not supposed to fight. Yet, if the NVA chanced to stumble onto the team they would find them to be a fearsome adversary.

Three team members carried M-14 rifles. Each Recon carried eight 20-round magazines on his web belt, although to prevent a possible failure-to-feed they had loaded only 18 rounds into each of them. In addition each man had two or three cloth bandoleers full of extra magazines in his pack, about 60 rounds per bandoleer. The standard M-14 was semi-automatic, but the armorer had worked on them. A selector switch gave Recons either semi-automatic or full automatic capability.

The team radioman, Cpl. Bachta, had a .45 caliber pistol for close combat, and he carried an M-79 grenade launcher instead of an M-14. Armed to the teeth, he also carried a one-shot M-72 Light Antitank Weapon (LAW). He used a gas mask pouch to carry about 30 rounds for the M-79, and each other team member carried five extra rounds for him. Each Recon carried six to eight M-26 grenades. Some had thermite grenades as well, plus red, yellow, and green smoke grenades for marking and signaling purposes. Each Recon carried the famous 1219C2 USMC knife, the Marine Corps fighting knife, the Ka-Bar. As a matter of personal preference, some wore it on their belt, and others wore it taped to suspender straps on their chest.

In addition to weapons, ammunition, food, and water, each man of Groucho Marx had other essential equipment. They carried spare batteries, encased in protective plastic, for their radios. When they could get it they carried C-4 explosive. Their warpaint came in tubes similar to lipstick tubes, and Recons painted their faces with camouflage lines of green, black, and white. They had several bottles of military issue "bug juice," an insect repellant slightly thicker than water and more effective than *6-12* or *OFF*. One Recon recalls: "We carried tons of it." Before a patrol they would soak their utilities and boots with it and rub it onto their arms, legs, faces, and into their hair. Highly effective. Whenever a land-leech chanced to latch onto them, they would spray bug juice on the creature. That always made it release its hold on the skin and fall away. When not on patrol they could touch the leech with the tip of a lighted cigarette. Instantly the bloodsucking invertebrate would curl up and drop off.

Helmets and flak jackets were too heavy. Recons simply wore a broad brimmed camouflaged boonie hat. They wore no skivvies (meaning, *underclothing*). In the high heat and high humidity any type of tee-shirt or undershorts would have stayed wet, resulting in jock-rot within a day. Their green fabric and leather jungle boots had drainage holes on each side and dried quickly even in a jungle environment. Dog tags were taped for noise discipline purposes, and Recons wore them on a leather cord in lieu of the customary metal chain. Most wore one around their neck, with the other laced into their right boot for contingency purposes.

The UH-1E *[Huey]* gunship was proved to be the most effective means of supporting a patrol in contact *[with the enemy]*. It is the only supporting weapon that can deliver fire safely within 10 meters of the patrol location.
[1st Force Recon, After Action Report, August 1966]

There were other necessities. A poncho was carried in each pack. Com-wire was used as a cord and to set up grenades as booby traps. One or two team members would carry claymores. Everyone carried a signal mirror, a rectangular device with an aluminum back and an aiming hole a person could see through. Someone had to carry a red panel. Spread out onto the ground, it could be used to signal aircraft. Each Recon carried a red lens flashlight, compass, pen flares, first aid kit, morphine syrettes, and two standard battle dressings. Altogether each man had about 80 pounds to carry. In addition, radiomen had to carry the heavy radios.

Contact with local Vietnamese civilians was not a concern. There were none living in the mountainous area where Recon teams would be operating. Cam Lo was on the frontier, and the wild territory to the west was largely uninhabited. There were two small and remote mountain villages, Khe Sanh and Lang Vei, 14 miles farther to the west near the Laotian border. Yet, for all practical purposes these two collections of thatched huts were "kingdoms unto themselves" and had no contact with the outside world.

The *[sparse]* local population in the areas west of Cam Lo are not to be considered as trustworthy or cooperative. The people in this area are montagnard *[mountain people]* and lowland Vietnamese. *[Task Force Delta, After Action Report, Operation Hastings]*

Razorback Valley, 7 August 1966, 1100 Hours: An hour before noon on 7 August the Recons of Groucho Marx again detected other men in the valley. Thin trails of smoke from cooking fires drifted up through the treetops 500 meters to the northwest along the streambed. Off and on the Recons could hear NVA soldiers talking and joking. Unlike their aural encounter the previous night, the sighting of smoke now enabled the Recons to visually pinpoint the enemy location.

071100H / XD-988597: The patrol heard talking and saw smoke *[in the]* vicinity *[of]* XD-982599. *[Groucho Marx Patrol Report, Team 61, 6th Platoon, 1st Force Recon, 7 August 1966]*

Cpl. Bachta tuned to 37.0, the radio frequency for Hotel Battery (call-sign, *Polish Hotel*) artillery at Cam Lo. Whispering into his PRC-25 mike, he requested a fire mission. As usual he "shackled" (letters substituted for numerals) target coordinates, for at battalion level and above the NVA had radios that could monitor Recon transmissions. For security purposes the shackle code changed often, and Recons would tape the current shackle code to their maps. Maps then were enclosed in plastic to protect them from rain and humidity.

"Polish Hotel, this is Groucho Marx."

"Groucho Marx, this is Polish Hotel, go ahead."

"Polish Hotel, this is Groucho Marx, fire mission."

Bachta radioed the shackled target coordinates, described the target, and then specified: "One round, Willie Pete *[meaning, white phosphorus]*, will adjust."

In less than a minute Marine artillery sent a 155mm shell arcing toward the valley. Both the men of Groucho Marx and the North Vietnamese could hear it coming. Ripping through the air, it sounded like someone tearing heavy canvas. Others have described the sound

```
d.  Shackle:

    1  2  3  4  5  6  7  8  9  0

    N  V  P  G  M  A  U  J  E  S
    C  Q  B  W  R  X  F  T  O  D
                H        L  K  Z
                Y                I

e.  Authentication:  Challenge; any letter;
    answer; any letter in the same column
    of the shackle.
```

One of the shackle codes used by the Groucho Marx patrol, per 1st Force Recon, Command Chronology, August 1966

as similar to the rustling noise of a gigantic squirrel running through dry leaves. The shell detonated about 200 meters east of the intended target area. Bachta radioed the necessary adjustment and stated: "Fire for effect." Moments later shells rained down onto the enemy.

Artillery was called with good coverage of the target. Gunships strafed the streambed where the smoke was located.
[Groucho Marx Patrol Report, Team 61, 6th Platoon, 1st Force Recon, 7 August 1966]

Bachta radioed "good coverage" of the target. When the artillery ceased firing, Deadlock gunships from Dong Ha took up the slack. Firing 2.75-inch rockets and four fixed 7.62mm electrically operated guns, plus two swivel-mounted machineguns fired by the crew chief and gunner, the gunships targeted the streambed area where NVA campfires had been spotted. After making six or seven strafing runs over the target the pilots turned to the east and headed back toward Dong Ha to rearm and refuel.

The Recons of Groucho Marx quietly congratulated themselves. They had located the enemy and had called artillery fire and gunships down onto him. But now, the four men of Groucho Marx realized, NVA commanders obviously knew that Marine spotters were in the valley with them, somewhere nearby.

Razorback Valley, 7 August 1966, 1600 Hours: The four men of Groucho Marx slowly and silently moved to a better vantage point roughly 100 meters to the west. There they settled into an observation spot closer to the streambed. They could hear NVA soldiers talking, hidden by the vegetation, to the north and east of them. The NVA apparently used water buffalo to transport ammunition and supplies, and also as food to supplement their ration of rice. The Recons could smell the pack animals.

> 071600H: The patrol moved 100 meters to the west of their previous position, where they heard more activity coming from the north and east. They also noted a distinct odor of livestock.
> *[Groucho Marx Patrol Report, Team 61, 6th Platoon, 1st Force Recon, 7 August 1966]*

Securely hidden in thick undergrowth and a mass of tangled vines at XD-988598, the men of Groucho Marx prepared for their second night in the valley. The NVA knew that Recons were somewhere nearby, and they sent out their own patrols to scour the valley for them. Recons could not see enemy soldiers in the dark, but they often heard them talking and searching through the undergrowth and thick elephant grass. Several times NVA soldiers passed within 100 to 150 feet of the concealed Recons.

<u>071600H / XD-988598</u>: The patrol set up its night OP and harbor site. Movement was heard all night, coming within 100 to 150 feet of the patrol position.
[Groucho Marx Patrol Report, Team 61, 6th Platoon, 1st Force Recon, 7 August 1966]

During the night Groucho Marx made radio SITREPS to Dong Ha and reported the nearby enemy soldiers. The NVA search party was close at hand, so at times Bachta had to substitute two clicks of his mike in lieu of an oral response. To ensure that radio contact was not lost an H-34 from HMM-161 (call-sign, *Barrelhouse*) orbited high overhead, 6,000 feet over the valley in the darkness. The helicopter provided radio relay capability. The H-34 crew chief, Sgt. Frank Bermudez, and the gunner, Sgt. Bill Bloomfield, could hear radio transmissions to and from Groucho Marx via the headsets in their flight helmets.

Razorback Valley, 8 August 1966, 0700 Hours: As daylight began to illuminate Razorback Valley on the morning of 8 August the Recons remained secure in their harbor site. Two slept or catnapped, and two remained on watch. The valley was huge, and the men of Groucho Marx were well hidden by thick vegetation. Unless enemy soldiers chanced to stumble right on top of them, their position would not be compromised. Meanwhile they could plot NVA locations and call for more artillery or gunship missions. Helicopters were waiting at Dong Ha to fly out and extract them if they needed to leave the hostile valley.

On the morning of the 8th the *[Recons]* saw 10 to 15 North Vietnamese troops moving in *[a]* skirmish line 100 meters away, apparently looking for the American patrol.
[Jack Shulimson, U.S. Marines in Vietnam: An Expanding War, 1966, 1982]

By 0830 Hours it was obvious that NVA soldiers were conducting on-line searches for the Recons. Cpl. Bachta spotted a group of enemy soldiers 100 meters away, moving on-line with fixed bayonets, walking up the hill toward the harbor site. Most of the hill had been bombed-out, but the harbor site was in a section of remaining thick vegetation and underbrush. The NVA were headed straight toward it, for they knew it was a likely spot to find the Recons. Bachta whispered to his teammates: "We've got company coming."

S/A *[meaning, small arms]* contacts were usually initiated at 10 meters or less. . . . Patrols gained fire superiority through the use of M-14 Modifieds, firing fully automatic.
[1st Force Recon, After Action Report, Aug.-Nov. 1966]

The Recons waited. They were camouflaged, concealed, silent, deadly, and overdosed on adrenalin. Lying prone, loaded and locked, they fixed their eyes and rifles on the approaching enemy patrol. NVA soldiers would not see them in the thicket until they were within 15 feet. The Recons had surprise on their side. Rifles set on full automatic, they would fire first, and they would take a horrible toll on unsuspecting tan-clad soldiers.

However, the NVA patrol went into the thicket 50 meters away, passed through it, and continued on up the hill without seeing the Recons. After the search party passed them, Donaldson directed artillery fire onto an enemy contingent 300 meters east of the team. Judging from screams of wounded enemy soldiers, the high-explosive rounds had impacted right on target.

080900H: Artillery mission was called on voices and movement down in the valley at XD-985598; *[the patrol heard]* movement 50 meters in front of the perimeter. It appeared that the NVA were on-line searching for the patrol.
[Groucho Marx Patrol Report, Team 61, 6th Platoon, 1st Force Recon, 8 August 1966]

Recons of the Groucho Marx patrol again congratulated themselves. Once again they had pinpointed the enemy and had called artillery fire onto him. They had undoubtedly done damage. Yet, they knew the North Vietnamese now would intensify the search for them, so it was time to radio for help from Deadlock gunships.

Remarks: There are two instances where air and artillery cannot be used simultaneously. One is when it is necessary for aircraft to

cross the gun-target line for attacking a target. The other is when it is desired to attack the same target with both air and artillery.
[2nd Bn., 4th Marines, Command Chronology, August 1966]

Dong Ha, 8 August 1966, 1000 Hours: Maj. Fred Seitz manned the MAG-16 (call-sign, *Rose-Ann*) Op's North GP tent south of the dirt airstrip. The Recon radioman at Dong Ha relayed to him a request from Groucho Marx: "Launch the gunships." Within five minutes a pair of Hueys was airborne and headed westward. The Deadlock pilots tuned to 49.6 on their FM radios and contacted Groucho Marx, unseen and concealed in the vast valley below.

> I recommended to Punctuate 6 *[the Task Unit Charlie infantry commander]* that the Recon team, 4 men, be retracted.
> *[Capt. Ben Meharg, USMC, typed account, 11 August 1966]*

Via his PRC-25 radio Cpl. Bachta explained that NVA soldiers were mainly to the west and north of the team. This information was of no value to the gunship pilots because they could not see where Groucho Marx was concealed. The Recons dared not "pop smoke" (meaning, *use a smoke grenade*), for that would mark their position for friend and foe alike. Finally they took a calculated risk. Using their M-14s, they fired white phosphorus marking grenades toward the enemy soldiers. Now the gunships had something to shoot at, so they flipped their arming switches and rolled in hot.

> Gunships were called on station. The patrol fired WP grenades to indicate locations of the enemy for the gunships to strafe the area.
> *[Groucho Marx Patrol Report, Team 61, 6th Platoon, 1st Force Recon, 8 August 1966]*

Concern was soaring at the Op's North tent at Dong Ha. Groucho Marx was doing an exemplary job, but they were under pressure. Perhaps it was time to extract the patrol. Not yet, the Recons radioed, because there was a potential helicopter landing area only 150 meters away. It was small but, one at a time, helicopters would be able to land there. If Marine reinforcements were flown to the valley they might be able to capture a prisoner, one of the original objectives of the Recon mission.

Captured Personnel: The term "prisoner of war" will not be used . .
. since this is not a declared war. For operations in Vietnam the
term "captive" will be used in reference to all prisoners . . . .
[Task Unit Charlie, Operational Order 1-66, 23 June 1966]

Every Marine, infantrymen and aircrewmen alike, knew the fate of captured NVA soldiers at Dong Ha. They would arrive bound with com-wire, their arms tied behind their backs. Their ankles would be tied together, and often their legs would be bent backwards and tied to their arms, bending their bodies like a bow. Such prisoners were totally immobile. They would be untied prior to interrogation and offered water and a cigarette. After lengthy questioning by Marine intelligence, aided by a Vietnamese interpreter, captives would be taken to an ARVN compound and turned over to South Vietnamese soldiers. They would promptly "die from malaria."

Dong Ha, 8 August 1966, 1320 Hours: A quick decision at Dong Ha involved Maj. Seitz from Op's North and Maj. Dwain Colby from 1st Force Recon. Also involved was Capt. Howard Lee (call-sign, *Pennant Winner Echo*), commander of Echo Company (the "Bald Eagle" company) from the 2nd Battalion, 4th Marines. They all agreed that Groucho Marx would be left in place. A "Sparrow Hawk" reaction force would be flown into the valley to link-up with the Recon team.

Marines in Vietnam had adopted the Sparrow Hawk concept. It consisted of a rapid reaction team of infantrymen that could be helicoptered into the field to exploit contact with the enemy. The concept drew its name from the small hawk of the genus *Accipitridae*. Known for its courage and ferocity, the miniature falcon could strike like lightning. Sparrow Hawk was a stone cold killer.

Maintain one platoon on 30-minute alert during daylight hours to reinforce/extract reconnaissance *[teams]* in *[enemy]* contact.
[Task Unit Charlie, Operational Order 1-66, 23 June 1966]

"Launch Sparrow Hawk!" Six H-46s from HMM-265 (call-sign, *Bonnie-Sue*) loaded-up with 40 infantrymen from Echo Company.

Unlike the Recons, these Marines were going into the valley to fight. Escorted by Deadlock gunships from VMO-2, the tandem rotor H-46s clawed their way into the afternoon sky and churned westward toward Razorback Valley.

Sparrow Hawk infantrymen riding in the helicopter cabins had no inkling of what lay in store for them during the next 21 hours. For those who would survive, those coming hours would prove to be an unforgettable time in their lives.

War is a rough, violent trade.
[Johann Schiller, <u>The Piccolomini</u>, 1799]

Two concealed Recons prepare to call artillery fire onto NVA troops. Note the old "grease gun" (photo courtesy of U.S. Marine Corps).

Two members of the "Touchdown" Recon team call for gunship fire support below the DMZ (photo courtesy of U.S. Marine Corps).

1st Force Recons killed this tiger that had crept too close to their harbor site (photo courtesy of U.S. Marine Corps).

Two compromised Recons from the 3rd Recon Battalion fire at NVA troops near Con Thien (photo courtesy of U.S. Marine Corps).

*A corporal from the 3rd Recon Battalion radios for an artillery fire
mission against NVA troops (photo courtesy of U.S. Marine Corps).*

A camouflaged Recon takes a helicopter ride toward his insertion coordinates (photo courtesy of U.S. Marine Corps).

Badly damaged by NVA fire, this H-46 landed in a river, the only clear area available. A maintenance team readies the helicopter for external lift by an H-53 (photo courtesy of U.S. Marine Corps).

One could reach the peak of the famous "Rockpile" by helicopter. At map coordinates XD-979558, it offered Marines an unparalleled observation post in Razorback Valley (photo by the author).

Members of a Marine patrol are almost invisible in the tall elephant grass as they make their way toward the top of a hill. This type of rolling terrain and thick ground cover was common in "Leatherneck Square" northwest of Dong Ha. The flat coastal plain lay to the east, and the rugged mountains and dense jungles lay to the west (photo courtesy of U.S. Marine Corps).

Two H-46 helicopter pilots from HMM-161 examine another tiger that decided to attack a Recon team harbor site. Recons won the battle (photo courtesy of U.S. Marine Corps).

Marines fire a 105mm howitzer in support of a Recon team (photo courtesy of U.S. Marine Corps).

This shot-down Huey was picked up as an "external sling load" and salvaged by a big H-53 (photo courtesy of U.S. Marine Corps).

The Groucho Marx Battle

I saw the battle-corpses, myriads of them,
And the white skeletons of young men – I saw them,
I saw the debris, and debris of all the dead soldiers of the war.
But I saw they were not as was thought,
They themselves were fully at rest – they suffered not;
The living remain'd and suffer'd . . . .
*[Walt Whitman, When Lilacs Last in the Door-Yard
Bloom'd, 1865]*

Razorback Valley, 8 August 1966, 1310 Hours: One at a time the
big Boeing H-46s flew down, landed in the tiny LZ, and dropped off
the Sparrow Hawk reaction force from Echo Company. Not a shot
was fired. The HMM-265 pilots pulled in collective pitch, and the
tandem rotor helicopters headed back toward Dong Ha, their jobs
over for the moment. Two Deadlock Huey gunships from VMO-2
remained in a racetrack orbit over the big valley. They waited to see
if Marine infantrymen or the four Recons needed help from their
7.62mm machineguns and 2.75-inch rockets.

1310H, Mission 8-7001: Two UH-1Es flew SAR *[meaning, search
and rescue]* for retraction of "Groucho Marx," did not make pickup,
put in reaction force instead.
[VMO-2, Command Chronology, 8 August 1966]

2ndLt. Andrew Sherman commanded the reaction force, and his
Marines quickly moved to the top of a nearby small knoll at XD-
986599. There was no contact with North Vietnamese soldiers. They
had melted away into the dense brush that covered the valley floor.
About 15 to 20 fighting holes, dug by either the North Vietnamese or
the Marines sometime during the past three weeks of fighting, circled
the crest of the little hillock.

The patrol moved back 100 meters, while *[a]* reaction force was
landed 200 meters to the west. The patrol linked up with the

reaction force and moved to the top of a hill at XD-986599. There they set up a defensive perimeter.
[Groucho Marx Patrol Report, Team 61, 6th Platoon, 1st Force Recon, 8 August 1966]

Seeing where the relief force had gone, the four men of Groucho Marx started toward them. They walked down a ridge, across some deep ravines, and within 30 minutes they linked-up with the Marines from Echo Company. With his equipment, weapons, and radio, Cpl. Bachta had humped over 100 pounds. The heat, exertion, and steep terrain had sapped his strength. He was exhausted when he got to the knoll. All his water was gone. HM3 Nick Tarzia, the corpsman with the Sparrow Hawk force, gave him a full canteen to perk him up.

SSgt. Donaldson, the Recon team leader, told Sherman where the Groucho Marx team last had seen NVA soldiers. Donaldson also stressed that many North Vietnamese troops were in the vicinity and that Echo Company had better be ready to fight. Sherman and his platoon sergeant, Sgt. Robert Pace (not to be confused with Cpl. James Pace), set up a defensive perimeter atop the little hill.

There were *[fighting]* holes already on the hill. That's the only thing that saved us.
[Robert Callaway, oral account, 23 January 2015]

Razorback Valley, 8 August 1966, 1355 Hours: Sherman and Pace sent one squad down to search the streambed where NVA soldiers had been sighted earlier in the day. For almost two hours the squad poked and probed through thick undergrowth within 150 meters of the knoll. They moved slowly, methodically, a few steps at a time. Their eyes flicked back and forth, lizard-like, scanning for almost invisible monofilament trip wires or electrical detonating cord. They found plenty of freshly dug protective holes, remnants of cooking fires that were still warm, and other evidence that North Vietnamese troops had been there. They also found several telltale trip wires where NVA soldiers had left their trademark booby traps. Grenades would be activated by snagging a thin wire stretched at ankle height across trails. When the squad completed its search of the streambed area it returned to the knoll.

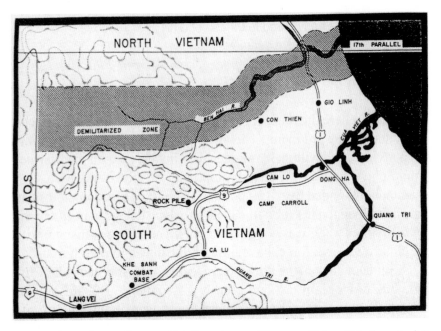

Map of northern Quang Tri Province. The small knoll is located 2 miles north of the Rockpile and 13 miles west of the Dong Ha combat base (map courtesy of U.S. Marine Corps).

[The squad] reported finding fresh signs of enemy activity and a few booby traps.
[Capt. Ben Meharg, USMC, typed account, 11 August 1966]

The North Vietnamese had gone, it seemed. They evidently had melted away somewhere into the surrounding jungle. Each Marine silently wondered to himself: "Where did the NVA go? How far away? Will they return? When?"

1445H, Mission 8-6001B: Two UH-1Es relieved TAC(A) on station *[over the valley]* in connection with Groucho Marx . . . .
[VMO-2, Command Chronology, 8 August 1966]

By now it was late afternoon. SSgt. Donaldson had been in the valley for over two days, so Lt. Sherman asked for his opinion. Donaldson opined that if Marines stayed atop the knoll the NVA eventually would hit them. He suggested that they be extracted.

Back at Dong Ha it had become "drop dead" time. Clouds had begun building in the west, and the forecast called for a solid overcast before nightfall. Clouds shrouding the valley would have invisible mountains for teeth. A low overcast would prevent use of fixed-wing close air support. At night even helicopters might not be able to get under the clouds and reach the knoll without slamming into an unseen mountain. If the reaction force and Recons were going to be pulled out of the valley, now was the time to start.

Razorback Valley, 8 August 1966, 1630 Hours: The H-46s had left Dong Ha to fly back to Marble Mountain. They had been replaced by eight Sikorsky H-34s from HMM-161 (call-sign, *Barrelhouse*) based at Phu Bai. At Op's North, Capt. Bob Mills (call-sign, *Rose-Ann Two*) assigned the extraction frag to the H-34s. Escorted by two Deadlock gunships, the eight helicopters arrived over the original landing area to which Sherman's infantrymen and the four Recons had returned. The small landing zone was supposedly secure, so one H-34 spiraled down alone to begin the extraction process.

Donaldson knew the Recon team axiom: stay together no matter what happens. He hated to split-up his team, but he believed that Echo Company *needed* him. He planned to put his two new Recons on one of the first H-34s. He and Cpl. Bachta, who had a PRC-25 radio, would ride out on the last helicopter.

The first H-34 landed and loaded-up with five Sparrow Hawk troops and the two new Recons. The H-34 took off and climbed skyward. As the Sikorsky warhorse cleared the treetops an enemy machinegun opened fire.

The chopper received heavy automatic weapons fire from the east. *[Groucho Marx Patrol Report, Team 61, 6th Platoon, 1st Force Recon, 8 August 1966]*

Three more H-34s swooped down, one at a time, but now the NVA opened up from another ridge north of the landing zone. One of the weapons firing was a 12.7mm machinegun. Marines could see its big green tracers and hear its heavy *thump-thump-thump-thump*. Rounds whipped through the air and tore through aluminum skins of the H-34s. Sherman and his Marines moved to the western side of the hill, trying to escape NVA fire from the east and north.

The two selected Recons and 18 infantrymen from the Sparrow Hawk force managed to get aboard four of the H-34s. The pilots cranked on full power and clawed their way over the treetops, heading eastward toward Dong Ha.

> The helicopters were getting hit. I watched the smoke roll out of two of them. . . . It looked like fuel was pouring out of one.
> *[Billy Donaldson, oral account, 29 January 1999]*

One of the helicopters targeted by the NVA was YR-22 (spoken, *Yankee-Romeo twenty-two*), and its two aircrewmen were alternates. Sgt. Jonah Waipa substituted for the regular crew chief, and Cpl. Ronald Belknap had volunteered to substitute for the regular gunner. Belknap, age 22, a Chicago native, was scheduled to rotate back to the United States the next month. He hunched over his door-mounted M-60 machinegun and scanned the terrain below him.

> The eight HMM-161 *[helicopters]* received overwhelming automatic weapons fire.
> *[MAG-16, Command Chronology, 8 August 1966]*

On the ground an NVA machinegunner aimed upward at YR-22 and squeezed his trigger. One of his heavy 12.7mm rounds tore through the fuselage, wounded two infantrymen passengers, and struck Belknap in the back of his neck and head. Belknap jerked, twitched, and then his body crumpled to the floor of the helicopter cabin. Waipa knelt by his friend and tried to help, but the young corporal was beyond mortal aid.

> Belknap, Ronald Lee, Cpl., KIA, Died 8Aug66 . . . result *[of]* missile wound to the right side of the neck and back of the head . . . .
> *[Cas.Card, Cpl. Ronald Belknap, USMC, 8 August 1966]*

On the ground the rate of incoming NVA fire intensified. Despite the danger the remaining H-34s started down to pick up the rest of the Marines, but Lt. Sherman waved them away. He and his remaining men made a dash back toward the knoll, where deep fighting holes waited for them. Over two hours of daylight were still left, and Sherman thought the small knoll would be easily defensible. He had plenty of ammunition, so he and his men reoccupied holes atop the knoll and waited for the NVA to make the next move.

> Further retraction was made impossible due to the volume of fire coming from North Vietnamese troops on all sides of, and as close as fifteen yards from, the Marine perimeter. *[and also]* Only three of the original eight *[H-34s]* were still operational . . . .
> *[USMC citation referencing 8 August 1966]*

Sherman, his men, and the two remaining Recons were on classic defensive terrain. They held high ground surrounded by gullies and ravines. The top of the little knoll was only about 15 meters in diameter. Yet, there were clear fields of fire on all sides, and there was almost no vegetation to block the defenders' view. Further, Marines were protected in fighting holes. Any attacking force surely would suffer horrible casualties. However, North Vietnamese commanders now knew exactly where the Americans were located. For almost a half-hour the NVA marshaled their forces and massed in ravines and gullies north and east of the knoll.

> The enemy, in company strength, tried to assault the Marine position.
> *[Jack Shulimson, U.S. Marines in Vietnam: An Expanding War, 1966, 1982]*

Razorback Valley, 8 August 1966, 1655 Hours: About 200 to 250 enemy soldiers charged the 24 Marines. Tan-clad North Vietnamese troops poured out of the surrounding jungle and ran up the eastern side of the knoll. Everyone was firing, yelling, screaming. Incoming rifle fire sent copper-jacketed death whistling toward Marines atop the small hill, and the rounds made quick sucking sounds as they zipped past. The din of battle rose to a deafening crescendo. One Marine later would write:

> They were screaming bloody murder during the first charge, like they were crazy drunk or something.

PFC Robert Callaway watched the onrushing NVA soldiers as they threw themselves against the tiny perimeter on the knoll.

> They hit us all of a sudden. I saw this one guy yelling and waving his arms around. He looked like a squad leader or platoon commander. I shot him. We were shooting them with pistols and throwing grenades like they were going out of style.
> *[PFC Robert Callaway, USMC, quoted in Pacific Stars and Stripes, August 1966]*

Tactically, Sherman had done well. He had put his men in wedge formation, one squad forward facing the expected attack from the east, and two squads back. He stood in the center with Donaldson and Bachta. Marines fought with M-14s, M-60s, M-79s, pistols, and grenades, everything they had. Donaldson knew the men did not have enough ammunition to continue firing indefinitely, so he yelled at the top of his voice: "Watch your ammo! Watch your ammo!"

> 081700H: *[The NVA]* were able to come within hand grenade throwing range. Most of the *[Marine]* casualties came from wounds inflicted by the fragments of the grenades.
> *[Groucho Marx Patrol Report, Team 61, 6th Platoon, 1st Force Recon, 8 August 1966]*

In response to the sudden onslaught from the east the Marines instinctively pulled back to the western slope of the hill. Attacking NVA soldiers had taken the hilltop. Many of them jumped into fighting holes that Marines had vacated only moments before. The two adversaries continued to fire and lob grenades at each other.

Lt. Sherman realized his plight. The enemy vastly outnumbered his men, the enemy now held the high ground, and the enemy had occupied the fighting holes. He and his Marines had to retake the hilltop. Otherwise they all would be dead men.

> They *[had]* pushed us off the hill. We had to take it back, or die.
> *[George Gibson, oral account, 26 February 2015]*

Sherman led the charge. His men followed him, firing from the hip, yelling blasphemous obscenities, and screaming like savages. They had no choice. No one faltered. One who charged up the slope was soft-spoken LCpl. George Gibson.

> Gibson leaped from protective cover and charged into the enemy fire. Although painfully wounded by a grenade he continued to press the attack until the original positions had been retaken. . . .
> He crossed 25 meters of fire-swept terrain.
> *[USMC citation referencing 8 August 1966]*

When they reached the hilltop, PFC Benjamin Hamrick stood beside Gibson. An NVA grenade bounced to a stop three feet away. Gibson dove aside and shouted: "Get down!" Hamrick remained on his feet. Perhaps he did not see the grenade. Maybe he did not hear the warning above the din of battle. The violent blast knocked him into the air and drove hot shrapnel into his torso.

Shocked by the unexpected Marine charge, the NVA retreated down the eastern and northern slopes of the hill. Marine infantrymen and the two Recons again held crucial high ground and its protective fighting holes. Sherman, standing erect atop the knoll, shouted to his men: "Cease fire! Cease fire!"

The Echo Company corpsman, HM3 Nick Tarzia, went from man to man, treating those who had been wounded. Stopping the bleeding was his immediate aim. Most wounds had come from hand grenades, not from rifle fire.

> Hamrick, Benjamin Neal, PFC, KIA, Died 8Aug66 result *[of]* multiple fragmentation wounds penetrating entire body . . . .
> *[Cas. Card, PFC Benjamin Hamrick, USMC, 8 August 1966]*

Gibson pulled Hamrick into a hole atop the hill as Marines set up a defensive perimeter. Hamrick was in agony. Tarzia worked on him and did his best, but the wounds were too severe. Hamrick slowly would bleed to death while lying in the hole with Gibson.

After the Marines reoccupied the hill and the firing slacked off, one man was missing. LCpl. Richard Iverson last had been seen standing his ground on the eastern slope and firing into the attacking horde. Marines looked down the slope. Iverson was still there, still alive, lying helpless, shot and bayoneted. In addition a grenade had shattered his femur between his pelvis and knee. He lay 35 to 40 feet below the Marine perimeter and only 30 feet above the NVA soldiers, who were concealed in thick brush at the base of the hill.

Iverson, Richard Leland, LCpl., WIA, 8Aug66, fragmentation wound left knee *[and other wounds]*.
[Cas.Card, LCpl. Richard Iverson, USMC, 8 August 1966]

The enemy could have killed Iverson when they took the hill. Now he was only 30 feet away from them, and they could finish him off at any time. Any woodsman, any hunter, and any infantryman would understand. To the NVA, Iverson was more valuable alive than dead. He was bait. North Vietnamese soldiers knew Iverson's Marine brothers would not leave him lying there.
"Covering fire! Covering fire!"

Retrieving wounded comrades from the field of fire is a Marine Corps tradition more sacred than life.
[Robert Pisor, The End of the Line, 1982]

Marines began a furious barrage, shooting into thick brush at the eastern base of the hill. The NVA fired back. Cpl. Douglas Van ignored the firestorm, jumped up, and dashed down the slope to Iverson. He grabbed the wounded man by his web gear and began dragging him up the hill. Maybe blind luck should get the credit, or perhaps divine intervention was involved. In either event Van did not get a scratch (his good fortune would end four weeks later on 9 September). Iverson was badly wounded, but he would survive.

Razorback Valley, 8 August 1966, 1730 Hours: For 30 minutes the North Vietnamese waited for reinforcements to trickle in from the east and north. Enemy soldiers around the knoll apparently did not have radios, for shrill whistles (similar to those a basketball referee would use) and verbal shouts were their main means of communicating. NVA troops regrouped and then charged the knoll again. They swarmed up the slopes toward the little perimeter, yelling and shrieking like demons.

Second assault . . . *[The NVA]* once again broke contact after throwing more grenades and firing into *[the]* position of the patrol. *[Groucho Marx Patrol Report, Team 61, 6th Platoon, 1st Force Recon, 8 August 1966]*

Marines also beat back the second attack, but not without cost. More infantrymen had been hit, mostly by shrapnel from grenades. However, one of the exceptions was the platoon commander, Sherman. While standing erect and directing the fire of his men, the Ohioan had been shot in the head. The young officer, a recently commissioned mustang, was dead before his knees hit the dirt.

On the second assault there was some hand-to-hand *[fighting]*. I saw Sherman get hit. He stood up, *[got]* shot in the face, *[and was]* killed instantly.
[Tom Bachta, oral account, 15 January 1999]

He *[Lt. Sherman]* did a whale of a job for the last few minutes of his life. He inspired everybody. . . . I was looking straight at him. He took a round in the head. He died instantly.
[Billy Donaldson, oral account, 29 January 1999]

Sherman, Andrew Marco, 2Lt., KIA, Died 8Aug66, result *[of]* gunshot wound to the head . . . .
[Cas.Card, 2ndLt. Andrew Sherman, USMC, 8 August 1966]

Razorback Valley, 8 August 1966, 1800 Hours: With the lieutenant dead, command of the beleaguered Americans passed to the platoon sergeant, Sgt. Robert Pace. None of the Marines panicked. They were military professionals. They had been through adversity before. This was not their first fight.

Soon the NVA charged the knoll once again, and this time they came from the west, north, and the east. Sgt. Pace, now in command of the platoon, stood atop the hill. He yelled to his men to stay in their holes and keep firing.

Pace, Robert Lynn, Sgt., WIA, 8Aug66, fragmentation wound face.
[Cas.Card, Sgt. Robert Pace, USMC, 8 August 1966]

Suddenly a Chinese stick-grenade bounced to a stop by Pace's feet. As he looked down, it detonated. The concussion knocked him into the air and momentarily numbed his entire body. Jagged steel ripped into his head below his left eye.

> I *[tried to]* put a battle dressing over my eye. I wasn't sure *[my eye]* was still there. I couldn't see out of it.
> *[Robert Pace, oral account, 10 February 2015]*

Donaldson saw that Pace was rattled. He was trying to tie a battle dressing over the wound, but in doing so he had covered both of his eyes. Donaldson grabbed Pace and pulled the dressing down so that he could see. Pace relaxed, got a mental grip, and went back into the firing line.

Suddenly a grenade rolled to a stop in front of Donaldson. He reached down, grabbed it, and hurled it back toward the NVA. As it left his fingertips it exploded. Hot jagged steel tore into the right side of his head and his right arm.

> Donaldson, Billy Marvin, SSgt., WIA, 8Aug66, fragmentation wound, right arm and head.
> *[Cas.Card, SSgt. Billy Donaldson, USMC, 8 August 1966]*

Standing nearby, Bachta had watched as the grenade detonated near Donaldson's head. He saw his friend, the Recon team leader, crumple to the ground like a child's limp rag doll. Donaldson lay on the knoll, unconscious for the moment.

> The grenade took off part of the right side of his head. It went off right by his head. His skull was wide open. . . . I escaped injury by the grace of God.
> *[Tom Bachta, oral account, 5 January 1999]*

Although stunned by the blast, Donaldson slowly regained his senses. He reached up where his right ear should have been. It was gone. The grenade blast had caused extreme neurological damage. Donaldson's hands were paralyzed. He could move his arms, but not his fingers. He could not grasp anything, and he could not stand up or crawl.

Bachta initially had thought his friend was dead, for the massive injury to the staff sergeant's head was obvious. Then Bachta noticed Donaldson as he began to thrash around. He keyed the mike on his PRC-25 radio and exclaimed:

Groucho Marx Actual is out of action! *[after a short pause]* No, he's just WIA!

The NVA again broke off the attack, but Marines on the knoll were in deep trouble. At least half of them were wounded, some from rifle fire, others from grenades. Ammunition was running out, and daylight was running out. The sun would set in little more than two hours. Worse yet, as minutes slowly ticked away more North Vietnamese reinforcements slipped in to join their comrades in the dense brush surrounding the small knoll. NVA troops massed to the east, north, and west of the little hill.

Leadership on the knoll had been ravaged. Lt. Sherman was dead. Sgt. Pace was severely wounded. SSgt. Donaldson was incoherent and could not walk or crawl. Bachta put a poncho under his friend's head "to hold it together" and put him in a deep hole. Marines atop the knoll knew they were in dire peril. Bachta keyed the mike on his PRC-25 and explained that more ammunition and more grenades were needed desperately. "Hurry!" he radioed.

Marines and the NVA around the little knoll continued to trade rifle fire and grenades. The Americans were protected in fighting holes, but that protection was not absolute. One of the infantrymen, Cpl. Dennis Schmidt, rose up and leaned forward to fire at the enemy below. That proved to be a fatal mistake. The NVA shot him. One enemy round struck him in the right shoulder. Another hit him in the lower chest.

Schmidt, Dennis Richard, Cpl., KIA, Died 8Aug66 . . . result *[of]* gunshot wounds penetrating right shoulder and lower chest . . . .
[Cas.Card, Cpl. Dennis Schmidt, USMC, 8 August 1966]

Schmidt had been born in East Chester, Canada, in 1945 and had enlisted in the Marine Corps in New York in 1964. Although shot twice, he did not die quickly. The corpsman, Tarzia, worked hard to save him, but Schmidt's lifeblood slowly oozed away. He died curled up in a fetal position in a shallow hole 12,000 miles from home.

PFC Callaway, a machinegun team leader on the eastern side of the knoll, had been wounded three months earlier in May. However, he eventually had recovered and had returned to duty.

Callaway, Robert Bruce, PFC, WIA, 4 May66, fragmentation wounds *[to]* both arms and right side of chest.
[Cas.Card, PFC Robert Callaway, USMC, 4 May 1966]

On the little knoll Callaway crouched in a hole with his gunner, Cpl. David Smith. They looked at each other without speaking, for both of them realized what they faced. They were professionals, but now it seemed that their time on Earth had almost run its course. Callaway finally spoke, almost in a whisper. There was no fear, just a statement of simple resignation.

"Well, Smitty – it looks like this could be it."

"Yeah, but I'm gonna' take as many with me as I can."

"Right," Callaway quietly agreed.

We were just stating facts. We had been surrounded by God only knows how many *[NVA soldiers]*. There was no way a relief force could reach us. Smitty and I figured we were gone.
[Robert Callaway, oral account, 21 January 2015]

Realizing the odds against them, Callaway and Smith wordlessly shared a prized possession, a *last supper* of sorts. Hunkering down deep in their hole, they opened a green tin of fruit cocktail that had been saved from a C-Ration box. Together they ate the delicacy.

All around the perimeter Echo Company infantrymen had reeled under the effect of NVA rifle fire and grenades. Most remained able to fire and fight. Others had suffered grievous incapacitating injuries. North Vietnamese attacks were taking a deadly toll.

Stevens, Tommy E., Sgt., WIA, 8 Aug66, Quang Tri Province, RVN.
[E/2/4, Unit Diary, August 1966]

Swartz, James Joseph, PFC, WIA, 8Aug66, fragmentation wounds
left wrist and left shoulder.
[Cas.Card, PFC James Swartz, USMC, 8-9 August 1966]

Some wounds were not life threatening and did not prevent a
Marine from defending the perimeter. Cpl. Danny Vance, whose
home of record was Cleveland, Ohio, had been hit by shrapnel in the
right leg and knee. He still could fight.

Vance, Danny Ray, Cpl., WIA, 8Aug66, fragmentation wound *[in]*
right knee.
[Cas.Card, Cpl. Danny Vance, USMC, 8-9 August 1966]

Razorback Valley, 8 August 1966, 1835 Hours: Pilots and aircrewmen from HMM-161 rushed to fly reinforcements, ammunition, and
water to fellow Marines on the knoll. With two H-34 cabins loaded
with troops and ammunition crates they flew westward to the
Rockpile, turned north, and then swooped down toward the encircled
Marines. Around the base of the knoll tall undergrowth covered the
terrain. The only clear place to land was right on top of the small
knoll and inside the perimeter, which was only about 15 meters in
diameter. NVA soldiers knew this, and they were waiting for the
helicopters. Sheets of fire tore into the Barrelhouse H-34s as they
approached. Landing on the knoll surrounded by the enemy would
have been suicidal. Nonetheless, the two helicopters made a low pass
over the hill. Crew chiefs kicked out crates of ammunition.

The helicopter squadrons were manned by saints and angels. . . .
The aircraft did a wonderful job of supporting us, absolutely superb.
[Dwain Colby, in a letter, 17 February 1999]

Dong Ha, 8 August 1966, 1840 Hours: At his command post at
Dong Ha the Echo Company commander, Capt. Howard Lee, a New
York native who had grown up in the Bronx, knew what had to be
done. Without more ammunition his trapped men on the little knoll
would not survive. There was no safe place for helicopters to land,
but he had to try. In the battalion GP tent he explained his risky plan
to LtCol. Arnold Bench, the experienced 2nd Battalion commander.

Bench approved the plan.

Back at Echo Company, Lee explained the danger and asked for six volunteers to fly with him to Razorback Valley. The sudden response brought tears to the eyes of many. The Marines of Echo Company all stood up and volunteered.

Two H-34 crews from HMM-161 got the frag for the hazardous resupply attempt. The 7.62mm ammunition came in metal cans, which were packaged inside wooden crates. With all the ammunition crates and grenades they could carry, Capt. Lee and his radioman, LCpl. Gary Butler, clambered aboard one of the helicopters. LCpl. Roger Baca and another Marine hopped in after them. Three more men packed additional ammunition into the second Sikorsky warhorse and then crawled aboard. The helicopters launched and headed westward in the company of VMO-2 Huey gunships.

I didn't want to abandon those men out there.
[Herb Kennedy, oral account, 14 October 1999]

The success or failure of this late afternoon resupply attempt could not be predicted in advance, and the dwindling hour of daylight remaining was crucial. Op's North prepared for a worst case scenario and flashed an urgent message to Marble Mountain: "Emergency medevac, four H-46s needed at Dong Ha ASAP."

Razorback Valley, 8 August 1966, 1850 Hours: H-34s carrying Capt. Lee and his six volunteers radioed the gunship pilots. There were two Huey pilots in command, Maj. Wayne Hazelbaker and 1stLt. Bud Willis. They tried to help H-34 crews figure out a place where they could land. The NVA had everything zeroed-in on the knoll, so trying to land there would be akin to insanity.

Any approach *[and landing on]* that hill by a resupply helicopter would have been tantamount to a suicide mission.
[Bud Willis, Marble Mountain, 2011]

The gunships and H-34s both tuned to the Recon radio frequency, 49.6. After getting radioed advice from Marines on the ground, the pilots made their best guess and zipped down toward the battle below.

In the cabins behind the cockpits the seven infantrymen were tightly strapped into web troop seats. They held their M-14s between their knees, muzzles up, butt plates resting on the metal floor.

In the helicopters headed down into the ongoing battle, Capt. Lee and his men had no control over their immediate fate. Like all infantrymen, they considered transportation by helicopter to be an occupational hazard, a mode of travel to be avoided when humanly possible. A Marine infantryman is in his element when he is on the ground in a firefight. There he has some control over his future, or at least the *illusion* of control. However, in a helicopter under fire he has no control whatsoever, not even the illusion of it.

> The only place in the world I wanted to be was off of that chopper. . . . It was the most helpless feeling in the world.
> [*John Hagler, quoted in <u>Marines, Medals, & Vietnam</u>, 2012*]

For these infantrymen, the helicopter ride into the hot LZ was terrifying. Strapped into troop seats, they were buffeted by vibrations from a twisting high speed autorotative descent. The metallic whine of the transmission combined with engine wail and the whop-whop-whop of the rotors. Battered by tooth jarring shudders from invisible rotor wash of a preceding helicopter, hearing the crackle of rifle fire below, infantrymen in the two helicopters were powerless to respond. Swept along by unseen aerodynamic and mechanical forces beyond their control and understanding, they prayed for the relative safety of a firefight on solid ground.

> We came in hot. We had rounds going through the chopper when we landed.
> [*Gary Butler, e-mail message, 26 February, 2015*]

1stLt. Herb Kennedy piloted the first H-34. He swooped down and managed to land on the steep southern slope of the knoll between the perimeter and the NVA soldiers. Capt. Lee and his three men leaped out. They and the crew chief began dragging out ammunition crates. Kennedy looked down from his cockpit and saw Sgt. Pace, the platoon sergeant who had been hit in the head by shrapnel.

I looked down and saw the Marine standing there, looking up at me. His face was covered with blood.
[Herb Kennedy, oral account, 14 October 1999]

Rounds whipped through the aluminum skin of the H-34. When Capt. Lee and his men got the ammunition out of the cabin the crew chief keyed his ICS: " Go! Go! Go! Go!"

As the pilot pulled in power the crew chief noticed Sgt. Pace standing by the helicopter. Blood was streaming from his head. The young aircrewman screamed above the noise of the engine and rotors: "Get in! Get in!" He reached through the open cargo door, grabbed the wounded man's arm, and snatched him into the helicopter cabin. The Sikorsky flying machine rose, shuddered through translational lift, and headed skyward.

As *[the H-34]* was lifting off the crew chief grabbed my arm and lifted me inside. We were under heavy fire.
[Robert Pace, handwritten note, 18 February 2015]

Both H-34s had been hit; they had been riddled. Trailing smoke, they clawed their way skyward and out of the valley. The pilots had done their jobs. They pointed the bulbous noses of their damaged helicopters eastward and raced toward Dong Ha.

Lugging ammunition crates, Capt. Lee and his three Marines ran into the tiny perimeter on the knoll. The NVA were shooting at the hilltop, and Marines were firing back. As he stumbled into the perimeter and jumped into a hole, Capt. Lee saw his radio operator, LCpl. Butler, take a round in the arm.

Butler, Gary Norman, LCpl., WIA, 8Aug66, gunshot wound right arm
[Cas.Card, LCpl. Gary Butler, USMC, 8 August 1966]

Butler's wound was in the fleshy part of his arm, and he was able to dive into a hole with Capt. Lee. His PRC-25 was undamaged. In a few minutes the firing tapered off. Capt. Lee took his silver metallic captain's bars off his shirt collars and tucked them into his pocket. The reason was obvious.

Resupply was made and a captain from Echo Company was
dropped off to take command.
*[Groucho Marx Patrol Report, Team 61, 6th Platoon, 1st
Force Recon, 8 August 1966]*

The other H-34 had landed on a narrow saddleback about 80
meters away. The three passengers had jumped out, but they found
themselves stranded. North Vietnamese soldiers were between them
and the Marines on the knoll.

We discovered that three men had been inadvertently dropped in
the wrong place *[behind the NVA]*.
[Capt. Ben Meharg, USMC, typed account, 11 August 1966]

Razorback Valley, 8 August 1966, 1910 Hours: The three men on
the saddleback were cut off, and they had no radio. Capt. Lee had
seen where the helicopter dropped the stranded men. He radioed the
Deadlock gunship pilots and asked if one of them could rescue the
three Marines.

Maj. Wayne Hazelbaker piloted one of the two gunships on
station. Deep shadows had settled over the terrain. Hazelbaker
talked it over with his copilot, 1stLt. Antony Costa, but they could not
spot the stranded men. Then they saw brilliant green smoke on the
saddleback – a smoke grenade! Hopefully it came from the three
Americans, not from North Vietnamese troops. Hazelbaker dumped
collective pitch, eased his cyclic forward, and the gunship dove
toward the valley floor.

We made two passes, and our door gunners were busy *[firing]*.
[Wayne Hazelbaker, in a letter, 12 December 1989]

On the third pass the gunship flared and plopped down onto the
saddleback. The stranded Marines leaped into the cabin. Hazelbaker
muscled his gunship into the air, then dove behind the saddleback so
that high terrain protected him from further NVA fire. He and his
wingman sped back to Dong Ha where they deposited the three
grateful infantrymen into friendly hands.

On and around the knoll both the NVA and Marines fired at any adversary they could see moving. When the enemy could not be seen in this war of attrition the combatants threw grenades toward likely places of concealment. Amid this maelstrom the corpsman, HM3 Tarzia, grabbed an M-14 from an unconscious WIA and fired back at the enemy below. Then, ignoring incoming fire all around him he repeatedly dropped the rifle, jumped to his feet, and rushed to assist wounded Marines.

> Tarzia repeatedly moved through withering enemy fire to aid the wounded. When his first aid pack was blown away by enemy fire, he used his own clothing for bandages. . . . He *[also]* gallantly helped defend his disabled comrades by manning a position on the defensive perimeter.
> *[USMC citation referencing 8-9 August 1966]*

Casualties on the hill continued to mount. By now over half of the Marines had been hit by rifle fire or grenade shrapnel. Sometimes the wounds were minor, and at other times they were incapacitating. Further, many Marines who had been wounded earlier were getting hit again. It was still daylight, and Tarzia treated those with minor and major injuries alike. The feared sucking chest wounds were evidenced by little pink bubbles that accompanied each labored breath and then burst within seconds.

> Corson, Richard, PFC, WIA, 8Aug66, gunshot wounds . . . left arm.
> *[Cas.Card, PFC Richard Corson, USMC, 8-9 August 1966]*

> Williams, Leroy, LCpl., WIA, 8Aug66, Quang Tri Province, RVN.
> *[E/2/4, Unit Diary, August 1966]*

> Smith, David A., Cpl., WIA, 8Aug66, Quang Tri Province, RVN.
> *[E/2/4, Unit Diary, August 1966]*

Marble Mountain, 8 August 1966, 1910 Hours: Seventy-five miles to the south at Marble Mountain, oblivious to fighting in Razorback Valley, standby helicopter crews in HMM-265 lounged on canvass cots in their hardback tents (known as, *hooches*). Tents housing the primitive O'Club and EM Club were not frequented by those on standby status for night missions. As long as base generators were running, each hooch could use its incandescent light bulb for late afternoon illumination. Some Marines on standby status wrote letters to their families in a faraway world. Others used small battery powered tape recorders in lieu of pen and paper.

The squadron duty officer banged on the side of several hooches: "Medevac at Dong Ha!" Affected men began gathering their flight gear, weapons, and body armor before trudging down to the ready room tent on the Marble Mountain flight line. In one hooch Capt. Ron Pfeifer, who was not one of the affected pilots, lay on his cot and lazily propped his head on his arm. Often called the Gentle Giant because of his soft-spoken demeanor and huge size, Pfeifer casually wished one of his five tentmates, 1stLt. Marion Sturkey, good luck on the flight. It probably would be quick and routine, he volunteered. The two pilots exchanged animated grins. Then for some reason Pfeifer turned deadly serious. He sat straight upright. Perhaps he had a vision, a premonition of things to come:

"Be *careful* up there tonight."

"See ya' in the morning," Sturkey quipped.

Although the young lieutenant had no way to know it, he would not see his friend the next morning. He *never* would see him again. Misfortune in Razorback Valley would delay his return for 116 days, and by then Pfeifer would be dead.

Pfeifer, Ronald Edwin, Capt., Died 6Oct66 . . . when the helicopter in which he was the copilot vanished. Body Not Recovered.
[Cas.Card, Capt. Ronald Pfeifer, USMC, 6 October 1966]

Crew chiefs and gunners went to the armory tent. Most of them chose two .50 caliber machineguns (affectionately called, *Ma Deuce*) for their helicopter. After mounting the guns they returned to the tent for load after load of ammunition. Meanwhile pilots gathered in the adjacent ready room tent. Only skimpy information was available. Marines were under attack and stranded on a small hill. The situation was fluid and evolving. Details would be worked out after the H-46s reached Dong Ha.

The four helicopters (call-sign, *Bonnie-Sue*) took off from Marble Mountain, flew out over the South China Sea, and paralleled the

Vietnamese coast as they flew northward. Within ten minutes they passed lofty Hai Van Pass. Next the city of Hue, on the coastal plain, fell behind them. Abeam of Quang Tri city the pilots angled north-westward, heading straight for Dong Ha and homing on its TACAN transceiver, Channel 46. The pilots tuned to 255.4 on their UHF radios and told Dong Ha Tower (in reality, *a traffic controller standing on the ground*) that they were inbound. Minutes later they squinted through swirling laterite dust and dim twilight as they landed in soft grass south of the dirt airstrip.

Dong Ha, Aerodrome Remarks: Electric *[runway]* lights *[are]* backed up by flare pots.
[VFR Enroute Supplement, Southeast Asia, 1967]

Dong Ha, 8 August 1966, 1950 Hours: In the cabin of Bonnie-Sue 9-3 the crew chief, Sgt. Herbert Murff, had been part of the Marine Corps H-46 program since its inception. Originally from Caruthersville, Missouri, the soft-spoken Murff was a skilled mechanic and a gutty career Marine. Back at New River, North Carolina, before the squadron had left for Vietnam, Murff had suffered a near fatal injury. He had fractured his skull when he fell from atop the open forward transmission clamshell doors on an H-46. From his hospital bed, Murff had pleaded with the squadron commanding officer not to leave for Vietnam without him (his wish was granted). LCpl. Luke Stephen, a relative newcomer, would assist Murff in the cabin, but already he had proved his mettle as a door gunner.

Time had become critical, for it was almost dark. The four helicopters taxied to the Dong Ha fuel pits to hot-point refuel. Crew chiefs topped-off the tanks with JP-4 jet fuel (essentially, *kerosene*). Per a radioed request from Op's North, pilots crawled out to go to a quick briefing. Copilots stayed strapped into their seats with both turbine engines running and rotors engaged.

Four minutes later each pilot returned, crawled in, strapped in, and used the helicopter ICS to explain the briefing to the rest of his crew. Crew chiefs and gunners made mental notes, while copilots filled in details on their kneeboard pads. Years later one of them would *find* that faded and long-lost kneeboard pad sheet with its skimpy details of Mission No. 591:

TIN — JOE R. ___166 -9-1___   #591
RICHEY — PAUL ___170-9-2___   steady dim
HARPO — SS ___163-9-3___
LEO — BUZ ___164-9-4___   ___

42.3 RoseAnn Alpha
49.6 Deadlock   280/10

MMRE to:	PAX	#
DONG HA	O	O
	15	O

Ridge to ESE
Fire — WNW
Bomb — Land

Copilot's kneeboard pad sheet, Mission No. 591, Bonnie-Sue 9-3: At Dong Ha the copilot added the FM radio frequency (42.3) for Op's North (call-sign, Rose-Ann Alpha) and the frequency (49.6) for Deadlock gunships and Marines on the knoll. He also added abbreviated notes about reported NVA positions. However, the mission would be interrupted at the knoll, and he never would get the chance to add further information.

Pilots told their crews that about 20 Marines were surrounded on a small and steep knoll. Some were dead, others were wounded, and they had fought off several attacks. H-34s earlier had tried to extract the infantrymen but had been driven away by heavy ground fire. Now the larger H-46s were going to land on or near the knoll and extract all surrounded Marines before complete darkness set in.

Bonnie-Sue 9-1, the flight leader, was ready to load-up with 15 reinforcements. Nine-dash-one would try to land on top of the knoll. According to the plan, the reinforcements would charge out of the helicopter and keep the NVA at bay. Dead and wounded men would be loaded aboard, and the H-46 would take off and head straight for the Dong Ha aid station. Then the remaining three helicopters would swoop down and land, one at a time. All remaining Marines would clamber aboard for a flight back to Dong Ha.

This rescue mission went downhill before it began. Nine-dash-one, flown by Capt. Dale Tinsley and Capt. Joe Roberts, fell prey to a major hydraulics problem. The helicopter would have to stay on the ground while mechanics tried to fix the malfunction. Pilots do not leave their wingman, so for the moment nine-dash-two would stay on the ground with nine-dash-one.

From Op's North, Maj. Fred Seitz ran to Bonnie-Sue 9-3, flown by Capt. Richard Harper and Lt. Sturkey. Seitz grabbed the external troop commander's ICS set. His voice remained steady, but the tension came through loud and clear:

"Get 'em out. You gotta' get 'em out."

"We'll get them."

Dong Ha, 8 August 1966, 2005 Hours: Nine-dash-three took the lead. The 15 reinforcements piled into the helicopter and strapped themselves into web troop seats lining each side of the cabin. The pilots pulled in full power and headed skyward into dim western twilight. Trailing behind was Bonnie-Sue 9-4, flown by Capt. Leo Farrell and Capt. Charles Joyner. In both helicopters the copilots reached down to their right and tuned to 49.6 on the FM radio so they could talk to Deadlock gunships and Marines on the knoll.

"Bonnie-Sue, you're gonna' take fire."

Deadlock pilots warned the H-46 crews. The NVA would target all helicopters that tried to land on or near the knoll. Further, there was no room for H-46s to land on top of the knoll because it was too small and steep. Besides, the NVA had everything zeroed-in on the crest of the little hill. But there was a relatively clear bombed-out area to the south-southwest about 25 meters from the top of the hill. One at a time, nine-dash-three and nine-dash-four probably would be able to squeeze down into it and land.

To be a Marine pilot is to be the chosen of the chosen.
[Jon Boule, quoted in Life on the Line*, 1988]*

According to Deadlock the heaviest NVA fire would come from the north and northwest. Whether or not the NVA also were in the bombed-out area was not known. The two gunships would stick with the H-46s and cover them on their approach, they radioed, but then the two big transport helicopters were on their own.

Razorback Valley, 8 August 1966, 2015 Hours: The two H-46s flew westward to the Rockpile, then turned north and slowed to 100 knots. The two gunships slipped in to join them, one on each side of Bonnie-Sue 9-3. In the faint twilight the gunships looked sinister and menacing while silhouetted against the sky.

It had become too dark to identify terrain features. The gunships and infantrymen would have to talk the H-46 pilots down. On the ICS, Capt. Harper again briefed his crew. In the cabin, Sgt. Murff manned the starboard machinegun. LCpl. Stephen manned the gun on the port side. After the Boeing helicopter landed, Murff would need to hustle the 15 reinforcements out in a hurry. Then the four-man crew would have to sit there and endure enemy fire until all dead and wounded Marines were loaded aboard.

The crew verbally rehearsed the plan via their ICS. Their voices were calm and steady. None of them had reservations despite the perils of their task. They had to succeed. Their only fear was the fear of making a dumb mistake, the fear of somehow letting their fellow Marines down. Their infantry brothers-in-arms depended upon them. Infantrymen rely upon helicopter crews in a way no men can fathom unless they have endured the crucible of warfare together. The crew of Bonnie-Sue 9-3 could not – *must not* – fail them.

"Get on here with me."

The copilot rogered Harper's request. For the record, Harper had elected to take the controls for this landing. Nonetheless, flying down into the maelstrom below the copilot would ride the collective, the cyclic, and rudder pedals with him – just in case.

Casualties were part of the profession of arms, the consequence of unsheathing a sword or aiming a gun.
[Michael Norman, These Good Men, 1989]

Guided by the gunships, Bonnie-Sue 9-3 turned eastward and

started down. This would be a power-on approach all the way, for the pilots could not yet see where they might land. Deadlock hung with them, radioing guidance. On the knoll the Echo Company radioman, LCpl. Butler, tried to help. His disembodied whispering voice was squeaky and several octaves too high. From experience the pilots knew why he was whispering. It was not a good omen.

The H-46 slowed to about 70 knots as it passed through 300 feet of altitude. Peering through the darkness, the pilots now could see the ground below. Dim twilight remaining revealed deep gullies and ravines all around the knoll. Where could they land? Where?

Buurrrrrppp!

Buurrrrrppp! Buurrrrrppp! Buurrrrrppp!

The gunships opened fire. Their tracers, beautiful at night, ripped downward and then seemed to slow, fade, and instantly vanish as soon as they struck the ground. Passing through 125 feet and about 60 knots the gunships no longer could maintain their nose-down firing attitude. They pulled in power, accelerated, and veered away. Now the crew of Bonnie-Sue 9-3 was all alone.

"Straight ahead, Bonnie-Sue."

"Roger."

Eighty feet above the ground the pilots could see the knoll and the nearby bomb crater, their intended landing area. Below lay a tangled mass of gullies, undergrowth, stumps, and felled tree trunks. In the dim twilight the pilots easily could have seen NVA muzzle flashes, but there were none. The copilot glimpsed a man as he jumped into a fighting hole on the western side of the knoll. Friend or foe? It was too dark to see clearly.

Down they went, lower and lower. Tree trunks littered the ground all around the bomb crater. The pilots glued their eyes to tree trunks standing south of the bombed area. They could not allow their rotors to rip into a large tree. Twenty-five feet over the crater the pilots hovered and began easing their helicopter straight down.

In the cabin manning the port gun, LCpl. Stephen peered through the faint twilight. Suddenly he noticed khaki-clad soldiers in the bomb crater below. They were lying prone below the crater rim, shielded from Marine rifle fire from the knoll. The next eight or nine seconds seemed like an eternity.

We were twenty feet above the ground when the firing started.
[Richard Harper, in a letter, 9 December 1989]

POP! POP! POP-POP-POP-POP!
Enemy rounds whipped through the cockpit. The pilots were mere seconds from landing among North Vietnamese soldiers. They were under the helicopter and all around it.

I was looking at the helicopter. I saw all Hell break loose. Then the helicopter gunner opened up . . . .
[Tom Bachta, oral account, 15 January 1999]

On the knoll LCpl. Butler watched the landing attempt. NVA fire suddenly erupted under and around the H-46. Butler saw the helicopter gunner on the port side open up with his machinegun. He watched as the gunner got hit and momentarily fell back into the helicopter cabin.
POP-POP-POP-POP! POP! POP! POP-POP-POP!
The port gunner, Stephen, got back on his gun and sprayed the NVA in the undergrowth at the base of the hill. Out of the corner of his eye he saw the crew chief, Murff, open fire from the starboard side. Murff suddenly crumpled to the helicopter floor.
POP! POP! POP! POP-POP-POP-POP-POP!
Suddenly a violent shudder wracked the helicopter. An invisible giant hand, it seemed, grabbed the fuselage. The collective dropped, the cyclic shook. Harper, the pilot, had been shot in the chest.
Sturkey clamped down hard on the cyclic. The terrible shaking stopped. He pulled in collective pitch and then felt Harper on the cyclic with him, shoving it forward.
"Turns! Turns! Watch the turns!"

The helicopter came under intense automatic weapons fire from North Vietnamese forces, wounding the entire crew and inflicting heavy damage on the aircraft.
[USMC citation referencing 8 August 1966]

Several bullets ricocheted off the sides and bottom of the pilots' armored seats: CLLAAANNGG! CLLAAANNGG!

The forward transmission, three feet above the cockpit, groaned in protest as six rotor blades chewed into the night air. The helicopter mushed upward and forward as the pilots struggled to steady the flight controls. Words could not help them now. Neither man spoke. They knew what they had to do.

"Go! Go! Go!" someone in the cabin implored via the ICS.

WHHAAAAMM!

A tremendous blow to Sturkey's right foot! Someone had taken a baseball bat – it *felt* like a baseball bat – and had swung it against the heel of his flight boot. The impact knocked his right leg upward. The inertia spun his torso sideways in his armored seat. He keyed the ICS: "I'm hit! I'm hit!"

The copilot's voice on the ICS side-tone sounded squeaky. He made no more needless exclamations and concentrated on controlling the helicopter – engines OK, turns OK, torque OK, pressures OK, full power, still flying. They floundered through translational lift and accelerated upward and forward. The shooting abruptly stopped. The entire nightmare had lasted less than ten seconds.

In the helicopter cabin the infantrymen passengers knew only that their helicopter had been drilled by enemy fire. They had felt the violent shudders, but they had no idea how badly the helicopter had been damaged. They had no way to know that, in addition to the crew chief and gunner in the cabin with them, both pilots had been shot. One passenger in the cabin would reminisce years later:

> We had been about to land in a gully. The *[helicopter]* floor came alive with bullets. All of us in the *[helicopter cabin]* had eyes as big as saucers.
> *[David Loosemore, oral account, 7 March 2002]*

In the cockpit the copilot reached up to the overhead console and flipped off all external lights. There was no sense in presenting a more visible target. They flew over the treetops, gathered speed, and then climbed skyward.

Richard O. Harper, Capt., WIA, 8Aug66, . . . wound, missile pene-
    trating left chest through and through . . . .
Marion F. Sturkey, 1stLt., WIA, 8Aug66, . . . wound, missile pene-

trating right foot . . . .

Herbert S. Murff, Sgt., WIA *[later, DOW]*, 8Aug66, . . . wound, missile penetrating abdomen . . . .

Luke A. Stephen, LCpl., WIA, 8Aug66, . . . wound, missile lacerating right forearm . . . .

[MAG-16, Casualty List, 8 August 1966]

On the H-46 instrument panel the Master Caution Light flashed on. Several individual caution lights winked at the pilots. They scanned the many black and white cockpit gauges that displayed the health of their flying machine. All gauges were still "in the green."

Back in the cabin Stephen keyed his ICS. He had been hit in the arm, he told the pilots, but he still could man his gun. Sgt. Murff was hit too, Stephen continued, and it looked bad. Murff was writhing on the cabin floor, shot in the stomach, unable to speak. Two passengers had unstrapped and were trying to aid the wiry crew chief. He was bleeding from his mouth and from the wound in his stomach.

Stephen grabbed another passenger, manhandled him to the port gun, and told him to return fire if anyone else shot at the helicopter. Then he knelt on the cabin floor and tried to help his friend, Murff.

One passenger, LCpl. Nathaniel Calvin, had been hit in the arm by NVA fire. Two other passengers were trying to aid him.

Calvin, Nathaniel Jr., LCpl., WIA, 8Aug66, gunshot wound upper right arm.

[Cas.Card, LCpl. Nathaniel Calvin, USMC, 8 August 1966]

In less than ten seconds 34 enemy rounds, fired at a point-blank range of 20 to 40 feet, had ripped into the helicopter. Disciplined NVA soldiers had aimed at the cockpit as they had been trained to do. Their rounds all had struck the forward fourth of the fuselage. The entire four-man crew plus one passenger had been wounded.

Harper keyed his ICS: "Sturk, where're you hit?"

"My foot."

A full 45 seconds passed without further comment while the pilots struggled to gain altitude and clear the ridge to the south. Then in his nasal subdued voice Harper explained that he had been shot in the hand and in the chest.

Unlike the copilot, Harper had not been wearing his recently issued Pilot's Armored Chest Protector (called, *bullet-bouncer* or *chicken-plate*). It was a helicopter pilot's equivalent of a medieval knight's breastplate. Without protection from a bullet-bouncer the enemy round had penetrated Harper's flak jacket and had ripped through his chest three inches below his heart.

If I should come out of this war alive, it will be because of simple luck, not because of my brains or my skills.
[Baron Capt. Manfred von Richthofen (the "Red Baron"), German Flying Service, in a letter to his mother, circa 1915]

Cam Lo River Valley, 8 August 1966, 2020 Hours: Bonnie-Sue 9-3 climbed up over Hill 549, reached the Song Cam Lo (aka, *Cam Lo River*), and sped eastward toward Dong Ha. The copilot's right foot felt totally numb. He knew the bullet had come up through the helicopter floor because it had knocked the rock-hard leather heel of his boot upward. Sheepishly, he now wondered if perhaps the round had lodged in the heel of his boot. Maybe he was not hit after all. Flexing his ankle, he wiggled his right foot inside his boot. His effort was rewarded by a wet squishy feeling. Now he knew.

Although heavily damaged, the H-46 seemed to be more or less flyable. The Automatic Trim System (ATS) had been shot away, and the Stability Argumentation System (SAS) control felt sloppy. The pilots checked each amber warning light on the Master Caution Panel. It looked like there were no problems that they could not handle.

However, the large Master Caution Light kept flashing. Then the pilots spotted the problem, their Number One Boost system. They helplessly watched the small gauge as hydraulic pressure gradually dropped toward zero.

An H-46 normally flies by using both of its 3,000 psi hydraulic boost systems. If one boost system fails, the helicopter still can fly using the remaining operative system. However, without at least one operative boost system, without its powerful hydraulic fingers to control the massive rotor head swashplates, the helicopter would literally rip itself apart in the air. It would assume the aerodynamic characteristics of a falling manhole cover. If the pilots lost both boost systems they, and everyone aboard, would be dead men.

It is impossible to control this helicopter with both boost systems inoperative.
[NATOPS Manual, CH-46A/D, NavAir Systems Command]

The vital Number One Boost slowly died, and soon the pilots could hear the empty pump cavitating. Sturkey reached to his right, raised the Control Boost switch out of the "Both" detent, and pulled it back to the "Boost 2" position. Now they were flying with only one boost system. The actuators and SAS links were hydraulicly separate, but mechanically common. How badly were they damaged? Would their helicopter hold together until they reached Dong Ha?

Neither pilot spoke. There was no need for conversation. They rotored eastward through the night at 1,500 feet, almost abeam of Marine artillery batteries at Cam Lo. They could make an emergency landing there. Their wingman, nine-dash-four, was behind them. If they landed at Cam Lo he could pick them up and fly them to the aid station at Dong Ha. On the other hand, each passing minute was precious. Stephen and Sturkey did not have life threatening injuries. However, Harper had a hole in his chest. Back in the cabin, shot in the stomach, Murff was lying in a growing pool of his own blood.

The pilot and copilot looked at each other in the eerie red glow from their instrument panel lights. The copilot did not have to ask, for he knew what the unspoken question would be. And he knew that they were a team. They might succeed, or they might fail, but they would succeed or fail together. There was no other Marine Corps way. The copilot had no choice, so he took a deep breath and keyed his ICS: "Don't stop; let's head for Dong Ha."

[We] thought about landing *[at Cam Lo]* but decided to bet on Boeing *[the airframe manufacturer]* and General Electric *[the engine manufacturer]*. If *[the helicopter]* held together for another four minutes we would be OK.
[Richard Harper, oral account, 9 March 1999]

Stephen, kneeling on the cabin floor by Murff, noticed a dark liquid dribbling down behind the cockpit. Was it hydraulic fluid? Transmission fluid? The gunner got up, stuck his head into the cockpit, and told the pilots. Neither of them spoke. Harper simply pointed straight ahead. They were committed to Dong Ha.

One of the passengers, PFC David Loosemore, wanted to help in any way he could. Stephen grabbed him and told him that both pilots had been shot. Loosemore eased his body through the passageway to the cockpit. In the red glow from instrument panel lights he could see shards of shattered plexiglass and winking caution panel lights. The two pilots *looked* OK, and the copilot gave him a thumbs-up. "Will they be able to land this thing?" Loosemore wondered.

> I kept sticking my head into the cockpit to check on the pilots. I told them: "Just get me over the runway and I'll jump out."
> *[David Loosemore, oral account, 7 March 2002]*

Strapped into a troop seat in the rear of the cabin, SSgt. Conrad Ortego silently endured the ride. He was a Korean War veteran, and the teenage Marines he accompanied considered him to be an old man. Ortego believed the young warriors *needed* him, so he had insisted on going with them on the flight to the knoll. Now, as the helicopter sped through the night toward Dong Ha he could see the three wounded men in the front of the cabin. Through the passageway leading to the cockpit he could see the amber flashing Master Caution Light. He also could see the small individual caution lights, in his words: "lit up like a Christmas tree."

Dong Ha, 8 August 1966, 2030 Hours: Deadlock radioed ahead to Maj. Seitz and Capt. Mills at Op's North. The reinforcement and extraction attempt had failed. Hearing this news, Capt. Tinsley knew that he and his wingman were needed desperately by Marines on the knoll. He might not succeed, but at least he had to try.

> The Devil take order now! I'll to the throng;
> Let life be short, else shame will be too long.
> *[William Shakespeare, Henry V, circa 1599]*

Ignoring his hydraulics problem, Tinsley took off in Bonnie-Sue 9-1 and sped westward into the night. He was followed by his wingman, Bonnie-Sue 9-2, flown by 1stLt. George Richey and 1stLt. Paul Albano. By now complete darkness had set in. Tinsley would have to attempt a landing right on top of the small knoll. Hopefully he could evacuate some of the critically wounded men.

Cam Lo River Valley, 8 August 1966, 2030 Hours: Meanwhile, Harper and his copilot raced eastward over the Cam Lo River toward the safety of Dong Ha. Harper suddenly jerked around sideways in his armored seat. Sturkey initially thought the pilot had gone into convulsions because of his chest wound, but Harper exclaimed:

"You've got it!" (meaning, *you fly the helicopter*).

Scalding hot liquid, either leaking hydraulic fluid or transmission fluid (the forward transmission, above the cockpit, had three bullet holes in it) was leaking down on Harper. Soon the copilot also got covered with the steaming mess. Nonetheless, they did not have a transmission "chip light" warning, so they forged ahead.

> Transmission oil temperature *[has a normal operating range up to]* 150° Celsius *[equal to 302° Fahrenheit]*.
> *[NATOPS Manual, CH-46A/D, NavAir Systems Command]*

The copilot tuned to 255.4 on his UHF radio, the frequency for Dong Ha Tower. Harper radioed ahead, and his steady voice did not betray any distress. The UHF transmissions were recorded:

"Dong Ha, Bonnie-Sue nine-dash-three."

"Bonnie-Sue, go ahead."

"Dong Ha, Bonnie-Sue is, uuuuhhhh four miles west, uuuhhh inbound with wounded, aaaahhhh we want the runway."

Under routine conditions helicopters did not take off or land on the dirt runway at Dong Ha. Instead they used the grassy area on the southern side of the airstrip so the runway would be available for fixed-wing aircraft. Only in an emergency would a helicopter need the added safety of a run-on runway landing. To the controller at Dong Ha, Harper sounded like a pilot on a routine medevac flight.

"Bonnie-Sue, cleared to land, use the grass, sir."

"We want the runway."

"Bonnie-Sue, use the grass, we've got fixed-wing holding."

Harper replied: "Dong Ha, Bonnie-Sue, aaaahhhh we're all hit."

"Say again?"

"We're all hit – we've been shot – we need the runway."
"Aaaahhh, Bonnie-Sue, cleared to land, your discretion."

When the H-46s got shot-up I was inside *[the Op's North tent]*
listening to the radio. I ran outside to see if *[the H-46 crews]*
would make it back alive.
[Larry Robinson, oral account, 16 April 1999]

Spurred onward through the night by a mixture of both hope and fear, the pilots sped toward Dong Ha and safety. They arced down out of the western sky and raced toward the parallel runway lights. Almost there! Then in the center of the instrument panel the dreaded Master Caution Light winked on again. The pilot and copilot both scanned the panel – the Number Two Boost!

The small rectangular warning light flashed out its message of impending doom. Immediately the pilots glued their eyes to the round pressure gauge above the center console. Their last remaining hydraulic boost system began to die, and the needle danced wildly in the gauge . . . 2800 . . . 2400 . . . 1900 . . . .

Disaster would be a few moments to late to snare them. The runway lights flashed past under the helicopter. With the collective bottomed and the nose of the H-46 pulled high into the air, they bled off airspeed and skimmed along five feet above the airstrip. Then they veered off to the right and softly settled onto the grass. As the nosewheel hit the ground Sturkey grabbed both Engine Condition Levers and pulled them back to the "Stop" position. Harper reached to the overhead console and flipped the electric Rotor Brake toggle switch. They had made it home alive.

Razorback Valley, 8 August 1966, 2040 Hours: Flying Bonnie-Sue 9-1, Capt. Tinsley and Lt. Roberts arrived over the valley and found that total darkness had settled over the terrain. They could see only a dim outline of mountaintops. Everything below was a black pit. In the cabin two veteran aircrewmen manned the .50 caliber machine-guns. SSgt. Edward Dusman was the port gunner, and when on the ground he was a skilled maintenance man. The crew chief, Cpl. John Hedger, manned the fifty-caliber on the starboard side.

The previous month Hedger, a native of Chaffee, Missouri, had become the first Marine in his squadron to be recommended for an award for heroism. His helicopter had landed under fire to pick up a critically wounded Marine. As another infantryman had carried the wounded man toward the waiting helicopter, he also had been hit by enemy fire. Both men fell to the ground, still alive and still under fire, but unable to move.

> Cpl. Hedger, the crew chief, . . . then ran from the helicopter under enemy fire *[and physically carried]* both wounded Marines into the helicopter.
> *[HMM-265, Command Chronology, July 1966]*

Hedger had made two trips. Bullets whipped through vegetation around him, but he did not get a scratch. They all safely made it back to the field hospital, and the wounded infantrymen had survived.

Tinsley orbited while talking on the radio with Capt. Lee in the darkness somewhere down below. After briefing his crew via the ICS, Tinsley radioed that he would try to land on top of the unseen knoll and evacuate some of the wounded men.

> We knew what had happened to Harper and Sturkey, but our four-man crew felt we had to try.
> *[Dale Tinsley, oral account, 24 March 1999]*

> We had a strong sense of duty.
> *[Joe Roberts, oral account, 12 March 1999]*

From a fighting hole, below ground level so the NVA could not see it, Lee switched on a flashlight and pointed it skyward. Tinsley spotted the light. Slowly and cautiously he started down into the dark dimensionless void below. Guided only by the pinpoint of light and Lee's voice on the FM radio, he headed for the knoll. In the dark there was no visual depth perception. Tinsley made a cautious and slow power-on approach. He had gone heads-up, looking out of the cockpit and focusing on the light, for nothing else was visible.

> I could dimly see tops of mountains *[silhouetted against the night sky]*, but it was too dark to see the knoll. I had no idea what it

looked like. I never saw it, only the light.
[Dale Tinsley, oral account, 24 March 1999]

Following protocol for such conditions the copilot, Roberts, kept his eyes riveted to the cockpit instrument panel. He was totally "on the gauges." His Radar Altimeter showed the helicopter's height above ground. His Attitude Indicator showed pitch and roll. As the height slowly decreased, Roberts kept up a running verbal narrative with his pilot, giving him guidance. The Radar Altimeter display reached 50 feet, and airspeed dropped below 20 knots.

Tinsley exclaimed: "I can see the ground!"

Now both pilots went heads-up for the landing. In the dark they could see a faint outline of the knoll straight ahead. There was no enemy fire. Tinsley hovered over the knoll and began easing the big H-46 down onto it. Five or ten feet above the ground, enemy rifle fire erupted and raked the helicopter.

[On the ICS] a crewman yelled: "I'm hit!" Then Joe *[Roberts]* got hit. Instant reaction, up collective and go! No need for debate.
[Dale Tinsley, oral account, 24 March 1999]

[The NVA] let us fly *[to the knoll]* without firing a shot. *[They were]* very disciplined. They were just a few feet from the left side of the helicopter.
[Joe Roberts, oral account, 12 March 1999]

NVA fire ripped through the fuselage of Bonnie-Sue 9-1. Tinsley pulled in collective pitch, and Roberts helped him keep the turns under control. The helicopter shuddered and then started scratching for altitude and airspeed. The shooting lasted only ten seconds.

Joseph T. Roberts, Capt., WIA, 8Aug66, . . . wound, missile lacera-
     ating left forearm . . . .
Edward R. Dusman, SSgt., WIA, 8Aug66, . . . wound, missile lacer-
     ating face . . . .
John A. Hedger, Cpl., WIA, 8Aug66, . . .wound, missile right and
     left thigh with nerve involvement.
[MAG-16, Casualty List, 8 August 1966]

Roberts took what he modestly called "just a little shrapnel" in his left arm. But back in the cabin the gunner, SSgt. Edward Dusman, got staggered by a round that tore through his flight helmet and ripped into his face.

The crew chief, Cpl. John Hedger, fared far worse. First, a bullet tore into his left leg above the knee, a flesh wound. Hedger stayed on his feet. Then a 12.7mm round ripped through both thighs, severing the sciatic nerves. Both legs instantly went numb, and Hedger crumpled to the cabin floor. Dusman, although shot in the face, knelt by his friend and tried to stem the massive loss of blood.

Mission 8-6001B: Two UH-1Es flew SAR for emergency extraction. Extraction incomplete. Attempted resupply of E-2 and Groucho Marx. Attempt unsuccessful.
[VMO-2, After Action Report, 8 August 1966]

The pilots hung on as their H-46 wallowed eastward through the night sky. They had their hands full because both SAS systems had been shot away. The fuselage began to vibrate. Neither the UHF nor the FM radio would work, and most of the cockpit instrument panel lights were gone.

Roberts, the copilot, had a relatively minor flesh wound. Via the ICS he talked with Dusman in the cabin. Although shot in the face, the gunner briefed Roberts on the seriousness of Hedger's wounds. He needed medical aid in a hurry.

Escorted by Deadlock gunships, Tinsley flew southeastward and reached old Route 9. If he had to put the helicopter onto the ground he wanted to be over the narrow dirt trail. They passed Cam Lo and forged on eastward toward Dong Ha.

Dong Ha, 8 August 1966, 2045 Hours: After Lt. Sturkey had shut down his engines at Dong Ha, Capt. Harper had reached to his right, twisted the emergency escape hatch handle, and lowered himself to the ground. The copilot then had opened the escape hatch on his side of the cockpit. The South Carolinian had swung his body through the opening and had eased himself out of the helicopter.

I helped lift the wounded *[men]* out of the helicopter cabin. We

thought Murff was gonna' die. He was gut-shot.
[Fred Seitz, oral account, 2 March 1999]

From the cabin, Capt. Mills and others had carried Sgt. Murff
outside. They loaded the pilots, the crew chief, and LCpl. Calvin
onto stretchers and took them 200 meters north of the runway. There
a small shabby masonry building, built by the French years earlier,
constituted the Dong Ha aid station grandiosely known as Delta-Med.
Stephen had wanted to stay with the helicopter, but Maj. Seitz had
seen blood on his arm and ordered him to report to Delta-Med.

The aid station was staffed by several U.S. Navy corpsmen who
were supervised by a Navy doctor. They constituted a field Shock &
Resuscitation Team. They were not equipped to perform complex
surgical procedures. The team would stabilize seriously wounded
men by stopping the bleeding and preventing or treating shock. Then
they would prepare them for aerial transport to more sophisticated
medical facilities such as Alpha-Med (at Phu Bai, 39 miles to the
south), Charlie-Med (at Da Nang, another 36 miles farther south), or
to the *USS Princeton* cruising 15 miles offshore.

HMC Ed Toland, the senior corpsman present, directed younger
corpsmen under his control. Toland, age 36, had joined the Navy in
1950 after a stint in the National Guard. After finishing basic training
and corpsman A-School he had received on-the-job experience in a
naval hospital.   Thereafter he completed several medical specialty
schools. Then he went though FMF Corpsman school to learn battlefield medicine. Eventually he got assigned to a Fleet Marine Force
combat unit. Toland was well trained and ready.

Corpsmen who worked with Toland now had a chance to do what
they had been trained to do, aid wounded Marines. Also they were
aware of the battle 13 miles to the west. They wanted to go there.

On eight and nine August most corpsmen at Dong Ha had pleaded
with me *[to let them]* fly to the hill.
[Edward Toland, oral account, 15 January 2015]

Like the Marines, corpsmen in Delta-Med were clad in filthy
utility uniforms. They busied themselves treating the most grievously
wounded fliers, Murff and Harper. Morphine gave each man a warm

and comfortable rush, a cozy and intoxicating high. Murff's face had turned ashen and blue-gray, almost a death mask. Harper sat on the floor and leaned back against the masonry wall. Corpsmen wrapped his chest with multiple layers of compress bandages.

Dong Ha, 8 August 1966, 2050 Hours: At the Dong Ha runway, Tinsley and Roberts landed in Bonnie-Sue 9-1. Several men helped carry Dusman and Hedger toward the aid station. Roberts initially refused to go, but a corpsman insisted that his arm wound be treated.

Several Marines with flashlights began circling the helicopter to look at battle damage. Their cursory check revealed 22 bullet holes, some made by big 12.7mm rounds. One man asked Tinsley to look at the holes in his flying machine, but Tinsley refused.

> I was happy to be alive. I didn't want to look.
> *[Dale Tinsley, oral account, 24 March 1999]*

At Delta-Med the two additional serious casualties, Dusman and Hedger, were carried into the room and placed on the concrete floor. Dusman had been shot in the face, and Hedger was bleeding profusely from enormous wounds in both thighs. After finishing with Murff, Harper, and Calvin the corpsmen turned to the two new critically wounded men. Hedger was losing a lot of blood.

> Doctors didn't last long at Dong Ha. They got a lot of experience real fast.
> *[Fred Seitz, oral account, 2 March 1999]*

Corpsmen worked on Hedger and Dusman simultaneously. With Hedger their primary concern was massive blood loss. Pressure on his wounds was their main tactic. Corpsmen wrapped Hedger and Dusman in multiple layers of white pressure dressings, and then it became Lt. Sturkey's turn. A sweat-soaked corpsman saw that the lieutenant was holding his bleeding right foot up off the floor:
"You hit anywhere else, lieutenant?"
"No."
"That boot's gonna' have to come off. Are you in pain?"
"Yeah."

Morphine eliminated all traces of discomfort. Lying on the floor while corpsmen plied their trade on his foot, the copilot looked at his discarded boot. In the bottom of the boot was a small hole, as though a pencil somehow had been rammed through the hard leather heel. Then the lieutenant saw the large exit hole in the back of the boot, two inches above the heel. It looked like a shotgun had been fired from inside the boot. No amount of money could have enticed him to look at the boot again.

Minutes later the wounded men were loaded onto a mighty-mite and driven to the runway. Marines carried them aboard a waiting C-130 Hercules, a four-engine fixed-wing turboprop, and placed them in litters stacked three-high along each side of the cabin. Capt. Harper lay in a center litter, and Sgt. Murff lay below him. Within a few minutes the other casualties were carried into the cabin. When all were aboard the C-130 raced down the runway, climbed up into the night sky, and headed for Da Nang 75 miles to the south.

Da Nang, Aerodrome Remarks: Due to possible small arms fire, pilots are cautioned not to descend below traffic pattern altitude until established on final approach. Final approach should be as steep as possible consistent with safety. Report to Da Nang Tower the specific locations of ground fire encountered.
[VFR Enroute Supplement, Southeast Asia, 1967]

Murff did not speak, but he was alive and semiconscious. Twice during the 20 minute flight he rolled his head to the side and vomited an evil crimson liquid onto the metal floor of the C-130 cabin. From the litter above, Harper reached down, grasped Murff's hand, and held it all the way to Da Nang.

LtCol. Arnold Bench commanded the 2nd Battalion, 4th Marines. He kept the regimental commander at Phu Bai abreast of developments. No one knew what would develop overnight. Nonetheless, the 4th Marines commander, Col. Alexander Cereghino, had begun readying more Marines and more artillery for a move to Dong Ha.

Alerted 4th Marines Command Group, "A"-3/4, to provide one company on one hour alert and the Battalion on three hour alert, 3/12 alerted to provide one battery on two hour alert.
[4th Marines, Command Chronology, 8 August 1966]

In the Fanciful Domain of the Armchair Warrior: Far from the din of battle many armchair military theorists might wonder why the Marine battalion commander, LtCol. Arnold Bench, did not send reinforcements to the knoll. Or, why not fly helicopters to the little hill, let everyone clamber aboard, and then fly back to safety? Those who have been in combat in a jungle environment at night know the futility of such efforts. Neither course of action was possible.

Bench and his officers at Dong Ha were experienced veterans. They understood that the battle was only 13 miles to the west. Yet, for all practical purposes it could have been on the back side of the moon. On the floor of Razorback Valley a tangled mass of vines, brush, thistles, and elephant grass rose to a height of eight to ten feet. Even during the daytime, combatants could not see, walk, or crawl through it. They had to chop and hack their way with machetes, propelled as much by their arms as by their feet. Above this nearly impenetrable undergrowth, deciduous trees and their lush canopies blocked out the sun. Troops on the ground had to stay in single file within arm's length of the man ahead. Even during daylight, anyone who fell behind in the shadowy darkness might be lost forever.

> That terrain! The bloody maddening uncanniness of it!
> *[Michael Herr, Dispatches, 1968]*

There was no way a ground relief force could *find* the knoll in the dark. Even if they could have pinpointed the knoll, no force could hack its way for miles through the jungle at night. There were no passable roads or trails northwest of Cam Lo. There was no way for helicopter crews to find a nearby place to land in the dark, exclusive of the tiny knoll.

> Tracked and wheeled vehicles cannot operate west of the north-south grid line YD-06.
> *[Task Force Delta, After Action Report, Operation Hastings]*

Helicopters were the only means of reaching the remote knoll. There was room for only one helicopter to land atop the little hill. Each helicopter would have to sit there and endure a hailstorm of fire while fresh troops debarked, or while wounded troops were loaded aboard. The enemy was only 35 to 90 feet away and "hugging the belt" around the tiny perimeter. Each helicopter and everyone in it would be a bull's-eye for several hundred NVA soldiers. The term *suicidal* comes to mind.

Via his radio Capt. Lee had been talking to the battalion CP. He had asked if a reaction force could be flown to some spot near the knoll. However, there was no known place for a helicopter to land, and no way to find such a place in the dark. Even if a suitable landing area could be found, NVA troops had filled most of them with 20-foot-tall anti-helicopter stakes, invisible at night. For the moment, neither a relief column nor extraction would be possible.

Lee briefly considered attempting to break-out to the south where NVA fire was less intense, but he soon dismissed the idea. If he and his Marines tried to leave the hill they would leave their protective fighting holes behind. They also would lose their fields of fire. They would have to carry their dead and critically wounded brothers-in-arms, and there were not enough walking-wounded Marines to do that. Even if some of them could break through surrounding NVA troops and reach the jungle, in the dark they would not be able to see each other amid the thick vegetation.

> We stumble blindly through the dark . . . . I cannot see the Marine
> only an arm's length in front of me.
> *[Philip Caputo, A Rumor of War, 1977]*

If some Marines left the knoll and survived, they would be unable to stay together. Where would they go? During the night nobody would be able to read a map. Even if they were able to see a map, terrain features would be invisible in the darkness. They also would lose their gunship support, for Deadlock pilots would have no way to locate them in the tangled undergrowth at night.

Staying on the knoll was the only viable option. There they had protection in fighting holes, an established perimeter, clear fields of fire, partial illumination, and gunship support.

> As long as we had ammo and illumination, no one was going to
> drive us off *[the knoll]*. . . . I told battalion that as long as they
> kept the ammo and illumination coming, we'd be OK. The NVA had

taken their best shots and hadn't overrun us yet.
[Howard Lee, oral account, 2 March 1999]

In the meantime, helicopters could drop more ammunition and water without landing. Gunships could continue to target ravines around the knoll. Additional options would be available nine hours later when the sun peeped over the mountains to the east.

North Vietnamese Reinforcements: Many laymen theorists might wonder why more North Vietnamese reinforcements did not arrive and overwhelm the small band of Marines on the knoll. After all, it later would be found that troops of the 812th, 803rd, and 90th NVA Regiments were in Razorback Valley, on Nui Cay Tre Ridge, on the Razorback itself, and along Route 9 from the Rockpile eastward toward Cam Lo. A layman might logically wonder why they did not join forces and overrun Marines on the small knoll. However, for anyone who understands warfare the reasons are simple: (1) military posture, (2) communications, and (3) night troop movement:

Military Posture: When not in attack mode the NVA would disperse its troops. Regiments, battalions, and companies did not bunch-up, for that would make them lucrative targets for Marine air-strikes and artillery. When in bivouac mode, NVA soldiers occupied widely separated defensive positions. Elements of regiments and battalions would be entrenched over a distance of several miles.

Communications: Each NVA battalion headquarters had a Type 71-B radio for voice contact with its regiment. Further, in bivouac and defensive mode, battalions and companies laid land-lines (distance and terrain permitting) to supplement the radios. Communication among companies, platoons, and squads required couriers (called, *runners*). During combat NVA companies, platoons, and squads used whistles (similar to those used by basketball referees) to communicate.

Night Troop Movement: The NVA and Marines shared the same problem. Night troop movements through the jungle are not feasible. Couriers face the same dilemma. Their task would be akin to blindly crawling through a pitch-black coal

mine. At night the jungle was a perilous land where Bengal
tigers lurked, waiting for warm-blooded prey to wander by.

> An unbroken mass of green stretched westward, one ridge-
> line and mountain range after another, some *[mountains
> were]* more than a mile high and covered with forests that
> looked solid enough to walk on. It had no end.
> *[Philip Caputo, A Rumor of War, 1977]*

During daylight on 8 August, NVA reinforcements had trickled-in
to bolster troops attacking the hill. However, the onset of darkness
changed everything. NVA soldiers 300 meters away, or a half-mile
away, or a mile away obviously heard the sound of battle. Yet, they
had no way to know what was afoot. They knew only that someone,
somewhere, was under attack. Were their comrades attacking? Were
they defending? Were they advancing? Were they retreating? What
were the opposing troop counts? If they made their way through the
jungle toward the sound of battle, who would they encounter first,
their comrades or the Americans? Would they be welcomed or fired
upon? Where were opposing combatants deployed? Was this an
enemy trap? An ambush?

Without radios or land-lines, potential NVA reinforcements had
no way to answer these questions. Even if they wanted to join the
fight, wherever and whatever it might be, there was no practical way
to make their way there through the jungle at night.

Razorback Valley, 8 August 1966, 2110 Hours: Cpl. Bachta, the
Recon radioman, shared a hole with Capt. Lee and the Echo radioman, LCpl. Butler. Knowing that two radiomen were not needed in
the same hole, Butler got permission to man the perimeter. The
gunshot wound in his arm did not materially slow him down. Armed
with his forty-five, Butler grabbed another pistol from the body of the
dead platoon commander, Lt. Sherman. Now armed with two pistols
he jumped into a hole on the perimeter.

Most of the holes were about three feet deep. In these holes
Marines did not sit on their buttocks. They had to squat with both
feet on the ground. By squatting with their feet under them they
could jump out instantly if a grenade chanced to bounce into their

hole. Squatting also allowed their heads to be level with the rim of the hole. They could see to fire, but they could duck down to escape flying shrapnel when grenades landed nearby.

Capt. Lee radioed that he had only 16 men, including those who were wounded, who were still able to fire and fight. Ammunition had run low again. Suddenly a grenade arced into the perimeter and bounced to a spot near the company commander. Lee had no time to roll away.

> The grenade that wounded me hit about two feet away. It exploded, but there was no pain.
> *[Howard Lee, oral account, 12 August 1990]*

To Lee the concussion was like a full speed block in a football game. The sheer force of the blast blew off his web belt, pistol, and canteen. The grenade sent jagged hot steel into Lee's right eye, right arm, and lower body. One piece of shrapnel tore into his buttocks and exited on the inside of his thigh. He was lucky, for no arteries were severed. However, he would lose blood and strength for the rest of the night. Steel that ripped into his elbow had numbed his whole arm. His right leg was partially functional. Yet, although maimed and blinded in one eye, Lee remained in command.

> Lee, Howard Vincent, Capt., WIA, 8Aug66, fragmentation wounds, right leg, back, and face.
> *[Cas.Card, Capt. Howard Lee, USMC, 8 August 1966]*

Artillery at Cam Lo had been firing illumination rounds toward the knoll. The artificial daylight partially illuminated the top and the southern and eastern sides of the knoll. Yet, the northern and western sides remained cloaked in darkness much of the time. A Marine C-117D flareship (aka, *R4D-8*) from Da Nang had been circling high overhead, but it was unable to get down through the thick clouds.

Meanwhile in a Faraway World: For Marines on the hill, the entire world was limited to Razorback Valley. Yet, there was another world during the summer of 1966. In that foreign world, England defeated West Germany 4 to 2 to win the World Cup. A musical group, The

Lovin' Spoonful, popularized *Summer in the City*. A professional pugilist, Cassius Clay (later known as Muhammad Ali), embraced pacifism, and his photograph graced the cover of *Esquire Magazine*. Alfred Hitchcock released another movie thriller, *Torn Curtain*. A British entertainer, John Lennon, claimed that he and his fellow musicians were more popular than Jesus Christ. Newspaper comic strips featured Little Orphan Annie and Steve Canyon.

Playboy Magazine expanded its peekaboo advertising campaign. Social activist Jesse Jackson announced plans for a rally in corrupt Chicago. At historic Fenway Park in Boston, the Red Sox beat the Indians 3 to 1. France tested its first nuclear bomb. Labor mogul Jimmy Hoffa voted himself a $25,000 pay raise. Sugar sold for eight cents per pound, and a new Ford Galaxie automobile cost $2,699. In that world the eighth day of August was a Monday.

Yet, to Marines in Razorback Valley neither the day of the week nor anything else in the foreign world had any meaning or relevance. Events in that world may as well have taken place on Mars.

Some Marines knew that a singer and songwriter, Tony Bennett, had left his heart in a mystical place called San Francisco. Some promised themselves that, if they chanced to survive the war, they would go there and wear flowers in their hair with the new-age unwashed masses. Perhaps San Francisco's fabled golden sun would bleach them clean and blot out all memories of close-combat.

Razorback Valley, 8 August 1966, 2120 Hours: Suddenly there was a lull in the firing of artillery illumination rounds toward the knoll. Total darkness shrouded the perimeter. Via his PRC-25 the Recon radioman, Cpl. Bachta, pleaded: "Don't let the lights go out!"

For a helicopter crew flying in the valley, light was life. Periods between flares posed a lethal peril for gunships. Flares would burn out suddenly. One second there would be light; the next second a pilot's world would become a dimensionless ebony pit. He could see nothing, not the ground, not the surrounding hills, not the sky. Up and down lost their meaning. Consequently, when making gun runs in flarelight the pilot would be heads-up, concentrating on his target and aiming his rockets and guns. The copilot would be totally "on the gauges" and oblivious to what was happening outside the cockpit. If a flare suddenly died he would take the controls and fly to safety.

Over the valley 1stLt. Lanny Ingvoldstad piloted a VMO-2 Huey gunship. After a long interval between flares he tuned to the artillery FM radio frequency and explained that Marines on the knoll needed "illum" immediately. He gave the map coordinates but was told that artillery at Cam Lo could not reach that far. "Well, at least get it over Dong Ha Mountain," he pleaded.

The batteries began firing again, and once again the illumination fell short. Light cast by white-hot burning magnesium flares offered faint illumination on the eastern and southern sides of the knoll. In dim flickering flarelight the NVA soldiers, when they could be seen, looked like phantoms or ghostly apparitions, escapees from Hades. Meanwhile the northern and western sides of the knoll remained cloaked in almost total darkness.

Ingvoldstad was already a veteran gunship pilot. He had been wounded three months earlier on 17 May 1966, had recuperated aboard the *USS Repose* (AH-16), and had returned to the cockpit.

Ingvoldstad, Orlando III, 1stLt., WIA, 17May66, missile wound perforating right arm.
[Cas.Card, 1stLt. Lanny Ingvoldstad, USMC, 17 May 1966]

Ingvoldstad knew that the Huey he flew had been modified since it had arrived in Vietnam. In the early days there had been no armored seats, no armor at all. However, squadron mechanics had *appropriated* armor plating from the U.S. Army. A piece was bolted onto the cockpit door below the window. Another piece was bolted onto the bottom of pilots' seats. Yet another section of armor was bolted onto the back of the seats. Pilots soon replaced their original soft body armor with new flak jackets that incorporated hard panels. Some began wearing the new Pilots Armored Chest Protector, called *bullet-bouncer* or *chicken-plate*. Thus equipped, a Huey pilot was ready to fly and fight.

Sometime early during the night LCpl. Edward McDermott got hit. Like most Marines this young man from Danbury, Connecticut, shared a hole with another infantryman.

There was a lot of smoke from all the shooting and the grenades,

and the NVA were all around the hill.
[Ed McDermott, oral account, 16 February 2015]

Out of the night a grenade arced down, hit McDermott's shoulder, bounced aside, and detonated. The sudden blast and concussion were deafening. Jagged steel sliced into McDermott's left leg and foot.

McDermott, Edward Joseph Jr., LCpl., WIA, 8Aug66, fragmentation wounds left thigh and left ankle.
[Cas.Card, LCpl. Ed McDermott, USMC, 8-9 August 1966]

Slowly clouds over the valley began to part. In a big C-117D flareship orbiting high overhead, the crew was able to spot Capt. Lee's flashlight on the knoll. The flareship began dropping magnesium flares, little mini-suns that cast light and dancing shadows onto the knoll and surrounding terrain. Each flare would ignite after a five second delay and float down under its small parachute. For Marine infantrymen down below, light was life, and gunship pilots could see well enough to target tangled undergrowth around the knoll.

The flareship crew had hundreds of flares aboard, but crewmen never wore parachutes. They would have been useless. If hostile fire ignited even one flare the whole plane would explode in a gigantic magnesium fireball that would light up the sky from the South China Sea to the Laotian border.

Even with the flareship providing illumination, Marine fixed-wing F-8 Crusader and A-4 Skyhawk pilots on station could not identify the knoll in the dancing artificial light. Soon they would begin stacking-up in a holding pattern over the ocean east of Dong Ha at around 24,000 feet (spoken, *angels twenty-four*). They would rely upon C-130 in-flight refueling to stay there. Their lethal close air support would not be possible until daylight.

Razorback Valley, 8 August 1966, 2200 Hours: The NVA made another mass attack. Screaming and swarming up three sides of the knoll, they fired rifles and hurled grenades as they charged forward.

[The NVA attacked] up 3 sides of the hill. They threw grenades and tried to penetrate the perimeter but were repelled by Marine rifle

fire. Ammunition supply at this time was critically low.
[Groucho Marx Patrol Report, Team 61, 6th Platoon, 1st Force Recon, 8 August 1966]

Two more Barrelhouse H-34s from HMM-161, with all volunteer crews, flew to the valley with water and ammunition. They saw no flashlight down below. They had no means of identifying the knoll. Overhead in his gunship Maj. Hazelbaker heard plaintive radio calls from Capt. Lee. His men on the little hill desperately needed more 7.62mm ammunition and grenades.

E-6 *[Capt. Lee]* radioed that the ammo supply was short and they would not be able to hold out much longer without resupply.
[Capt. Ben Meharg, USMC, typed account, 11 August 1966]

Twice a Deadlock Huey made a low pass over the knoll, and the crew chief kicked out crates of rifle ammunition. On both attempts the crates missed the knoll and fell into surrounding ravines occupied by NVA soldiers. The Marine perimeter was *so small*, and enemy troops were *so near*. A more accurate delivery was necessary. Time was running out. Worse yet, the flareship pilot radioed that he had only two flares left.

Hazelbaker decided to try to sneak his gunship to the perimeter by flying low through a steep ravine on the southeastern side of the knoll. Walls of the ravine and a nearby saddleback would shield him from enemy fire, he hoped. With aid from a flareship and a little luck he might make it to the perimeter and drop off his linked machinegun ammunition. The plan worked.

He flew his aircraft through the suicidal curtain of enemy fire and landed at the Marine position, delivering 3,000 rounds of 7.62mm ammunition he had on board for use by his helicopter guns.
[USMC citation referencing 8 August 1966]

With the light from a flareship, Costa *[the copilot]* and I slipped our gunbird up the backside of the small hill and passed our remaining ammo into a foxhole. The last flare went out just as we were making our departure and turning into the uphill drainage – really

one of the more exciting moments.
[Wayne Hazelbaker, in a letter, 12 December 1989]

Hazelbaker was right. When the flare died the world turned jet black. For helicopter crews in the age before night vision goggles, this was akin to being locked in a deep coal mine. Literally, one could not see his hand in front of his face. Overhead, Capt. Ben Meharg piloted a gunship zipping through the valley, and suddenly he could not see surrounding ridges and mountains. Hazelbaker was trying to take off from the knoll, and he could not see high terrain that surrounded him. Potential disaster reared its ugly head.

The last flare burned out *[when]* I was at the bottom of a gun run. In the ensuing darkness both aircraft nearly crashed attempting to get around the hills in pitch dark with no visual references.
[Capt. Ben Meharg, USMC, typed account, 11 August 1966]

The flare had died. Enemy fire had stopped because nobody, neither friend nor foe, could see anything. Perhaps it was a blessing in disguise. Both helicopters avoided crashing into surrounding hills.

Emboldened by his success, Hazelbaker decided to try again. To him it seemed logical that a Huey slick, with aid from a replacement flareship, could slip up the ravine, unload more crates of sorely needed ammunition, and evacuate some critically wounded Marines. He termed the risk factor to be "acceptable." Years later when asked to define *acceptable* he would muse in a letter: "Don't ask what that is, I don't know."

Meanwhile, a half-hour before midnight at the regimental CP at Phu Bai, preparations to reinforce the task force at Dong Ha swung into high gear.

At 2330 Hours directed 3/4 to prepare to displace one company to Dong Ha *[on the]* morning of 9 August 1966, on arrival chop OPCON *[meaning, operational control]* to 2/4.
[4th Marines, Command Chronology, 8 August 1966]

Dong Ha, 8 August 1966, 2330 Hours: Hazelbaker flew back to Dong Ha and exchanged his Huey gunship for a Huey slick, a cargo hauler. The slick was loaded with crates of 7.62mm ammunition, M-79 rounds, grenades, and water cans. The risky plan called for flying back to Razorback Valley, sneaking up the ravine in the dark, landing, and kicking out ammunition and supplies to fellow Marines on the knoll. Hopefully the Marines on the hill would load their most critical casualties aboard, and Hazelbaker would fly them back to Dong Ha. For this perilous task he asked for a volunteer crew.

Hazelbaker and Costa would go because they had discovered the hidden route to the knoll. There was no shortage of VMO-2 volunteers to fly as gunners, but the first two Marines to step forward were Cpl. Eppie Ortiz and LCpl. Jim McKay.

Jim McKay: The fact that he volunteered to fly to the knoll with Hazelbaker defies logic, almost defies belief. Earlier that day McKay had flown as a gunner aboard another Huey gunship from VMO-2. That flight had been McKay's last scheduled combat mission. His combat tour in Vietnam had come to an end. He was supposed to return to the United States.

A short, slightly built, and soft-spoken Marine, Jim McKay had joined the Marine Corps in June 1964. In early 1965 he had arrived in Vietnam with the 3rd Shore Party Battalion. That duty had proved to be too tame, so in December he had requested a transfer to Force Recon. McKay, an armorer by trade, spent the next couple of months in the field on patrol with Recons. However, by February 1966 he had less than a month remaining on his standard 13-month tour in Vietnam. McKay wanted more.

From the ground McKay had watched the gunships darting and swooping around. Yes, that was the role he wanted, and it would allow him to stay in Vietnam. McKay had arranged a deal with the Marine Corps. He volunteered to extend his combat tour for six more months in exchange for reassignment as a helicopter gunner in a VMO-2 gunship. The Marine Corps had granted the request in March 1966. For the following six months McKay daily had lugged his M-60 machinegun and ammunition to the designated Huey. He served as a gunner when airborne and as a loadmaster while on the ground. He had his share of narrow escapes. Most recently, five days earlier on 3 August he had manned his M-60 behind 1stLt. Richard Drury when an NVA 12.7mm round nearly severed the lieutenant's arm.

Now it was late at night on 8 August 1966, McKay's last day for combat missions. After his afternoon flight he had been scheduled to turn in his gear and catch the first available flight to Da Nang. He had been promised a ten day R&R (meaning, *rest and recuperation*) in Singapore as a reward for volunteering for the six month extension in Vietnam. Then he would be flown back to "the world" (meaning, *the United States*).

> Yes, that's right, I was due to start my ten day R&R to Singapore on August the ninth.
> *[Jim Mckay, oral account, 26 July 1990]*

Yet, after turning in his gear at Dong Ha, McKay refused to catch one of the many available flights to Da Nang. Some of his Recon buddies were in the Groucho Marx patrol. McKay's friends were surrounded on the knoll in Razorback Valley, vastly outnumbered by the enemy, in desperate need of more ammunition, and fighting for their lives in the dark.

> I did only what my duty demanded. I could have taken no other course without dishonor.
> *[Gen. Robert E. Lee, CSA, 1807-1870]*

McKay was supposed to go home, but he refused to leave Dong Ha. He would not abandon his Marine brothers. As soon as he got the chance he volunteered to fly with Maj. Hazelbaker.

McKay and the other three Marines piled into the slick, Bureau No. 151290, which was loaded with ammunition and water. They fired up the powerful T-53 Lycoming turbine, launched into the hot August night, and headed toward their destiny in Razorback Valley.

Razorback Valley, 9 August 1966, 0005 Hours: Five minutes after midnight the Huey slick arrived over the valley in the darkness, and Hazelbaker made radio contact with Capt. Lee down below. He had done almost the same thing before in a gunship. He planned to sneak down to the ravine in the slick. Protected by walls of the deep ravine he would air-taxi to the knoll, slip up its dark side, kick out the ammunition, and evacuate some of the casualties.

Hazelbaker and his crew would not be alone. Three gunships had accompanied his slick to the valley. 1stLt. Shepard Spink piloted the first gunship. He had been in the air almost constantly since noon on the previous afternoon. Now he would be the decoy, a feint to divert enemy fire away from Hazelbaker.

With all his external lights turned on bright so that he would be highly visible, Spink dove toward the knoll, twisting and jinking to avoid the rounds reaching up for him. Drawing fire in this manner was not for the faint of heart. Spink made a high speed pass over the little hillock, then turned and climbed away. Before the battle at the hill would end his logbook would reflect 14.8 hours of flight time, including 4.4 hours of night VFR time.

> The high volume of enemy fire coming out of the *[ravines and gullies]* was almost unbelievable.
> *[Shepard Spink, oral account, 30 April 2015]*

Two more gunships, piloted by Capt. Jack Enockson and Capt. Ben Meharg, followed the decoy. With external lights turned on bright they made simultaneous gun runs and fired into ravines around the little hill, pitting their flying skills against NVA marksmanship.

Amid the fireworks with his external lights turned off, Hazelbaker and Costa crept down into the shadows. They entered the safety of a ravine southeast of the knoll. So far, so good. Perhaps they would not be noticed. Sneaking through the ravine, Hazelbaker put his right skid next to the ground and eased his helicopter up the side of the knoll, shielded from NVA fire. Near the top he put the right skid on the ground next to a fighting hole and hovered with the other skid hanging in mid-air over the ravine.

> Maneuvering through darkness and braving intense fire by North Vietnamese troops from all sides and as close as fifteen yards from the Marine position, he landed at the Marine position with 800 lbs. of ammunition.
> *[USMC citation referencing 9 August 1966]*

Ortiz and McKay began kicking out their ammunition crates. However, now their Huey was visible to the NVA. A storm of fire erupted from gullies surrounding the small knoll, and it all zeroed-in on the Huey. One Marine on the hill later would explain that the incoming tracers "looked like the fourth of July."

LCpl. Butler, the Echo Company radioman, saw a brilliant "flash" in the NVA-held brush beyond the southern slope of the hill. No one had to explain to him what happened two seconds later.

BBLLAAAAMM!

An NVA rocket struck the helicopter and detonated. The impact high atop the rotor mast tore off the pitch control rods.

Mission 8-5001: Received intense small arms, automatic weapon, and .50 cal. fire from all around the zone. Wingman *[Maj. Hazelbaker]* made resupply *[but]* was shot down in the LZ.
[VMO-2, After Action Report, 9 August 1966]

Chopper came in for resupply. While on the LZ enemy grenades or 3.5 rocket hit the rotor blade and downed the chopper.
[Groucho Marx Patrol Report, Team 61, 6th Platoon, 1st Force Recon, 9 August 1966]

The concussion and blast knocked McKay up onto the console between the two pilots. Stunned, Ortiz fell back onto the web seats, his flight helmet shattered. In the cockpit in the left seat, Costa had hot shrapnel in his leg.

Costa, Anthony D., 1stLt., WIA, 9Aug66, RVN.
[VMO-2, Unit Diary, August 1966]

Costa had a big tear in his leg, in the flesh by the shin.
[Jim McKay, oral account, 27 September 2000]

Although dazed, Hazelbaker was otherwise unhurt. He hit the rotor brake and shut down the wildly vibrating and bucking Huey. Years later he would explain in a letter: "I still don't know why we didn't roll down the hill."

McKay had three shrapnel holes in his back. Hot steel had ripped through his protective flak jacket, but he crawled out of the helicopter and stumbled toward two infantrymen in a nearby fighting hole. From down below the knoll the NVA continued to fire. McKay felt no impact or pain, but he inexplicably fell down. He got up, then fell again. "What's wrong with my legs?" he wondered. Trying to get back on his feet, he tumbled down the slope and lost consciousness. When he regained his senses he found that the shooting had stopped. Why had he fallen? What was wrong?

McKay, James E., LCpl., WIA, 9Aug66 . . . missile wounds left knee and back right side.
[MAG-16, Casualty List, 9 August 1966]

Almost a quarter-century later McKay would explain in a letter: "I ran my hands down my leg and located the injury, then understood what my problem was." McKay had been shot through the left knee. The bullet had shattered his kneecap. Worse yet, it had severed the tendons, and his lower leg flopped around like a warm wet noodle. He could not walk or stand up.

McKay heard Vietnamese voices about 40 feet below him in the ravine. He heard Marines talking 30 feet above him on the knoll. Although shooting had stopped the adversaries were tossing grenades back and forth. McKay pulled out his pistol and started crawling up the hill. He dared not chamber a round, for he knew both the Marines and NVA would hear it and would shoot him in the dark. However, one of the Marines had seen McKay tumble down the slope, and he crawled down to help him. They both made it back into the perimeter and dropped into a fighting hole with another Marine.

0015H, Mission 8-6001B: Attempted resupply of Groucho Marx and E-2; *[attempt was]* unsuccessful.
[VMO-2, Command Chronology, 9 August 1966]

The hole seemed secure, McKay reasoned. The two men in the hole with him, LCpl. Jesus Daniels Jr. and Cpl. Richard Strock, had stacked bodies of three dead NVA soldiers around the rim of their hole. One corpse blocked fire from the NVA-held ravine west of the knoll. The other two enemy bodies effectively sandbagged the sides. Daniels put a battle dressing around McKay's knee, and Strock tied it in place with a strip of his shirt.

<u>0025H</u>: One UH-1E conducted airstrike against . . . enemy positions around hilltop of encircled Marines. Enemy ground fire *[was]* received and returned.
[MAG-16, Command Chronology, 9 August 1966]

Razorback Valley, 9 August 1966, 0025 Hours: In a few minutes McKay realized that Cpl. Ortiz, the Huey crew chief, was missing. An infantryman crawled to the downed helicopter, found Ortiz lying unconscious on the ground, and dragged him back into a fighting hole. The back of his flight helmet was crushed. There was little bleeding, but there was a huge open gash in the side of his head. McKay tried to get a response from Ortiz, who mumbled that he wanted to go to sleep. McKay and others discussed taking off the flight helmet but decided against it. They reasoned that the helmet was helping to hold the crew chief's head together. Although Ortiz would mumble incoherently at times throughout the night, he would not regain consciousness.

Ortiz, Eppie, Cpl., WIA, 9Aug66, . . . concussion, head, received from shrapnel.
[MAG-16, Casualty List, 9 August 1966]

Marines on the knoll breathed a little easier for the first time in several hours. The resupply helicopter had been shot down, but now the infantrymen had fresh water, crates of sorely needed ammunition, and grenades. They also had two M-60 machineguns from the Huey.

Capt. Lee, his strength slowly ebbing, still crawled among his men, encouraging them and calming them.

Major Hazelbaker and his copilot joined the fight on the ground.
[Jack Shulimson, <u>U.S. Marines in Vietnam: An Expanding War, 1966</u>, 1982]

Lt. Costa helped to man the perimeter. He crawled from hole to hole to distribute ammunition, grenades, and water from his downed Huey. From time to time he relieved Capt. Lee and Maj. Hazelbaker on the radio and directed fire of gunships circling above. When not needed elsewhere he shared a hole with LCpl. Timothy Roberts.

The Lt. *[Costa]* first treated some of the wounded. . . . He brought along an M-79 with ammo, AR-15 with ammo, and an M-14. *[He]* crawled to the chopper and drug back some more much needed ammo.
[LCpl. Tim Roberts, USMC, typed account, 11 August 1966]

Roberts, who hailed from Portland, Oregon, was a rifleman with the standard "Grunt" 0311 MOS (military occupational specialty). He spent much of the night in a hole with Costa, but hour by hour his injures mounted. A finger on his left hand had been ripped open. Then he would be hit in the left side, and hit again in the left leg. Nonetheless, he continued to fight.

Roberts, Timothy A., Cpl. *[sic]*, WIA, 9Aug66, laceration, left second finger, wound left side and left leg.
[Cas.Card, LCpl. Timothy Roberts, USMC, 9 August 1966]

Hazelbaker initially wondered why Marines were not shooting at the concealed NVA, for they were only about 45 to 80 feet away. The young infantryman with whom Hazelbaker shared a fighting hole explained that, in the darkness, they would not fire unless they could see their target. Otherwise the NVA would shoot back at the muzzle flashes. That made sense, so Hazelbaker waited and listened.

Hazelbaker took the ground-to-air FM radio and talked to Capt. Enockson, his erstwhile wingman circling overhead. The downed Huey pilot would coordinate air and artillery support for much of the night. The following day when documenting the ill-fated mission the VMO-2 operations clerk would make a short entry in the "remarks" column of Hazelbaker's flight logbook: "Shot Down In Zone."

Major Vincil W. Hazelbaker was our Angel and Savior; had he not made that last flight with lots of ammo – we were all dead!
[Robert Callaway, on a questionnaire, 2 February 2015]

Hazelbaker reflected on his dilemma. At 37 years of age he was old and old-fashioned. Born in 1929 near rural Grangeville, Idaho, he had been educated in a one-room schoolhouse. His parents ran a farm powered not by tractors, but by horses. After high school he had joined the U.S. Navy and later had gone to the University of Idaho courtesy of the federal G.I. Bill. He had been selected for flight training during the Korean War, got commissioned as a second lieutenant in 1953, and became a Marine Corps fighter pilot. Later he had transitioned into helicopters. Yet, now his past experiences counted for little. He was in a hole atop a Godforsaken little hill in Indochina. A radio provided his only contact with the outside world.

The Huey crew chief, Eppie Ortiz, was in bad shape. Shrapnel had penetrated his skull. He had been born in Puerto Rico and had grown up in New York. Now he lay curled up in a shallow hole. He was unconscious and unable to fight. The Huey gunner, Jim McKay, had shrapnel in three places in his back, and his left leg did not work. He could not stand or walk. However, one of the Marines had brought him an M-60 from the downed Huey. McKay still could fire and fight, and he helped to defend the perimeter.

LCpl. Roger Baca, an Echo Company rifleman (not to be confused with Cpl. Tom Bachta, the Recon radioman), had arrived at the knoll with Capt. Lee late on the previous afternoon. Now the Huey had been shot down, and Baca realized it was full of ammunition. Ammunition was life. Between flares, Baca joined others and low-crawled to the Huey. They helped themselves to boxes of grenades and 7.62mm rounds.

Baca, Roger J., LCpl., WIA, 8Aug66, Quang Tri Province, RVN.
[E/2/4, Unit Diary, August 1966]

By now Baca had shrapnel wounds in both legs, but he still could man the perimeter and fight. He and his Marine brothers knew they were surrounded. They knew the odds against them. Baca was too proud to let it show, but he and his comrades were scared. Fear is a hard thing to dominate, especially in the dark. Like a child who hears a bump-in-the-night, imagination can play cruel tricks on an adult's mind in the darkness.

Faced with a known peril in the dark, the human mind conjures images of the worst possible outcome, the greatest evil, the greatest horror. One mentally *sees* what he fears the most. This is what psychologists call "Scenario Fulfilment Syndrome." It can override reason and logic. Panic can follow, and panic among warriors in combat is usually lethal.

> **Note:** *Perhaps the best example of "Scenario Fulfillment Syndrome" occurred 22 years later in the Strait of Hormuz on 3 July 1988. The* USS Vincennes *was in a running gun battle with Iranian gunboats. On radar the warship crew saw an unidentified aircraft, a bogey. They "truly believed" that the bogey was an Iranian Air Force F-14 warplane. They fired two SM-2 missiles and shot the bogey down. In reality the bogey was a civilian Airbus A-300 passenger plane, Iran Air Flight 655. All 290 people aboard were killed.*
>
> USS Vincennes *was a Ticonderoga class Aegis cruiser with a state-of-the-art automated fire control system. It functioned perfectly. The electronic data trail showed that the bogey was not a threat. The failures were human, not electronic. In the chaos of battle the crew fell prey to emotional frailty and cruel illusion. They "saw" their worst nightmare. Scenario Fulfillment Syndrome took control.*

Under circumstances existing on the knoll, only an idiot would not have been impacted by fear's chilling breath. Yet, Marines on the hill kept Scenario Fulfillment Syndrome at bay. None of them panicked. Controlled fear can be an asset in combat. Conversely, fighting alongside *fools* is dangerous. All warriors understand the wisdom embodied in the old infantryman's witticism: "Never share a fighting hole with anyone braver than you are."

> No sane man is unafraid in battle. But discipline produces in him a form of vicarious courage.
> *[Gen. George Patton, USA, quoted posthumously in* War As I Knew It, *1947]*

There would be no more mass frontal assaults against the knoll. However, all night the NVA would probe the small perimeter, lob grenades at the Marines, and shoot at any target of opportunity.

> You could hear *[the NVA]* dragging off the bodies. Some would come right up to the brush line and just start talking. Every time we

shot at them another grenade would come in.
[HM3 Nick Tarzia, USN, quoted in U.S. Marines in Vietnam:
An Expanding War, 1966, *1982]*

Capt. Lee, blind in one eye, continued to lose blood and strength. Lt. Costa stayed with him and helped him throughout the night. Costa concentrated on stopping the bleeding, and he repeatedly assured Lee that he would survive. Years later Lee would remember Costa's calm voice as he tried to help: "Captain, le'me see if I can plug up your holes."

Marines Over the Knoll: Marine infantrymen on the hill knew that helicopter crews were not mere aerial prima donnas. With respect to ground combat and tactics, most Marine flyers had *been there*. Capt. Meharg and Capt. Enockson had been infantry officers before they transitioned into aviation. In a weird coincidence, Capt. Enockson had served as executive officer of Echo Company, 2nd Battalion, 4th Marines (E/2/4), the same company to which Marines on the knoll were attached. Originally an enlistee, he had earned a commission, had become a mustang, had become an infantry platoon commander, and eventually was assigned as executive officer of E/2/4. He later completed flight school and became a Huey pilot.

> The helicopters kept trying to get in to help us, but they kept getting shot-up. If it wasn't for the aviation elements, we would have been overrun.
> *[Howard Lee, oral account, 12 August 1990]*

Other Marine pilots had followed a different path to the cockpit. Originally they had enlisted, had completed boot camp and infantry training, and had served thereafter for a few years. As young NCOs they had been selected for the MARCAD (Marine Aviation Cadet) Program. Marines who could complete the regimented four-month preflight syllabus, and then the year-long flight training program, earned a commission and the coveted Naval Aviator designation.

Helicopter crew chiefs and gunners were a diverse lot. All had completed boot camp and infantry training prior to technical schools for their aviation MOS. All had become skilled aerial gunners with the swivel-mounted M-60 and M-2 Deuce. Most of them, like LCpl. Jim McKay who had served in the field with Recon teams, were well acquainted with infantry tactics and concerns.

> *[On 8-9 August 1966]* everyone in VMO-2 was up all night to support the Marines on the hill.
> *[Shepard Spink, oral account, 6 May 2015]*

Regardless of their route to the cockpit or to the machineguns in the cabin, all Marine helicopter crews knew their primary job. They supported Marines on the ground, the Grunts who depended upon them. In the Marine Corps the Grunts are considered the elite, the tip of the spear, the best of the best. Marine flyers, like tank crewmen and artillerymen, exist to empower and support the Grunts, the lethal gunfighters. Regardless of their MOS, for Marines there is no higher military calling than "the Grunts."

Dong Ha, 9 August 1966, 0100 Hours: 1stLt. Larry Robertson, an H-34 pilot assigned TAD to HMM-161, had flown on the extraction flight the prior afternoon. Despite taking hits he had made it back to Dong Ha. Extensive battle damage, including one round through the helicopter's Wright radial engine, prevented him from flying the craft during the long night.

> I loved the H-34. It had that big radial engine under your feet to stop the bullets. In the H-34, unless *[hostile fire]* killed the pilot, or it caught on fire, it would bring you back alive. It would shudder and shake, spit and pop, but I felt safe in the H-34.
> *[Larry Robinson, oral account, 16 April 1999]*

With his H-34 too badly damaged to fly again, Robinson hung around Op's North and listened to the radio. About an hour after midnight VMO-2 ran out of copilots. Robinson had never been checked-out in a Huey. He had never even ridden in one. Yet, this was a chance to contribute, so he hopped into the copilot's seat of Bureau No. 152421. The pilot showed him where the radio cords and switches were and helped him strap himself into the copilot's seat. Before the night was over he would log 4.1 hours with VMO-2.

Flying in a gunship was a new experience for Robinson.

> The gunsight swung down, and they had grease pencil marks on the windshield to aim with. . . . Tracers look like they go into slow motion as they near the ground. If they ricochet, they speed up. It's all an optical illusion.
>
> *[Larry Robinson, oral account, 16 April 1999]*

An explanation is necessary. When an enemy soldier aims and fires directly at a helicopter in flight at night, the crew can see the tracers. Thirty caliber tracers look like blazing golf balls. Larger 12.7mm tracers look like fiery beer cans. They first appear to move slowly, for they are headed straight toward the crew. There is no visual indication of relative motion, no visual indication of speed. But as the helicopter flies forward (away from where it was when the tracers were aimed and fired), the tracers continue to move upward in a straight line. The relative motion is obvious. The tracers appear to be (1) curving behind the helicopter and (2) speeding up.

Unfortunately, if an enemy soldier *leads* the helicopter and aims ahead of it (so that his tracers and the helicopter will arrive at the same spot at the same time), the reverse is true. The helicopter crew first will see tracers moving upward in a straight line toward a point *ahead* of the helicopter. Because the tracers are angling ahead, relative motion makes it appear that they are moving fast. However, as the helicopter flies forward (toward the point in the sky where it will meet the tracers), the angle decreases, and relative motion decreases. To the crew, it looks like the tracers are slowing down. In the split-second before the helicopter and tracers meet, there is no relative motion, for the tracers are headed straight toward the crew. The tracers appear to have stopped.

Robinson was right (see his quote, above). Gunship tracers seem to be in slow motion as they near the ground. The gunship has four fixed forward-firing machineguns. There is no relative motion as gunship tracers continue straight ahead, and the gunship follows. However, if a tracer hits the ground and ricochets, gunship pilots instantly detect the relative motion. The ricocheting tracer is angling away from the helicopter's path, so it appears to speed up.

Razorback Valley, 9 August 1966, 0145 Hours: Clouds over the valley continued to break, and soon infantrymen on the knoll would get a new weapon. The World War II-vintage Douglas C-47 had found a new role. Fitted with General Electric SUU-11 7.62mm miniguns, the former transport became an AC-47, a gun platform. "Puff" (often called, *Spooky*) could fire an incredible 6,000 rounds per minute. This magic dragon in the sky finally was able to get down under the cloud layer.

Maj. Hazelbaker got a flashlight and, from the bottom of his hole so the NVA could not see it, aimed it skyward at Puff. Yes, the pilot radioed, he saw their light, and he knew their position. He could rain down destruction to within 50 meters of the knoll. In the hole with Capt. Lee, the Recon radioman, Cpl. Bachta, began yelling: "Puff is on the way! Puff is on the way! Puff is coming!"

LCpl. Butler had never heard of Puff. What was happening? He noticed that Huey gunships had flown away. Why? Overhead he heard the drone of a strange kind of aircraft. All shooting stopped. An eerie and spooky quiet settled over the hill.

Puff's miniguns suddenly belched flame and emitted an unearthly moan. One Marine described it as a terrifying roar. Another related the deafening whine to the sound of a mammoth buzz saw.

A long wide undulating ribbon of fire appeared from the sky. I knew we all were dead.
[Wayne Hazelbaker, in a letter, 12 December 1989]

Infantrymen, the two Recons, and stranded helicopter crewmen on the knoll could not see individual tracers, just a solid finger of fire, a blinding tendril of flame slicing down from the sky. For Marines on the small knoll it looked too terrifying, too close.

Marble Mountain, 9 August 1966, 0230 Hours: For the Marines trapped in Razorback Valley more help was on the way. Far to the south at Marble Mountain, the HMM-263 (call-sign, *Powerglide*) duty officer began waking selected pilots and aircrewmen. They shuffled down to the ready room tent and entered through homemade saloon type swinging doors. Overhead was the famed handpainted sign: "Dunphy's Tavern." Beneath that moniker was the squadron logo and slogan: "Bluebird Taxi: You Call, We Haul."

At a quick briefing few details were available. Eight H-34s were needed at Dong Ha. Plans would be formulated after they arrived. The 50-minute flight would be led by the squadron commanding officer, LtCol. Jerry Goebel. For this mission he had handpicked his most experienced pilots and aircrewmen, the heavy hitters.

> HMM-263 sent 8 *[helicopters]* to Dong Ha today for support of Operation Prairie.
> *[HMM-263, Command Chronology, 9 August 1966]*

Goebel and his copilot, 1stLt. Tom Holmes, crawled into Bureau Number 149318. The eight H-34s launched and headed up into the dark night. There was no moonlight, no starlight, no illumination at all. Following IFR procedures the pilots tracked outbound on the Da Nang TACAN, Channel 37. They switched to 278.4 on their UHF radios and called "Panama" (IFR Departure Control) for radar vectors past the invisible 3,907-foot peak of the mountain at Hai Van Pass. Once vectored past the unseen mountain they all monitored 315.5, Phu Bai Approach Control. They rotored on northward paralleling the coastal flatlands and tracked inbound on the Dong Ha TACAN, Channel 46.

Over the South China Sea, 9 August 1966, 0315 Hours: In the left seat of the first H-34, Lt. Holmes peered ahead into the night. He could not see the land, the sea, the moon, or stars. Exclusive of external lights on the other helicopters he saw nothing as he flew IFR into an endless and dimensionless black hole. There were no lights below. The world outside his cockpit was an ebony void. Exclusive of his Airspeed Indicator and the roll of his DME (distance measuring equipment) display on the instrument panel, he had no sensation of speed or motion.

> It is impossible to describe the sheer blackness of a night *[over]* the ocean with no moon, no stars, no lights, thick clouds, and an overcast. It is the blackest of black.
> *[Roy Stafford, "Heart Stopper," 2013]*

Off to his left where the mountains should be, Holmes suddenly saw a brilliant beam, a bright shaft of light. Obviously originating from some type of aircraft, the beam flickered on and off. Holmes and Goebel watched in fascination. What could it be? Later they would learn they had been watching the faraway deadly finger of fire from Puff's miniguns in Razorback Valley.

Dong Ha, 9 August 1966, 0330 Hours: The eight H-34s landed at Dong Ha. Walking to the Op's North tent, Powerglide crews drank hot coffee and learned that the situation was stable for the moment. Marines on the knoll had ammunition from the Huey that had been shot down. Also, remaining flyable Hueys and H-34s had made low and slow passes over the knoll and had kicked out a limited amount of ammunition. Most of the fighting had turned into a grenade battle.

> During the night the NVA kept launching grenade attacks; they were within grenade range.
> *[Howard Lee, oral account, 12 August 1990]*

Razorback Valley, 9 August 1966, 0340 Hours: Marines on the knoll knew where the encircling NVA troops were. And, of course, the NVA knew exactly where the surrounded Marines were. Both adversaries would shoot at anything they could see moving. The North Vietnamese had everything zeroed-in on the knoll, obviously waiting for another helicopter to land. The NVA waited for more helicopters, and Marines waited for dawn. Deadlock gunships stayed in a racetrack pattern over the knoll and fired at the thick brush surrounding the little hill.

> Hueys piloted by Capt. Ben Meharg, Capt. Jack Enockson, and Lt. Jose Melendez, remained on station all night long, conducting airstrikes within 50 meters of the besieged Marines and providing suppressive fire of their own.
> *[VMO-2, Command Chronology, 8-9 August 1966]*

Infantrymen on the knoll watched the flashing red anticollision lights on Huey gunships as they prepared to make strafing runs. The Hueys used a wagon wheel tactic. To thwart NVA gunners they never approached from the same direction twice in a row. As they began strafing runs they would turn off all external lights and become invisible to both the NVA and Marines down below. After a gun run the lead gunship would turn, climb away, and turn his lights on again. His wingman, following behind, would turn off his external lights and strafe the same area to suppress enemy fire.

Received intense small arms, automatic weapons, and .50 cal fire from all around the *[hill]*.
[VMO-2, Command Chronology, 9 August 1966]

Between grenade attacks the downed gunship copilot, Lt. Costa, stayed busy. The flesh wound in his lower leg did not materially hinder him, and he made rounds of the perimeter making sure that Marines in each hole had enough ammunition to continue the fight. At times he also relieved Hazelbaker on the radio, and he never got rattled. His fellow lieutenants in the gunships overhead dispensed with radio protocol and addressed him as "Tony," the common name by which he was known.

When an NVA grenade thumped down onto the hill and bounced to a stop on level ground, nearby Marines would yell: "In the hole!" This signaled all Marines to hunker down as low in their holes as possible to escape the blast and flying shrapnel. Conversely, when grenades bounced down *into* a hole the occupants would shout: "Out of the hole!" This verbal warning system was not perfect. From Washington, DC, Sterling Fletcher had enlisted in the Marine Corps. Now a lance corporal, he helped to man the perimeter atop the besieged knoll.

Fletcher, Sterling Aloysius, LCpl., WIA, 8Aug66,. . . fragmentation wounds face, neck, right leg, both ankles, and both buttocks.
[Cas.Card, LCpl. Sterling Fletcher, USMC, 8-9 August 1966]

Fletcher's wounds, although not life threatening, were agonizing. HM3 Tarzia insisted upon injecting Fletcher with morphine to kill the pain, but the wounded infantryman refused to take it. He could still fight, he yelled. The enemy soon would storm the perimeter again, he reasoned, and he did not want to be wrapped in morphine's warm embrace when the attack came. Before he became a Marine he had seen Washington's inner-city teenagers and young adults stoned and strung-out on drugs, unable to cope with reality, mentally wasted. Fletcher insisted that his mind had to remain clear. He would ignore the pain and tune it out. He wanted to fight.

One by one Marines on the knoll were falling prey to rifle fire or shrapnel, and often both. LCpl. Roger Davis had sustained minor shrapnel wounds in his back the previous month on 23 July. On the hill he had been aggressive, crawling from hole to hole to make sure everyone had ammunition and grenades, and he helped wounded men load magazines in the dark. Then his luck ran out.

Davis, Roger A., LCpl., WIA, 8Aug66, Quang Tri Province, RVN. *[E/2/4, Unit Diary, August 1966]*

The previous afternoon PFC Fred Rode had been standing about ten feet from Lt. Sherman, the platoon commander, when the lieutenant was killed. Rode escaped injury. He was a rifleman, and he had been in Vietnam for only two weeks. Yet, for Rode and all Marines on the hill, sooner or later their good fortune would end. During the night a grenade detonated by the Pennsylvanian's hole and sent hot steel into his left elbow and arm.

Rode, Frederick, PFC, WIA, 8Aug66, Quang Tri Province, RVN. *[E/2/4, Unit Diary, August 1966]*

Dong Ha, 9 August 1966, 0345 Hours: VMO-2 ground crews stayed busy. Like helicopter crews in other squadrons, VMO-2 crews at primitive Dong Ha wore their nomex flight suits 24 hours per day. They worked, flew, ate, and slept in them. They had no need for other attire. When a Huey returned to Dong Ha to rearm and refuel, the crew chief took charge. He would drag a fuel line to the flying machine and top-off the tanks. Then he would rearm the six 7.62mm machineguns (he would fire one of them, another would be fired by the gunner, and the four forward-firing guns would be electrically fired by the pilot). Then the crew chief would supervise loading of 2.75-inch rockets into rocket pods on each side of the helicopter. The entire process would take about 20 minutes.

The venerable Huey was the first true helicopter gunship. Cobras and Apaches would come years later, but in 1966 the Huey gunship was state-of-the-art. A overhead swing-down gunsight, fabricated in the squadron metal shop, served as the pilot's rear sight. He would align its crosshairs with a grease-pencil mark on the windshield. Lined up on a target, he could fire his four fixed forward-firing guns and his 2.75-inch rockets, high-tech in the 1960s.

When time was of the essence, Hueys could be refueled with the Lycoming jet engine running and rotor engaged. With the engine running, the crew chief had to be careful not to overfill the tanks and spill JP-4 fuel (essentially, *kerosene*) that could ignite. Around 0330 Hours while hot-point refueling, jet fuel sprayed out over the top of a Huey and gushed over the windshield. The pilot, 1stLt. Lanny Ingvoldstad, frantically shut down the Huey, threw off his straps, and leaped out of the cockpit.

A pressure surge had caused the spill. I waited for *[the Huey]* to blow up. It didn't.
[Lanny Ingvoldstad, oral account, 12 August 1999]

Every Marine at Dong Ha knew their brothers on the knoll were in grave danger. Everyone wanted to help in some way, but they were frustrated. One pleaded to Ingvoldstad: "What can I do? I want to hump ammo or something!"

1stLt. Al Barbour was the VMO-2 scheduling officer at Dong Ha. When Op's North needed Huey gunships or slicks, Barbour normally assigned the helicopters and crews. However, after midnight Barbour delegated that job to others. He elected to fly a gunship and would do so for the remainder of the night.

This is what the Marine Corps is about. We had a total commitment to the Marines on the ground.
[Alan Barbour, oral account, 4 November 1999]

While gunships were flying, most Powerglide H-34 crews sat on the grass near the Op's North tent and waited, perhaps the hardest thing to do. From time to time they wandered inside and listened to radio contacts between gunships and Marines on the hill. However, that usually proved to be too nerve-wracking. Most crewmen crawled back into their H-34s, curled up on top of nylon troop seats, and tried to get some sleep.

Hours earlier SSgt. Conrad Ortego had been aboard Bonnie-Sue 9-3 when it had tried to land in a bomb crater at the base of the knoll. Enemy fire had wounded all four crewmembers, but they had been able to flounder back to Dong Ha. Ortego did not abandon his effort to reach the knoll. The surrounded young Marines there needed his combat experience and leadership. Fourteen years earlier he had fought in Korea with the 2nd Battalion, 1st Marines. There he had tasted the sting of battle and had been seriously wounded on 7 April 1952. Yet, the Corps was his life. He had a wife in San Diego and parents in Opelousas, Louisiana, but now his Corps had sent him to Vietnam. After midnight he had hopped aboard an H-34 for another attempt to reach the knoll.

I was aboard two different helicopters that tried to land on the knoll and reinforce the Marines fighting there. On both occasions the pilots were forced to turn back by the heavy enemy fire.
[Conrad Ortego, quoted in <u>Marines, Medals, and Vietnam,</u> 2012]

On both attempts to land on the knoll the helicopters had been riddled. Nevertheless, Ortego survived without injury. He had no way to know it at that time, but his good luck would end ten days later on 19 August 1966.

Razorback Valley, 9 August 1966, 0400 Hours: Capt. Lee finally relinquished command. All night he had crawled among his men to encourage them, but now the loss of blood had taken its toll. He lay slumped against the side of his fighting hole. He no longer had the strength to crawl out of it. Now semiconscious, Lee relinquished command of his men to Maj. Hazelbaker.

Our C.O., Capt. Lee, was wounded and incapacitated due to numerous wounds inflicted by rockets and grenades.
[Cpl. David Smith, USMC, typed account, 11 August 1966]

LCpl. McKay, the downed Huey gunner, remained in a hole with two men from Echo Company. The wounds in his back were not causing pain, but his shattered knee was beginning to stiffen up and ache. It had not bled very much. No one had given him morphine. McKay's main concern was not pain or the wound in his leg. He had been coughing-up blood for two hours. Had shrapnel in his back punctured a lung? He knew a relief force could not arrive before daylight, and he knew of no way to stop internal bleeding.

McKay shared his problem with LCpl. Jesus Daniels, one of the two Marines in the hole with him. Daniels replied in essence: "Don't worry, if you smoke a cigarette it will dry it up." Perhaps that was a psychological ploy, or perhaps it was good medical advice. McKay pulled a poncho over his head and upper torso to conceal the flame and glow. Then he lit and smoked a cigarette. Within 15 minutes he was no longer spitting-up blood (later he would learn that his internal bleeding had been caused by rocket blast concussion, not by puncture of internal organs).

The Hispanic guy in my hole *[LCpl. Jesus Daniels]* did a great job. He made several trips back to the *[downed]* helicopter to get ammo, and he distributed it to the other guys.
[Jim McKay, oral account, 27 September 2000]

Daniels, called "Jes" by friends in Echo Company, had a Yaqui and Mexican heritage. He had been born in rural Buckeye, Arizona, but had been living in Hollister, California, when he enlisted. He often had told his Marine brothers that, after his time in the Corps, his lifelong dream was to become a cowboy (although badly wounded, he would survive and accomplish that goal).

Cpl. Strock, the other Marine sharing the hole with McKay and Daniels, had concentrated on the ammunition supply. He and Daniels had stripped the downed Huey of its ordnance and guns. Strock had crawled to PFC Hamrick's body and had taken his M-14 magazines. While gathering more ammunition an NVA grenade had detonated nearby and had sent hot shrapnel into his left arm, leg, and back.

Strock, Richard Alvin, Cpl., WIA, 8Aug66, fragmentation wounds.
[Cas.Card, Cpl. Richard Strock, USMC, 8-9 August 1966]

Although wounded, Strock still could contribute to defense of the hill.   He crawled from hole to hole to distribute ammunition and grenades.   However, the ordnance supply gradually dwindled, and eventually many Marines were down to their last magazine.   When all ammunition was gone their only weapons would be their bayonets, Ka-Bars (fighting knives), and fists.   By now most infantrymen on the hill knew that time might soon come.   One by one they unsheathed their Ka-Bars.   Hilts up, they jabbed them into the ground in front of their holes so they instantly could grab them.   They would be ready if a North Vietnamese charge breached the perimeter.

> We were committed to each other and resolved that in the end we were going to prevail. . . . Training takes over, and the only thing that really matters is the Marine next to you.
> *[Richard Strock, e-mail message, 2 March 2015]*

There was no more water.   All battle dressings long ago had been used.   Marines and their corpsman, HM3 Tarzia, began removing the compress bandages from those with relatively minor wounds and from KIAs who no longer needed them.   They re-used the battle dressings on Marines with new grievous wounds.

Maj. Hazelbaker crawled to each hole every 30 minutes or so, trying to reassure everyone and keep their spirits up.   He had no more ammunition to distribute, but between flares when it was dark he would scurry around the hilltop.

> *[In the dark]* we would hear *[Hazelbaker's]* voice saying: "Hey, Marines, tell me where you are; I'm coming to see you." He had his thirty-eight *[revolver]* in his hand.
> *[Richard Strock, oral account, 2 March 2015]*

By now Marines on the knoll, the gunships circling above, Op's North, artillery at Cam Lo, and battalion headquarters were on the same radio frequency, 49.6.   Hazelbaker stayed busy on his radio, communicating with Op's North and the gunships.   Before he had lapsed into listlessness, Lee had been giving radio updates to LtCol. Arnold Bench, his battalion commander at Dong Ha.   Now no longer able to communicate effectively, he told Cpl. Bachta to use the company commander call-sign, Echo Six, and maintain radio contact with the battalion commander. Despite the danger on the knoll this led to some humorous moments.

In good faith Bachta began identifying himself as Echo Six. He kept LtCol. Bench and Maj. Colby updated and responded to all radio transmissions to Groucho Marx and Echo Six. To most Marines, on the radio Bachta had *become* Echo Six. With all that was going on, LtCol. Bench initially did not realize he was no longer talking with Capt. Lee. After a while he radioed Echo Six and asked: "What's your profile like?"

Such command terminology was not familiar to Bachta, so an awkward silence ensued. Then a Deadlock pilot, orbiting overhead in the night sky, keyed his mike and radioed in the blind: "He wants to know how you are doing."

"I'm doing fine, sir, how are you?" Bachta naively radioed.

"Who am I talking to?"

"This is the Groucho Marx radioman."

"Where's my company commander?"

"He's here, but he's out of it."

Bachta explained that Capt. Lee's wounds were incapacitating, and that he was merely doing what the captain had asked him to do, just following orders. Bench asked: "Well, who is in charge?"

"I am," Bachta gamely replied.

> When Lee *[had gotten]* to the hill, he *[had taken]* over the radio. He was the one we talked to until he was no longer able to function. Then Bachta took over. . . . Bachta was calm on the radio, professional, *[he]* never got rattled.
> *[Dwain Colby, oral account, 23 March 1999]*

Dawn was still over two hours away. If they could hold out until dawn, Marine fixed-wing pilots could see the knoll and could pound surrounding terrain with bombs and napalm. Helicopter crews could find landing spots and bring in reinforcements. For the moment the NVA seemed content to probe the perimeter with grenades and small arms fire. Although Marines had gotten a Huey full of ammunition when Hazelbaker had been shot down, most of it had been expended.

I remember running out of ammunition a couple of times.
[Rick Rode, oral account, 4 June 2015]

The night seemed to be a living entity. Nobody slept. Minutes crawled slowly by as in an interminable waking nightmare. Could the men on the hill survive until daylight? Words of Capt. Francis West Jr., USMC, written about another group of besieged Marines, were applicable to surrounded men on the knoll.

The living took the ammunition of the dead and lay under a moonless sky, wondering about the next assault.
[Capt. Francis West Jr., USMC, Small Unit Action in Vietnam, 1967]

Down in the dark ravines and gullies below the knoll the North Vietnamese soldiers kept as close to the perimeter as possible. They followed doctrine for fighting the Americans and "hugged the belt." The closer they got to the top of the knoll, the safer they were from Puff and the gunships circling above. Earlier in the night they had tried human wave attacks up the steep knoll. Entrenched Marines had clear fields of fire and had thrown back each assault. The NVA now were content to creep within throwing distance, lob in a grenade or two, and then fire a few AK-47 rounds before scurrying for cover. Both the Americans and NVA were low on ammunition, and between grenade exchanges an eerie silence prevailed.

No one was shooting. It got real quiet. The gunships were circling high *[over the valley]* with lights on. The radio operator was silent. Flares were drifting down. *[It was]* peaceful.
[Wayne Hazelbaker, in a letter, 12 December 1989]

The eastern side of the hill was different. Twenty feet beyond the perimeter was a mini-cliff, a steep drop-off. It was only about four feet high. Yet, below the drop-off, protected and unseen in defilade, NVA soldiers had crawled up to within 20 feet of the perimeter. Hunkered down and concealed by the terrain they could accurately lob grenades onto the Marines.

Nearby on the eastern slope PFC Callaway and his gunner, Cpl.

David Smith, had their M-60 set up to defend the perimeter. NVA soldiers who jumped up and charged uphill over the drop-off would run into their machinegun field of fire. Twenty feet away Cpl. James Pace had another M-60 to defend the eastern slope.

> *[During attacks]* Callaway was yelling and hollering. That was the cowboy in him. He was like a wild man.
> *[Richard Strock, oral account, 20 February 2015]*

LCpl. Butler, the erstwhile Echo Company radioman, shared a hole above the drop-off with another Marine from Echo Company. Several NVA were 20 feet away below the lip of the steep terrain. Butler could hear their sing-song voices below him, but out of sight. He and his comrade quietly debated the possible wisdom of flanking the enemy below. Butler theorized that they could leave the safety of their hole, crawl parallel to the slope, double back below the drop-off, and rake the enemy with close range fire.

However, caution prevailed. If they tried the flanking maneuver in the dark they most likely would be shot, maybe by the NVA below, and maybe by Marines above. They elected to stay in their hole, where they hoped to survive until daylight.

Razorback Valley, 9 August 1966, 0500 Hours: SSgt. Donaldson, severely wounded nine hours earlier, lay in a fighting hole with a young Marine who looked not a day over 16 years of age. He had loose 7.62mm rounds that had come from the downed Huey, and he asked Donaldson to load them into a magazine for him. Donaldson tried, but he could get only four rounds into a magazine. He could not use either paralyzed hand, so he had to roll each round into position with his arms and then try to squeeze it into the magazine with his wrist in the dark.

Donaldson knew that he likely would be killed by the NVA before daylight, but possibly they might *capture* him. The futility of his dilemma became comical to him. He could not walk. He could not stand up. He could not crawl. He could not use his hands. If he were to be captured he only would be able to curse the NVA soldiers and kick at them. He began laughing like a crazy man.

LCpl. Gibson, a native Texan, crouched in a hole on the eastern side of the perimeter. The NVA were in front of him and in defilade below the drop-off. According to his peers, Gibson had been fighting like a man possessed. He had humped ammunition from hole to hole and had almost worn out the barrel of an M-60. When an NVA machinegun team had threatened the perimeter, Gibson did not ask others to help him.

Gibson moved out on the fire-swept slope in full view of the enemy, flanked the weapon, and single-handedly knocked it out, killing its crew.
[USMC citation referencing 8-9 August 1966]

The mild-mannered Gibson was a gunfighter, pure and simple. To supplement his M-14 he had picked up two more rifles from KIAs. He had a stack of magazines and grenades. However, like all mortals Gibson was not invincible. Between flares during a period of darkness he sat up on the side of his hole, trying to get a better view. An NVA soldier promptly shot him.

Gibson, George Ronald, LCpl., WIA, 8Aug66, . . . gunshot wound right shoulder.
[Cas.Card, LCpl. George Gibson, USMC, 8-9 August 1966]

Obviously both the NVA and Marines were short of ammunition. During dark predawn hours no one fired unless he had a clearly visible human target. They no longer could waste ammunition by shooting at shadows and apparitions. Marines defending the knoll long ago had rummaged through clothing and web gear of their dead brothers, searching for ammunition and grenades. After that supply had run out they low-crawled downhill between flares to scrounge rifles and ammunition from dead NVA soldiers. On several such trips in the shadowy darkness a Marine suddenly found himself face-to-face with an enemy soldier who was doing the same thing.

Every five minutes or so the adversaries would toss grenades back and forth. In the interludes NVA soldiers could hear Marines talking, and Marines could hear sing-song Vietnamese voices down below them, only 35 to 90 feet away. In Vietnamese culture, laughing is a part of communication. The NVA in ravines below injected laughter into their vocabulary.

NVA soldiers down below the perimeter obviously did not speak English, but they had memorized a few words and phrases. Often one of them would shout: "Marine you die!" or "Marine num-bah ten!" On the western slope a highly vocal North Vietnamese soldier often screamed: "Jone-son you num-bah ten!" (*Jone-son* referred to the U.S. President, Lyndon *Johnson*).

Marines responded in kind. They would shout in reply: "Ho Chi Minh number ten!" and "Ho Chi Minh bo coo dinky dow!" (*bo coo dinky dow* is an Americanized corruption of *beaucoup dien cai dau*, which means, *very crazy*). Yet, the most common Marine pejorative was a simple shout: "Ho Chi Minh sucks dicks!"

> The NVA mounted many assaults on the recon position throughout the night. . . . The gunships continued to provide CAS *[close air support]* for the rest of the night.
> *[Capt. Ben Meharg, USMC, typed account, 11 August 1966]*

One has to have been there to understand, but in the midst of peril the most trivial matters prompted serious debates. LCpl. McKay, badly wounded in his back and knee, shared a fighting hole with LCpl. Daniels. By now Daniels had a concussion, and shrapnel had torn into his elbow and buttocks.

> Daniels, Jesus Jr., LCpl., WIA, 8Aug66, fragmentation wound left buttock and concussion.
> *[Cas.Card, LCpl. Jesus Daniels, USMC, 8-9 August 1966]*

Daniels had another injury. While jumping into his hole he had fallen onto his bayonet, which stabbed him in the buttocks. In the morning darkness between incoming grenades and rifle fire, Daniels and McKay debated Purple Heart policy. Daniels would, of course, be awarded a Purple Heart for shrapnel wounds and the concussion. Absent those wounds, the two Marines wondered if Daniels would be awarded a Purple Heart due to the *accidently-self-inflicted* bayonet wound in his buttocks. They were undeniably in combat. The ethical debate continued for a half-hour. McKay opined that a Purple Heart was warranted. Daniels modestly disagreed.

Razorback Valley, Death of Pvt. Vernal Martin: Sometime before daylight Pvt. Vernal Martin, a rifleman, lost his life on the besieged knoll. Based solely upon military records, very little is known about him. His name, service number, and MOS would appear on the 2nd Battalion, 4th Marines, Unit Diary for August 1966. He is listed with other Echo Company men who were killed-in-action on the knoll. However, his Casualty Card would not be prepared until 4 January 1968, over a year later. Contrary to convention it does not list his date of birth, place of birth, home of record, place of entry into the Corps, or date of entry. His parents, next of kin, or other relatives are not included. Instead the Casualty Card contains the entry: "Miss Laura L. Kelly, address unknown, friend." Typewritten entries in the identification and casualty sections of the card are brief:

> Martin, Vernal Glen, Pvt., KIA, Died 9Aug66.
> *[Cas.Card, Pvt. Vernal Martin, USMC, 9 August 1966]*

Civil records agree that Pvt. Martin was in 2nd Platoon, Echo Company, and was killed-in-action on 9 August 1966. These civil records show that his home of record was Marshfield, Wisconsin. He had been born on 9 March 1945 and was 21 years of age when he was killed. He died due to "multiple fragmentation wounds."

> Pace, James, Cpl., WIA, 8Aug66, Quang Tri Province, RVN.
> *[E/2/4, Unit Diary, August 1966]*

Cpl. James Pace (not to be confused with Sgt. Robert Pace) was one of the squad leaders. He had been active on the perimeter all night. To him it seemed that daylight never would come. Daylight would allow fixed-wing *fast movers* to strafe and bomb the enemy around the hill. Daylight would enable helicopter crews to spot nearby landing areas and bring reinforcements. Until the sun peeped over the ridges to the east, he and others on the hill were in dire peril. Would they survive until dawn?

> All of us were wounded . . . . We were low, extremely low, on ammo, and we were surrounded by the enemy.
> *[Cpl. James Pace, USMC, typed account, 11 August 1966]*

Dong Ha, 9 August 1966, 0515 Hours: Daylight was still an hour away, but already the regimental commander, Col. Cereghino, was on the way to Dong Ha. He wanted to *be there*. Also, Mike Company, 3rd Battalion, 4th Marines, would be on the way within the hour.

> At 0515 Hours, Regimental Commander and S-3 *[meaning, operations officer]* departed *[Phu Bai]* CP en route to 2/4 CP at Dong Ha, via helicopter. At 0551 Hours, began lifting M/3/4 to Dong Ha via fixed-wing aircraft, on arrival chopped OPCON *[to]* 2/4.
> *[4th Marines, Command Chronology, 9 August 1966]*

Before daylight 1stLt. Larry Robinson was no longer needed as a volunteer copilot with VMO-2. He had flown the previous afternoon, had flown 4.1 hours in the predawn darkness, and had not slept in over 24 hours. He first tried to sleep on helicopter troop seats, but mosquitoes were feasting on him. He had no protective bug-juice.

> Shortages still exist in aerosol and liquid insect repellants.
> *[4th Marines, Command Chronology, August 1966]*

Robinson crept into the Val-Pac tent where razor blades, soap, and edible goodies were stored. There he curled up on the ground, covered himself with a mosquito net, and fell asleep immediately.

Robinson awoke when he felt something clawing on his left arm, pulling at the sweat-soaked leather band of his wristwatch. A huge wharf rat! He screamed and slung the toothy rodent off. He dashed outside, regained his composure, crawled onto helicopter troop seats, and slept with the mosquitoes.

Razorback Valley, 9 August 1966, 0620 Hours: The eastern sky beyond Hill 549 grayed and then brightened, and the first faint rays of dawn slowly illuminated Razorback Valley. Soon the rising sun would burn away shrouds of night mist that had cloaked the valley. Maj. Hazelbaker busied himself on the radio while Deadlock Huey gunships buzzed overhead. In one of them, 1stLt. Spink had been in the air almost continuously during the past 16 hours.

The morning sky belonged to the Marines. Fixed-wing close air support arrived over the valley: Oxwood 63 and Oxwood 67 (A-4

Skyhawks from Chu Lai) plus Condole 55, Condole 56, and Condole 57 (F-8 Crusaders from Da Nang). Survivors on the hill, perilously low on ammunition, had help from above. Marine jet pilots flying over the valley now could see the knoll, and they emptied their explosive and incendiary bowels onto the North Vietnamese.

> The jets flew up the valley right over the trees, very low. I could see the pilots in the cockpits.
> *[Gary Butler, oral account, 2 March 2015]*

> One UH-1E of VMO-2 directed *[ground attack jets]* on airstrike around area of encircled Marines on hilltop.
> *[MAG-16, Command Chronology, 9 August 1966]*

NVA soldiers were famed experts at digging-in for protection against artillery, hard bombs, and rifle fire. However, as the minutes ticked by and the sky continued to brighten, their probes against the perimeter faded away. They withdrew northward toward their big fortress on the jungled Nui Cay Tre Ridge (later, *Mutter Ridge*).

SSgt. Donaldson found himself in a hole on the side of the knoll ten meters from the top. How he got there he did not know. He tried to crawl uphill but could not do so. He looked behind him. Ten meters away and below the perimeter was a 12.7mm machinegun with five dead NVA soldiers sprawled around it.

LCpl. Butler crawled out of the hole where he had spent the past four hours. He was wounded, dehydrated, exhausted, wasted, had not slept, had not eaten, and had nothing to drink. He tried to stand up, and he fainted.

Razorback Valley, 9 August 1966, 0700 Hours: A lone green H-34 arrived high over the valley, out of the effective range of small arms fire. The pilot, LtCol. Goebel, had replaced his regular copilot. LtCol. Bench, commander of the 2nd Battalion, 4th Marines, was riding in the copilot's seat as an observer. He and Goebel were visually checking potential nearby landing areas where a large relief force could be helicoptered into the valley.

At 0735 Hours a silver-gray Marine A-4 Skyhawk sliced down out of the sky and leveled, heading westward through the valley. The pilot laid down a white phosphorus smoke-screen between the knoll and the enemy ridge to the north. Lethal WP particles corkscrewed their way to the ground. The drop was close to the knoll. PFC Callaway and several others got minor burns when corrosive white phosphorus particles sprinkled onto their bare skin.

> Mission 8-7001: Two UH-1Es acted as TAC(A) in support of company (240 troops) . . . controlled and supported medevac pickup at XD-988598. Ran LZ prep and smoke screen for lift. Controlled Oxwood 63 & 67 flights, Condole 55, 56, & 57 *[airstrikes against]* enemy troops in bunkers at YD-999598. Received fire on passes.
> *[VMO-2, Command Chronology, 9 August 1966]*

At 0740 Hours, south of the smoke-screen and one at a time, Powerglide helicopters spiraled down onto a tiny landing spot 300 meters west of the knoll. The H-34s discharged the first wave of relief troops from Foxtrot Company. Again flying as copilot in the first helicopter, Lt. Holmes realized the smoke-screen was highly effective. It appeared that a thick white curtain had been drawn between the knoll and the enemy ridge to the north. Soon the helicopters returned with the remainder of Foxtrot Company plus a small contingent from Echo Company. This relief force linked-up with exhausted Marines on the knoll. There was no enemy fire.

> There were NVA bodies all over the top and side of the hill. . . . It was difficult for me to set the *[Huey]* skids down on the ground without *[putting them]* on a body.
> *[Al Barbour, e-mail message, 5 October 1999]*

Capt. Lee, still alive and semiconscious, lay in his hole. He was too wasted to crawl out of it. He called for his radioman, LCpl. Butler. In a course whisper the captain asked Butler to retrieve the two metal rank insignia from his pocket and pin them onto his collar. The radioman complied. However, the chore was foreign to him, and he inadvertently pinned the bars on sideways.

Razorback Valley, 9 August 1966, 0830 Hours: H-34s had been circling overhead, and now they flew down to land right on top of the knoll itself. They had to land one at a time because the little hill was so small and steep. There was room for only one helicopter.

In the first H-34, Lt. Tom Holmes had made a careful power-on approach. The knoll appeared only about 30 to 35 feet high, he had estimated, and in a recorded narrative years later he would explain.

> It had been hand-to-hand during the night. When we *[landed]* you could see all of the *[NVA]* bodies, all in tan uniforms, the dead North Vietnamese. The dead guys were lying all over, all over the hill. It was hard to find a place to put the *[helicopter]* landing gear down without putting it on top of one of them.
> *[Tom Holmes, recorded account, 11 July 1989]*

The first H-34 picked up only dead Marines. As other helicopters flew down and landed, troops in the relief force loaded wounded men aboard for the 13-mile flight back to Dong Ha.

> I was *[mentally]* in and out of it. Next thing I knew I was being manhandled into an H-34.
> *[Howard Lee, oral account, 2 March 1999]*

PFC Callaway crawled out of his hole and began looking around the hilltop. The ground was littered with dead North Vietnamese. In a macabre twist a Marine had stuck an unlit cigarette between the lips of one dead soldier from the north. They all exhibited a gray pallor, a death mask, a tallow-like sheen that made them appear to be wax dummies. Exclusive of their tan khaki uniforms and web gear they looked like dead Marines.

One soldier from the North had no right arm. Another had only the stump of a leg; the rest had been scythed off. Yet another still had most of his head, but little of his face was left. Callaway saw that the eyes of one dead NVA were still wide open and staring up into a sky that he never again would see.

Callaway prodded the soldier with the tip of his bayonet, just to confirm that he indeed was dead. Then he noticed papers in the dead man's shirt pocket. Also in the pocket was a wrinkled photograph of a young woman and a baby.

I'll never forget that picture!
[Robert Callaway, oral account, 23 January 2015]

Like the Marines, the dead soldier had been mortal. Presumably he had parents, a wife, a baby, and aspirations for a joyful reunion after the war. Although transit time averaged over three months, perhaps recently he had written to his wife. If so, his letter may have mirrored the unmailed letter dated 25 March that had been written by another NVA soldier. That letter was among documents seized when American forces overran an enemy base camp. Translated into English, it is quoted below in part:

My Dearest: . . . We belong to a generation that is advancing speedily forward and scoring achievements on the battlefield. . . . I've given all my love to you. As long as I continue fighting under the Party flag, I'll remain your own. Self-respecting and loving people will remain faithful to the ones they love. This is proof of their dignity. I'll wait for you and remember you forever. . . . Sometime in the future, or when the country is reunified, you and I will be reunited. How precious will our love be then! Do you agree, my love? I'm going to stop here. I send you my unspoken but profound and faithful love.   Yours, *[name redacted]*

Razorback Valley, 9 August 1966, 0840 Hours: The relief force fanned out and searched the ravines, gullies, and jungle below the knoll, but the NVA had melted away to their fortress on Nui Cay Tre Ridge. The North Vietnamese had fought fiercely, for they were disciplined soldiers. They loyally had carried most of their dead comrades away with them. Marines found plenty of blood trails and drag marks, but they found no NVA bodies down below the knoll. Yet, the NVA had been unable to retrieve their comrades who had fallen atop the hill. Thirty-seven dead North Vietnamese soldiers lay sprawled in and around the tiny perimeter.

No tongue can tell, no mind *[can]* conceive, no pen *[can]* portray the horrible sights I witnessed this morning.
[Capt. John Taggert, USA, after the battle at Sharpsburg (aka, Antietam), Maryland, 17 September 1862]

Most Marines boarded helicopters and headed eastward toward Dong Ha. Thousands of huge blowflies with swollen bellies already had descended onto the dead North Vietnamese, attracted by the dawn and a repugnant odor of death and human feces. Not yet bloating, the corpses would be left where they had fallen. Soon maggots would begin taking their grim toll.

> Mission 8-6001B: Escorted H-34s to retract E-2 *[from the knoll]*.
> *[VMO-2, Command Chronology, 9 August 1966]*

Dong Ha, 9 August 1966, 0900 Hours: Capt. Larry McDonald, the pilot, and Capt. Bob Porter, copilot, had flown from Marble Mountain to Dong Ha during the night. They had flown Bureau No. 152514, an H-46 "slick" assigned to HMM-265, the Bonnie-Sue squadron. The slick could function as a regular transport helicopter, but it had a special capability. It was a heavy-hauler. All excess weight had been removed: the armored seats were gone, cargo rails were gone, engine armor was gone, etc. Thus lightened, the slick could lift much more weight. During the flight to Dong Ha the slick had been loaded with 2.75-inch rockets for the gunships. Each gunship was equipped with two multi-shot rocket pods, and the supply of rockets at Dong Ha almost had been exhausted.

However, the slick had been needed at Dong Ha for an additional reason. The heavy-hauler would be used to "external" the downed Huey from the knoll back to Dong Ha. An aircraft recovery team already had been flown to the valley. They had affixed a heavy cargo sling to the downed craft.

Razorback Valley, 9 August 1966, 0925 Hours: McDonald and Porter launched from Dong Ha and flew to Razorback Valley. Once again an A-4 Skyhawk laid down a smoke-screen between the knoll and the enemy-held Nui Cay Tre Ridge to the north.

> The Huey was in a small depression about halfway down the hill .
> … I *[flew to the knoll]* very low, right as the A-4 made the smoke run. We had it hooked up in about 15 seconds.
> *[Larry McDonald, in a letter, 2 December 1999]*

As McDonald zipped in and hovered over the Huey, a Marine from the recovery team slammed the sling connector onto the slick's cargo hook. McDonald pulled in full power and slowly flew back to Dong Ha with the Huey dangling on the sling below. Exhaustive and major repairs would be needed before it could fly again.

Lt. Costa, the downed Huey copilot, had an ugly shrapnel wound in his leg, but he had insisted upon staying on the knoll with his erstwhile pilot, Maj. Hazelbaker. Now that what remained of their Huey had been picked up and helilifted back toward Dong Ha, they crawled into one of the H-34s for the eight minute ride to the aid station. As the Sikorsky flying machine climbed eastward, Costa unholstered his .38 caliber revolver, aimed out of the port hatch at the NVA-held ridge to the north, and cranked off a single round. Perhaps he simply wanted to take the final shot.

Dong Ha, 9 August 1966, 0930 Hours: Covered with a filthy and grimy combination of red mud and blood, SSgt. Donaldson had been carried into the third helicopter for a flight to safety. As soon as his helicopter landed at Dong Ha, Marines put him on a stretcher and rushed him toward Delta-Med north of the dirt runway. Two of his Recon buddies met him on the way there and tried to shake his hand, but his fingers still would not work. His Recon brothers simply held his thumbs and squeezed them tightly.

HMC Toland took charge as a stream of wounded Marines was carried to Delta-Med. The small room looked like a charnel house, a butcher shop. Mutilation from rifle fire and grenades presented a horrible sight. Among the many wounded men, Toland recognized his company commander, Capt. Lee, semiconscious and caked with blood and grime. Toland checked him. The captain was in shock, and his blood pressure was extremely low. Nonetheless, corpsmen were able to resuscitate him.

Delta-Med was the epicenter of activity at Dong Ha. Wounded men packed the little room, and other casualties lay on the ground outside waiting to be treated. Their entrance wounds were usually small, but one could put his fist into many exit wounds.

Corpsmen plied their medical trade with skill, hemostats, insulin, morphine, and compress battle dressings. They had no collegiate degree from a medical school. Yet, to Marines the corpsmen were doctors. They labored in an environment of unspeakable gore and shattered bodies that would have broken lesser men. When they had tagged along on a Marine patrol they had been fearless. In a firefight when someone yelled "Corpsman up!" they always had run toward the sound of the guns. Marines did not know first names, surnames, or military rank of their corpsmen. They did not care. To them all corpsmen were simply "Doc."

Trust among Marines and corpsmen was very tight, and respect was mutual.
[Ed Toland, oral account, 15 January 2015]

In Delta-Med, corpsmen injected pain-killing morphine into those who were in agony. They used a grease pencil to mark anesthetized men's foreheads with a cautionary "M." The paper tag attached to each casualty also noted the injection and the time it was given. After all wounded men had been stabilized they would be flown southward to Alpha-Med or Charlie-Med for surgery in a hospital environment. Depending upon the nature and extent of their wounds, some would recuperate in Vietnam. Others would be flown to American military hospitals in the Phillippines or Japan. Still others would be flown to military hospitals in the United States.

There was a final task for corpsmen at Dong Ha. They had five young Marines for whom time no longer mattered (another wounded Marine would die later). Corpsmen would complete the paperwork required. Identification and cause-of-death data would be compiled for each dead Marine. This information would be forwarded to the base (Phu Bai, Da Nang, or Marble Mountain) where the decedent's service record book was maintained. Corpses would be flown 75 miles southward to Da Nang. There each body would be packed in ice and placed inside a silver metal coffin in preparation for a final flight to the United States. Everything the dead men had, their memories, their accomplishments, their loves, their dreams, and everything they ever would have been was gone forever.

A day or two later and 12,000 miles away, parents or a wife would answer a knock on their front door. A Marine officer in Dress Blues, usually accompanied by a minister or chaplain, would tell them that their son or husband was dead. The years they had loved him, the aspirations they had for him, their plans for him; all of that was wiped away. His education, his training, his role in society and in his family, all of that also was gone.

> Not for fame or reward, not for place or rank,
> Not lured by ambition or goaded by necessity;
> But in simple obedience to duty as they understood it,
> These men suffered all, sacrificed all,
> Dared all – and died.
> *[Randolph McKim, CSA Chaplain, later inscribed on the Confederate Memorial at Arlington National Cemetery]*

Dong Ha, 9 August 1966, 0940 Hours: Somewhat surprised that he was still alive, Maj. Hazelbaker had crawled out of an H-34 cabin at Dong Ha. Caked with filth and grime, he wandered into the Op's North tent and found that the VMO-2 relief detachment had not yet arrived. He began wondering how he was going to get back to Marble Mountain. Then Lt. Costa, newly bandaged, hobbled in and reported that he had arranged for them to be flown home in an H-46. Hazelbaker, a Huey pilot, had never ridden in one of the newfangled H-46s, and to him the novel prospect was "exciting."

> 7 UH-34Ds of HMM-161, 4 CH-46As of HMM-265, and 8 UH-1Es of VMO-2 received damage from small arms fire. Of the 7 UH-34Ds, 3 are still flyable. Of the 4 CH-46As, 2 are still flyable. Of the 8 UH-1Es, 6 are still flyable.
> *[MAG-16, Command Chronology, 9 August 1966]*

MAG-16 maintenance crews went to work repairing helicopters that had suffered battle damage during the previous day and night. One H-34 with extensive damage had managed to fly away from the hill, but had run out of steam and had autorotated down onto Route 9 between the Rockpile and Cam Lo. Another was forced down and landed in the wide riverbed near Cam Lo. Yet another almost made it back to Dong Ha, but it ran out of oil due to battle damage leakage. The engine froze, and the pilots autorotated down a mile west of the Dong Ha airstrip. Only three of the eight Barrelhouse H-34s from HMM-161 were still flyable. Two Hueys from VMO-2 and two H-46s from HMM-265 would be unable to fly until extensive repairs were made. Maj. Seitz, the Op's North commander, reflected upon the past day and night.

> I sent out 17 helicopters. I got only 13 back. We lost one H-34 in sight of Dong Ha. He was boiling smoke, ran out of oil, autorotated *[to the ground]*. A Huey came down and picked *[the crew]* up.
> *[Fred Seitz, oral account, 2 March 1999]*

Bureau Number 152498, Bonnie-Sue 9-3, still squatted in the grass where its four wounded crewmen had left it. The warhorse had taken 34 hits. Incredibly, all of those hits had been in the cockpit and gunner's station areas. The forward transmission had three holes in it, both hydraulic systems were inoperative, and big structural and electrical repairs would be needed. Even the sync-shaft between the forward transmission and aft transmission, the H-46 equivalent of the so-called "Jesus Nut," had a bullet hole in it. Yet, although crippled, the tough flying machine had brought its crew home alive.

Capt. Roberts, a U.S. Naval Academy graduate in the Class of 1962, had been the copilot in Bonnie-Sue 9-1. By the morning of 9 August he had been treated for his minor arm wound. He wandered around south of the runway and looked at battle damage.

> The helicopters were all shot-up. Bullet holes everywhere. I saw two fifty-cal. holes in the *[blade]* spar of one helicopter. Between the cockpit seats were a bunch of holes, and more in the instrument panel and windshield.
> *[Joe Roberts, oral account, 26 November 1989]*

Upon their return to Dong Ha most Echo Company warriors with minor wounds collapsed onto the soft grass near the runway. None spoke unless spoken to. Their hollow eyes and gaunt faces said more than any words ever written. They were covered from head to foot with red grime. The smell of cordite permeated what was left of their tattered utilities. Parts of their clothing torn away revealed flesh covered with jungle-rot, infected leech bites, and insect whelps. But they had cheated the Grim Reaper. Many slept in the morning sunlight. Eyes of others evidenced the fabled "thousand yard stare" and chronic mental and physical exhaustion that no amount of sleep ever could erase. They had lost the bloom of youth.

> His clothes were mud caked, and the telltale signs of war reflected in his eyes.
> [*Pacific Stars & Stripes, describing PFC Robert Callaway, USMC, an Echo Company survivor*]

Lt. Holmes wandered over to a young Marine who had been flown back from the knoll. Sitting on the ground, Holmes asked the teenage gunfighter about events during the long night. Holmes later would explain in a recorded interview.

> One Marine got out *[of the helicopter]*, about eighteen *[years old]*, covered with dirt and gunpowder, black under the eyes. They were glassy. He was exhausted. Man, he looked bad, real bad. He said he had his bayonet fixed all night. I asked if he had been scared, and he said, "Yeah." Right before daylight he had one bullet left. One bullet. Just one bullet. So he started throwing rocks at the NVA in the dark – you know – tryin' to make 'em think the rocks were grenades. Only one bullet left. He was saving it for the final charge. He told me he realized he was gonna' die. Then, once he accepted that, he wasn't scared anymore.
> [*Tom Holmes, recorded account, 11 July 1989*]

Cpl. Bachta, the Groucho Marx radioman and assistant patrol leader, stumbled into the Recon GP tent to be debriefed. There was little he could add to radio reports he had made from the knoll. After the debriefing he would *crash* and sleep for two days.

Regiment needed a photograph to accompany documentation of the struggle on the hill. The picture would have to be taken at Dong Ha, of course. Four Echo Company infantrymen, all wounded, had been treated at Delta-Med. Thereafter they were "still walking," so they were selected:

1. Cpl. Timothy Roberts had one finger lacerated to the bone and deep shrapnel wounds in his left side and left leg.
2. LCpl. Leroy Williams had various shrapnel wounds (and would be KIA 31 days later).
3. LCpl. Roger Davis had minor shrapnel wounds (but would

be seriously WIA six days later and flown to CONUS).
4.   LCpl. Roger Baca had shrapnel wounds in both legs but, like Davis, he would be critically wounded six days later and flown to CONUS).

LCpl. Baca (third from the left in the first picture at the end of this chapter) later recalled how he and the other three Marines were "cleaned up" for the photograph. As can be seen in the picture, they donned clean utilities, bloused their trousers, tucked their shirts, and put on their steel pot helmets. Williams and Roberts draped belts of M-60 ammunition over their shoulders in Mexican bandit style. Each man carried an M-14 rifle, and Williams even inserted a magazine into his weapon. They posed for the picture, and it would go into official records as USMC Photo A-187657.

Casualties at the Hill: Marines with relatively minor wounds were patched-up at the aid station, Delta-Med. After several days of light duty they would return to Echo Company. Those in need of more extensive medical care had been flown 39 miles southward to Alpha-Med at Phu Bai. Those with grievous wounds were flown to the *USS Princeton.* Others had been flown 75 miles southward to Charlie-Med at Da Nang.

Medical facilities at Da Nang were fully equipped for major surgeries. Neurosurgery for brain trauma was available at the huge Naval Support Activity (NSA) hospital nearby. The NSA hospital also had what doctors called the "White Lie Ward." It was for those who would survive, but who had been horribly maimed, blinded, dismembered, disfigured, or otherwise crippled for life. "You'll be OK," doctors promised them. Yet, in reality their disabilities would forever limit their role in mainstream America.

> Some Marines had been so badly mangled that there seemed to be no words to describe what had happened to them.
> *[Philip Caputo, A Rumor of War, 1977]*

Critically wounded Marines who needed many months or years of hospital care were flown out of Vietnam. Many were sent to the huge U.S. Naval Hospital at Yokosuka, Japan, and others went to the big hospital at Clark Air Force Base in the Phillipines. Others were flown back to the United States and sent to the U.S. Naval Hospital nearest to their family or next of kin.

Jim McKay, the downed Huey gunner, was hospitalized at Clark Air Force Base in the Philippines. The Marine in the bed next to him had been on the knoll, and he had multiple wounds from a grenade that had detonated right in front of him. He had a wrenched pelvis, two mangled and broken legs, and numerous shrapnel holes in his abdomen. However, he was a blissfully happy young man.

The blast spared his genitals, so he was ecstatic!
[Jim McKay, oral account, 27 September 2000]

In total, on 8-9 August the Marines suffered 36 casualties at the knoll. Of those, six died (4 infantrymen and 2 helicopter crewmen). Thirty more were wounded (20 infantrymen, 9 helicopter crewmen, and 1 Recon). The following list of casualties at the knoll is based upon (1) Casualty Cards, (2) Unit Diary entries, and (3) Command Chronology casualty listings:

Rank	Name	Casualty	Primary Source
LCpl.	Baca, Roger J.	WIA	Unit Diary
Cpl.	Belknap, Ronald L.	**KIA**	Casualty Card
LCpl.	Butler, Gary N.	WIA	Casualty Card
LCpl.	Calvin, Nathaniel Jr.	WIA	Casualty Card
1stLt.	Costa, Anthony D.	WIA	ComChron.
LCpl.	Daniels, Jesus Jr.	WIA	Casualty Card
LCpl.	Davis, Roger A.	WIA	Unit Diary
SSgt.	Donaldson, Billy M.	WIA	Casualty Card
SSgt.	Dusman, Edward R.	WIA	Casualty Card
LCpl.	Fletcher, Sterling A.	WIA	Casualty Card
LCpl.	Gibson, George R.	WIA	Casualty Card
PFC	Hamrick, Benjamin	**KIA**	Casualty Card
Capt.	Harper, Richard O.	WIA	Casualty Card
Cpl.	Hedger, John A.	WIA	Casualty Card
LCpl.	Iverson, Richard L.	WIA	Casualty Card
Capt.	Lee, Howard V.	WIA	Casualty Card
Pvt.	Martin, Vernal S.	**KIA**	Casualty Card
Cpl.	McDermott, Edward	WIA	Casualty Card
LCpl.	McKay, James E.	WIA	Casualty Card

Sgt.	Murff, Herbert S.	**DOW**	Casualty Card
LCpl.	Ortiz, Eppie	WIA	Casualty Card
Cpl.	Pace, James	WIA	Unit Diary
Sgt.	Pace, Robert L.	WIA	Casualty Card
Capt.	Roberts, Joseph T.	WIA	Casualty Card
LCpl.	Roberts, Timothy A.	WIA	Casualty Card
PFC	Rode, Frederick W.	WIA	Unit Diary
Cpl.	Schmidt, Dennis R.	**KIA**	Casualty Card
2ndLt.	Sherman, Andrew M.	**KIA**	Casualty Card
Cpl.	Smith, David A.	WIA	Unit Diary
LCpl.	Stephen, Luke A.	WIA	Casualty Card
Sgt.	Stevens, Tommy E.	WIA	Unit Diary
Cpl.	Strock, Richard A.	WIA	Casualty Card
1stLt.	Sturkey, Marion F.	WIA	Casualty Card
PFC	Swartz, James J.	WIA	Casualty Card
PFC	Vance, Danny R.	WIA	Casualty Card
LCpl.	Williams, Leroy	WIA	Unit Diary

10 August 1966: Gen. Wallace M. Greene Jr., Commandant of the Marine Corps, happened to be in Vietnam at the time. The day after Groucho Marx Battle survivors returned to Dong Ha, Gen. Greene made a scheduled stop at the 4th Marines CP at Phu Bai. After a quick briefing he insisted on flying to Dong Ha to meet ambulatory survivors who had battled through the night in Razorback Valley.

> At 1140 Hours, CMC and party arrived *[at]* Hue Phu Bai Airfield. *[He]* departed at 1345 Hours to *[fly to]* Dong Ha via fixed-wing to visit 2/4.
> *[4th Marines, Command Chronology, 10 August 1966]*

13 August 1966: More Marines were needed at Dong Ha, and the build-up began immediately. Within weeks the primitive Dong Ha complex would expand and feature over 174 hardback tents, marston-matting to cover the dirt runway, and a wooden mess hall that would seat over 500 men.

> Elements of the 4th Marines Headquarters were airlifted from Phu Bai to Dong Ha to establish a forward CP. In addition, 1st Battalion,

4th Marines, was moved from Phu Bai to Dong Ha by Rough Rider
[meaning, via truck]. 2nd Battalion, 7th Marines, was airlifted
from Chu Lai by KC-130. Other supporting elements were lifted to
Dong Ha by LCU.
[4th Marines, Command Chronology, 13 August 1966]

13 August 1966 – The Meat Grinder Continues: Elusive NVA
troops obviously had returned to Razorback Valley. Echo Company,
two more 2nd Battalion companies, and M-48 tanks pushed westward
from Cam Lo along Route 9 toward the Rockpile on 13 August 1966.
They encountered an enemy fortress.

Airstrikes and artillery missions had little effect on enemy concrete
and metal-plated bunkers dug into the solid rock of Hill 252.
*[Jack Shulimson, U.S. Marines in Vietnam: An Expanding
War, 1966, 1982]*

The 803rd Regiment, 324-B NVA Division, had dug-in. Their
12.7mm and 37mm AAA guns belched fire and lead at any Marine
helicopter within sight. The NVA had turned the massive Razorback
into an almost impregnable bastion. The 1,000-foot-high stone ridge
was honeycombed with caves, some natural and some manmade, and
the NVA had fortified them.

During the first month of fighting west of Cam Lo the Marines
suffered 121 severe casualties. Among them was the new Echo
Company commander, Capt. Edwin Besch (not to be confused with
LtCol. Arnold Bench, the battalion commander), who had replaced
Capt. Lee. However, during combat on the Razorback, Besch's right
arm had been shattered on 23 August. His command of Echo
Company had lasted only two weeks.

Theirs not to make reply,
Theirs not to reason why,
Theirs but to do and die . . . .
[Alfred Tennyson, The Charge of the Light Brigade, 1854]

North Vietnamese soldiers and the Marines became locked in a
war of attrition below the DMZ. Their artillery duels could have been

mistaken for the World War II siege of Stalingrad. Their infantries clashed in the inland rolling hills and in jungles and mountains to the west of Dong Ha. Battlefield names became part of Marine Corps lore: Con Thien, Gio Linh, Helicopter Valley, Razorback Valley, Leatherneck Square, Mutter Ridge, Dai Do, Khe Sanh, and others. This brutal meat grinder would continue for two years before the Marines finally would persevere.

And when he gets to Heaven,
To Saint Peter he will tell:
One more Marine reporting, sir,
I've served my time in Hell.
[Tombstone epitaph, PFC William Cameron, USMC, (H/2/1), killed-in-action near Lunga Point on Guadal-canal, Soloman Islands, 10 September 1942]

"Posed" photo at Dong Ha. It depicts four Echo Company survivors of the battle on the knoll. See chapter text for infantrymen's names and details (photo courtesy of U.S. Marine Corps).

10 Hours of fierce battle makes for a long night

Article headline, <u>Pacific Stars & Stripes</u>, in reference to the battle on the knoll. The article text begins:

Private First Class Robert Callaway climbed out of the helicopter at Dong Ha. Several belts of machinegun ammunition were slung across his shoulders; an M-14 rifle was in one hand, and an M-60 machinegun *[was]* in the other. His clothes were mud-caked, and the telltale signs of war reflected in his eyes. "They hit us all of a sudden," he said. "I set up my machinegun on the slope of a hill and began firing. I didn't even have to pick out a target; just shoot anywhere to the front. I was bound to hit one of them . . . ."

Marine infantrymen wade through a stream 400 meters south of the DMZ on Operation Prairie (photo courtesy of U.S. Marine Corps).

After dropping a bomb, a Marine F-8 Crusader circles around for a follow-up strafing run (photo courtesy of U.S. Marine Corps).

The Marine artillery firebase at Gio Linh, north of Dong Ha and south of the DMZ (photo courtesy of U.S. Marine Corps).

Marine infantrymen from 1/5 board H-34 helicopters for a strike mission south of Da Nang (photo courtesy of U.S. Marine Corps).

With his M-79 in his lap, an exhausted Marine infantryman rests in the sunshine (photo courtesy of U.S. Marine Corps).

On patrol, Marines cross a stream as Vietnamese children try to sell food products to them (photo courtesy of U.S. Marine Corps).

Four Marine H-34 pilots from HMM-263 pose for the camera at Dong Ha during mid-1966 (photo courtesy of Tom Holmes).

Shot down and destroyed, the front of this H-46 helicopter has been carried back to Marble Mountain by an H-53 (photo by the author).

As one helicopter burns (right background), an H-46 lands to reach stranded Marines. A mirror-image of this photo is on the cover of the author's book, <u>Bonnie-Sue</u> (photo courtesy of U.S. Marine Corps).

The rear fuselage of an H-34 extends toward the maintenance tents of HMM-263 at Marble Mountain (photo by the author).

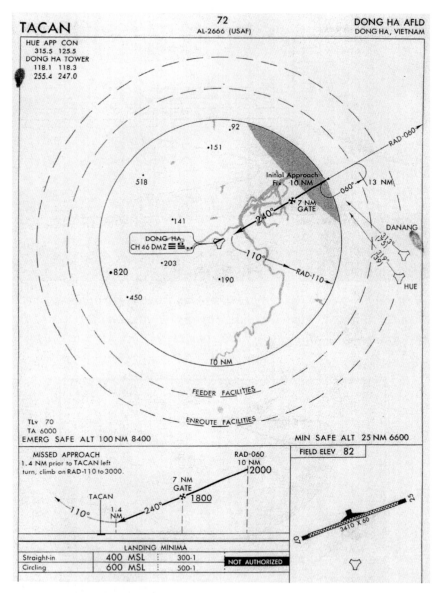

Dong Ha had a primitive dirt airstrip in the summer of 1966. Yet, Marine pilots could land day or night in all weather conditions. This TACAN Approach Chart enabled IFR inbound aircraft to make an instrument approach. In addition a GCA radar controlled approach was available, and also an ADF radio beacon approach could be made (from Low Altitude Instrument Approach Procedures, Pacific and Southeast Asia *courtesy of U.S. Department of Defense).*

A Marine fires his machinegun from the hip during combat in the rolling hills below the DMZ (photo courtesy of U.S. Marine Corps).

A Marine infantry company has geared-up in preparation for combat in "Leatherneck Square" (photo courtesy of U.S. Marine Corps).

With a lance corporal chevron pinned to his boonie cover, a Marine prepares for a patrol in the bush. Note his handwritten credo: "God is with the Point Man" (photo courtesy of U.S. Marine Corps).

YR-31, an H-46 from HMM-161, eases down to land on a small hill near the DMZ. Terrain in this landing area is typical of the rolling hills west of the coastal plain. Note the crew chief leaning out of a starboard hatch to help his pilots avoid tree stumps and other obstacles. The whirling rotor blades could rip through foliage and medium sized limbs without suffering damage, but striking a large tree trunk would bring disaster.

In this photo the special sand filters (known as "barrier filters"), elongated black cylinders on top of the fuselage in front of the aft pylon, are visible. These filters covered the engine air intakes and prevented sand erosion of the jet turbine blades. Protective armor plates (bolted to the outside of the fuselage between the barrier filters and the jet exhaust port) are visible. These armor plates helped to protect the engines from enemy gunfire.

Exclusive of the bomb crater (center background), the small hill depicted in this photo is similar to the knoll at XD-986599 where Marines battled through the night on 8-9 August 1966. The knoll was denuded, but the surrounding ravines and gullies were heavily vegetated (photo courtesy of U.S. Marine Corps).

Marines based an infantry company here on Hill 55 overlooking the fertile rice basin south of Da Nang (photo by the author).

Over eastern Laos, an H-46 from HMM-265 flies westward to insert a team of Nungs (Chinese mercenaries) into rolling terrain near Ban Houei Sane at map coordinates XD-646356 (photo by the author).

Loaded with a full field pack and weapons, two Marine infantrymen climb up a steep slope in the jungled mountains west of the coastal plain. The slope is almost vertical, so they are propelled by their arms as well as their legs (photo courtesy of U.S. Marine Corps).

Between missions at Dong Ha, three pilots from HMM-265 relax on the loading ramp of an H-46 (photo courtesy of the author).

By the runway at Phu Bai, infantrymen board H-46 helicopters to fly to an ongoing battle on the coastal plain (photo by the author).

An H-46 "slick" externals a shot-down Huey back to the helicopter base at Marble Mountain (photo by the author).

An "Air America" C-47 at Dong Ha (note the CIA airline name painted on the aft fuselage). Air America's silver C-47s, C-46s, and Hueys shuttled through Dong Ha each day (photo by the author).

Parting Shots

The cause for which he suffered was lost; the people for whom he fought were crushed; the hopes in which he trusted were shattered. But his fame, consigned to the keeping of time which, happily, is not so much the tomb of virtue as its shrine, shall in years to come, fire modest worth to noble ends.
[Inscription on a Confederate Veterans Memorial in Lake Eola Park, Orlando, Florida]

12 August 1966: Cpl. Eppie Ortiz had been wounded on the knoll after midnight on 8-9 August 1966. The previous week he had been the crew chief on a medevac flight. His helicopter had picked up a young Marine whose abdomen had been ripped open by shrapnel. Ortiz had knelt in the Huey by the wounded Marine, who said his name was John, and had held his hand on the flight to Delta-Med.

On 12 August 1966 in Charlie-Med at Da Nang, three days after neurosurgery to remove shrapnel from his brain, Cpl. Ortiz regained consciousness. He saw John, heavily bandaged, propped on an elbow in the adjacent bunk and smiling at him.

I woke up in Charlie-Med, and John was there beside me. He remembered me. He was watching over me.
[Eppie Ortiz, oral account, 8 November 1999]

=======================

15 August 1966: LCpl. Roger Baca, an Arizona native who had been a rifleman on the knoll, had received shrapnel wounds there on 8-9 August 1966. Delta-Med corpsmen patched him up, and within a week he was back in the bush. His 2nd Battalion, 4th Marines, began an assault westward from Cam Lo toward the Rockpile. They faced concrete and metal-plated NVA bunkers along Route 9.

Fragmentation wounds in both legs.
[Cas.Card, LCpl. Roger Baca, USMC, 15 August 1966]

On 15 August 1966 during a battle along Route 9, Baca was hit in both legs. His multiple wounds were severe. Five days later on 20 August 1966 he would be evacuated to the U.S. Naval Hospital at San Diego, California.

=====================

15 August 1966: Seventeen days before the battle on the knoll, LCpl. Roger Davis had received shrapnel wounds in his back on 23 July 1966. He had recovered quickly. Two weeks later during the battle on the knoll he again had been slightly wounded. He again recovered. By mid-August he was once again in Razorback Valley when Echo Company tangled with the 803rd NVA Regiment.

> Fragmentation wounds both legs with compound fracture *[of]* tibia.
> *[Cas.Card, LCpl. Roger Davis, USMC, 15 August 1966]*

During a firefight on 15 August 1966, Davis suffered shrapnel wounds in both legs and a compound fracture of the larger of the two bones between his knee and ankle. Due to the extent of his injuries he would be evacuated to the U.S. Naval Hospital at Pensacola, Florida, five days later on 20 August 1966.

=====================

17 August 1966: A few days before he had been shot and killed on the knoll, 2ndLt. Andrew Sherman had addressed his platoon. He had told them the local Vietnamese church needed financial help, and he asked for donations. Sherman had collected money but had been killed-in-action before he could deliver it. Nonetheless, on 17 August 1966 the money was delivered to the Vietnamese priest.

> A memoriam donation of $60.00 was made to the Eqlise Catholique Church, *[to]* Father Etchatten. This collection was taken by 2d Lt. Sherman from his 2d Platoon, Company E, just prior to his being killed, and members of his platoon wounded.
> *[2nd Bn., 4th Marines, Command Chronology, 17 Aug. 1966]*

=====================

18 August 1966: Capt. Richard Harper, an H-46 pilot, had been shot while trying to land at the knoll on 8 August 1966. He survived. Ten days later on 18 August 1966 in the huge NSA hospital, he was visited by a schoolgirl, Pham Thi Ne. She attended Phan Chu Trinh High School in Da Nang. She gave Harper a personal note:

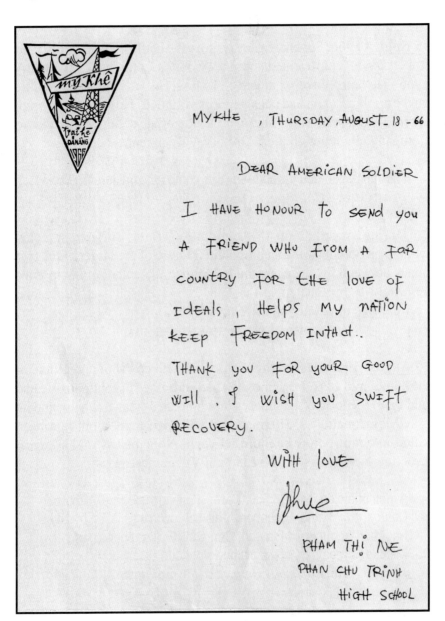

MY KHE   , THURSDAY, AUGUST 18 - 66

DEAR AMERICAN SOLDIER

I HAVE HONOUR TO SEND YOU A FRIEND WHO FROM A FAR COUNTRY FOR THE LOVE OF IDEALS , HELPS MY NATION KEEP FREEDOM INTACT.. THANK YOU FOR YOUR GOOD WILL . I WISH YOU SWIFT RECOVERY.

WITH LOVE

[signature]

PHAM THI NE
PHAN CHU TRINH
HIGH SCHOOL

19 August 1966: In his words, PFC Frederick Rode had been "a rifleman in a hole" on the knoll on 8-9 August 1966. He had been hit by shrapnel several times. Yet, his wounds were minor, and within 10 days he was with Echo Company near the Razorback.

> Gunshot wounds buttocks.
> *[Cas.Card, PFC Frederick Rode, USMC, 19 August 1966]*

On 19 August 1966 near Route 9 west of Cam Lo, Echo Company discovered NVA troops in a large bunker complex. During the fight Marines suffered 2 KIAs and 14 WIAs. Rode got shrapnel wounds all across his back and torso (not "gunshot" wounds as stated on his casualty card). The wounds proved to be extreme, so five days later on 24 August 1966 he would be evacuated to the U.S. Naval Hospital at Yokosuka, Japan.

=====================

19 August 1966: The seasoned veteran, SSgt. Conrad Ortego, had been aboard two helicopters that had tried to land reinforcements at the knoll on 8-9 August 1966. Both flying machines had been badly shot-up, but the pipe-smoking Ortego had escaped injury. However, his luck would run out in less than two weeks.

> Fragmentation wound right elbow.
> *[Cas.Card, SSgt. Conrad Ortego, USMC, 19 August 1966]*

On 19 August 1966 along Route 9 far west of Cam Lo, Ortego was with Echo Company when it battled NVA troops in reinforced bunkers. Shrapnel tore into Oretgo's right arm and elbow. Within several hours he was on a C-130 with other casualties bound for Charlie-Med at Da Nang.

=====================

22 August 1966: Cpl. Eppie Ortiz is the VMO-2 crew chief who had been critically wounded on the knoll on 9 August 1966.

> Shrapnel to the head.
> *[Cas.Card, Cpl. Eppie Ortiz, USMC, 9 August 1966]*

After neurosurgery in Vietnam, Ortiz was evacuated to hospitals at Clark AFB and later Travis AFB. On 22 August 1966 he arrived at the U.S. Naval Hospital on Long Island, New York, to begin an extremely lengthy recovery process.

========================

23 August 1966: The struggle on the knoll on 8-9 August 1966 had critically wounded the Echo Company commander, Capt. Howard Lee. He had been replaced by Capt. Edwin Besch, who had recovered from wounds suffered the previous month.

Abrasions lower back and left knee and contusions left side of chest, right arm, and right leg.
[Cas.Card, Capt. Edwin Besch, USMC, 23 July 1966]

Exactly a month later on 23 August 1966 the new commander led two platoons as Echo Company tried to drive NVA soldiers out of caves in the Razorback.

Gunshot wound and fragmentation wounds *[to]* right arm.
[Cas.Card, Capt. Edwin Besch, USMC, 23 August 1966]

Besch's right arm was shattered. Three days later he was evacuated to the U.S. Air Force hospital at Clark AFB in the Phillippines. His command of Echo Company had lasted only 13 days.

========================

23 August 1966: On 8 August 1966, Cpl. Daniel McFarren had flown to the knoll as part of the Sparrow Hawk reaction force from Echo Company. Later in the afternoon an H-34 had plucked him from the knoll during a partial extraction of the reaction force. However, 15 days later his good luck would end.

Gunshot wound back, and fragmentation wounds left leg, right forefinger, and both buttocks.
[Cas.Card, Cpl. Daniel McFarren, USMC, 23 August 1966]

On 23 August 1966, McFarren was with Echo Company when

Marines battled NVA soldiers entrenched on the Razorback. As his squad searched a cave, an enemy 12.7mm gun opened fire. McFarren was hit, but he survived and was hospitalized at Alpha-Med.

===================

9 September 1966: LCpl. Leroy Williams, a rifleman, had survived the battle on the knoll on 8-9 August 1966. He had become a mini-celebrity after his inclusion (extreme left) in USMC Photo A-187657 with three other survivors. His wounds had been minor, but a month later he would be dead.

Williams was with Echo Company when Marines attacked the 90th NVA Regiment north of Con Thien on 9 September 1966. Shrapnel tore into his left ankle and left arm. He continued to fight until an enemy round struck him squarely in the upper torso.

> Died . . . result *[of]* fragmentation wounds penetrating left ankle, left arm, and gunshot wound to the chest . . . .
> *[Cas.Card, LCpl. Leroy Williams, USMC, 9 September 1966]*

Williams clung to life in the aid station at Dong Ha. Corpsmen loaded him and other casualties onto a C-130, and it sped southward toward Charlie-Med, the field hospital at Da Nang. During the 20-minute flight Williams' life slowly slipped away. He was dead when the airplane landed at Da Nang.

===================

9 September 1966: On the knoll on 8 August 1966, LCpl. Douglas Van had dashed down the slope to rescue a comrade crippled by the enemy attack. Under heavy fire he had dragged the wounded Marine up the knoll and into a fighting hole. Both of them had survived.

> WIA, Hostile, Vicinity of Quang Tri, Republic of Vietnam . . . .
> *[Cas.Card, LCpl. Douglas Van, USMC, 9 September 1966]*

The next month on 9 September 1966, Van and his comrades battled soldiers of the 90th NVA Regiment. Van was shot twice, once in the left thigh, and once in the right knee. His injuries were severe, so five days later he was evacuated to the U.S. Naval Hospital at Yokosuka, Japan.

========================

25 September 1966: At the start of helicopter flights west of Dong Ha all pilots checked-in via radio with "Sav-A-Plane." This liaison was designed to keep all aircraft away from the trajectory of 105mm and 155mm Marine artillery shells.

No system is perfect, and it failed on the evening of 25 September 1966. YR-3 (spoken, *Yankee-Romeo-Three*), an H-34 from HMM-161, flew westward from Dong Ha to evacuate wounded Marines. The four-man helicopter crew was supplemented by a corpsman from HMM-265:

    Capt. Phillip A. Ducat. . . . . HOR: Fort Wayne, Indiana
    1stLt. Dean W. Reiter. . . . . HOR: Manchester, Missouri
    Cpl. Vernon H. Parker. . . . . HOR: Secane, Pennsylvania
    LCpl. Arthur W. Greene. . . HOR: Chicago, Illinois
    HM3 Peter R. Bossman. . . . HOR: West Seneca, New York

At 1915 *[Hours]* on the 265 degree radial at 12 miles from Dong Ha TACAN, YR-3 was hit by friendly artillery . . . .
[HMM-161, Command Chronology, 25 September 1966]

Over the southern edge of Razorback Valley the helicopter flew into the path of a Marine 155mm artillery shell. The high-explosive shell and the 115/145 aviation fuel detonated in an enormous orange fireball. The explosion blasted the Sikorsky flying machine apart. Like fireworks, hundreds of sparkling wreckage fragments rained down into the jungle below. Everyone aboard had died instantly.

========================

28 September 1966: Brutal fighting raged on Nui Cay Tre Ridge (aka, *Mutter Ridge*), the northern rim of Razorback Valley. Carnage there drew worldwide attention. In Rome, Pope Paul VI called for negotiations to stop the horrible slaughter. *Krasnaya Zuezda*, the Soviet Union defense ministry newspaper, warned of repercussions because Russian "advisors" were endangered.

On 28 September 1966 on Nui Cay Tre Ridge the 3rd Battalion, 4th Marines, faced a reinforced North Vietnamese regiment. The

Marine battalion was accompanied by renowned journalist Arnaud de Borchgrave, a *Newsweek Magazine* reporter. Although wounded on the ridge, he would survive. Portions of his scribbled notes would be published by his employer two weeks later.

> Machine guns keep up intense fire. NVA now have us almost surrounded. I have a terrible feeling I will never see my family again. . . . We've run out of battle dressings. Air strikes coming every 30 seconds. The ground trembles continuously. Once again I feel the end is near – at least for me. I get an uncontrollable case of the shakes. I wonder if I ever had what it takes to be a Marine, and conclude that I never did, and don't now.
> *[Arnaud de Borchgrave, "The Battle for Hill 400" in News-*
> *week Magazine, 10 October 1966]*

==================

14 October 1966: LCpl. James Hager, a Recon, had been lucky on the Groucho Marx patrol. The Sparrow Hawk relief force had linked-up with his team on the afternoon of 8 August 1966. Later that day he and another Recon from his team, and half of the relief force, were being extracted when the NVA attacked. Unwounded, Hager had gotten into an H-34 and had been flown back to Dong Ha. However, his good fortune would end nine weeks later on 14 October 1966.

> Fragmentation wound left arm.
> *[Cas.Card, LCpl. James Hager, USMC, 14 October 1966]*

==================

23 December 1966: 1stLt. Larry Robinson, an H-34 pilot in HMM-161, had flown 4.2 hours in Bureau No. 148069 during missions to the knoll on 8-9 August 1966. Thereafter, battle damage to his helicopter rendered it unflyable. Undaunted, Robinson volunteered and flew another 4.1 hours as copilot in a Deadlock gunship during the rest of the long night. He came through unscathed.

Robinson later became a Forward Air Controller (FAC) with the 3rd Battalion, 7th Marines. He always wanted to be *up front* where he could more effectively help his infantry brothers. His fitness report dated 24 March 1967 would explain:

As FAC he volunteered to accompany the point companies. He was where the action was heaviest; his personal bravery was demonstrated on numerous occasions. *[and also]* In the heat of close combat he retains his composure and judgement.

While a FAC, Robinson would be wounded twice, once on 23 December 1966 and again five weeks later on 1 February 1967. He survived the war. Thirty-two years later he would reminisce:

[I] enjoyed my service in Vietnam and would do it all over again in a second. *[I]* met friends who will remain with me for life and thereafter. *[Yet,]* it still haunts me that some very good men didn't come home.
[Larry Robinson, handwritten account, April 1999]

===================

21 February 1967: Dr. Bernard Fall, a French professor and writer, had evolved into the world's most respected analyst of the Vietnam dilemma. He had first gone to Vietnam in 1953 to chronicle the death struggle of the French Army. Among his many books, *Street Without Joy* (1961) and *Hell in a Very Small Place* (1966) had become international military classics.

Marine infantrymen unofficially adopted Fall. They loved him. He empathized with them and thrived on their camaraderie. Alpha Company, 1st Battalion, 9th Marines (aka, *The Walking Dead*) began a search-and-destroy sweep 14 miles north of Hue, and Fall tagged along. The area was the same enemy hotbed that had been the backdrop for his acclaimed book, *Street Without Joy*.

That's my area. That's my home ground.
[Bernard Fall, French historian, early February 1967]

On 21 February 1967 as they approached a helicopter LZ, Fall triggered a booby trap, a buried artillery shell. The blast vaporized his lower body below the waist. His friend, GySgt. Byron Highland, died with him. From unfinished notes Dr. Fall's final treatise, *Last Reflections on a War*, would be published later that year.

===================

22 March 1967: PFC Roger Dewald had been part of the Sparrow Hawk reaction force flown to the knoll on 8 August 1966. He had been fortunate, for he had been helicoptered back to Dong Ha late in the afternoon. His luck would hold for seven more months.

> Fragmentation wounds, right calf and right foot.
> *[Cas.Card, LCpl. Roger Dewald, USMC, 22 March 1967]*

By 22 March 1967, Dewald had been promoted to lance corporal. During a firefight that day he suffered debilitating shrapnel wounds to his right leg and foot. The injuries were extreme, and he was evacuated to the U.S. Naval Hospital at Philadelphia, Pennsylvania.

===================

23 June 1967: Capt. William Buchanan, a VMO-2 pilot, and LCpl. John Bornemann, a VMO-2 gunner, had provided air cover over the knoll during the night of 8-9 August 1966. Their Hueys had been holed repeatedly, but both flyers escaped injury. Both eventually had returned to the United States and had joined VMO-1 at MCAS New River, North Carolina.

Buchanan and Bornemann had been living on borrowed time. On 23 June 1967 they crewed a Huey (call-sign, *Yazoo-Four-One*) on a VMO-1 training flight. At 0903 Hours they took off from Runway 23 at New River. Five-hundred feet above the ground their climbing Huey collided with a descending Sikorsky H-53.

> The tower controller . . . did not accurately perceive the impending conflict until it was too late.
> *[Naval Aviation Safety Center Investigation No. 70-67]*

The rotor head ripped off of the Huey. The airframe dropped like a manhole cover, hit the ground inverted, and burned. Buchanan and Bornemann died upon impact. Most of the narrative on the Casualty Cards for both Marines is identical:

> Died 23Jun67, MCAS New River, NC, result *[of]* extreme multiple injuries sustained . . . in midair collision with another helicopter.

===================

7 January 1968: Cpl. Danny Vance, a rifleman, had been wounded in the right knee during fighting on the knoll on 8-9 August 1966. The West Virginia native recovered. Eighteen months later he was attached to a Marine unit that provided security for villagers in Thua Thien Province far to the south.

On 7 January 1968 the enemy attacked the hamlet that Vance and his Marine brothers were protecting. During the attack Vance was killed-in-action.

> Died 7Jan68 . . . result *[of]* third degree burns to entire body from explosive device while engaged in action against hostile forces.
> *[Cas.Card, Cpl. Danny Vance, USMC, 7 January 1968]*

=======================

2 February 1968: Then a lance corporal, Huey gunner Jim McKay had been shot down on the hill after midnight on 8-9 August 1966. After a long recovery at Clark AFB Hospital in the Phillippines and at the U.S. Naval Hospital at Oakland, California, he had returned to duty in early 1967.

A year later Sgt. McKay was back in Vietnam. During fighting near Camp Carroll, west of Dong Ha, he was wounded by artillery shrapnel on 2 February 1968.

> Enclosed is the Purple Heart Medal for wounds received in combat action . . . on 2 February 1968.
> *[3rd Marine Division letter dated 16 May 1968 to Sgt. James E. McKay, USMC]*

=======================

14 April 1968: For almost two years after the battle on the knoll the NVA and Marines had struggled amid the coastal rolling hills and mountainous jungles below the DMZ. Finally at Khe Sanh combat base far to the west, 5,772 Marines were cut off and surrounded. Outnumbered roughly seven-to-one, they faced 38,400 to 43,100 encircling NVA soldiers.

> Somewhere Out There, within artillery range of the Khe Sanh combat base, concealed, silent, and ominous, lay five full divisions

of North Vietnamese Regulars.
[Michael Herr, Dispatches, 1968]

A titanic firestorm began on 21 January 1968. NVA artillery and 122mm rockets rained down onto Khe Sanh for 77 days. Marine infantry and NVA infantry clashed all around the base. Slowly the Marines decimated surrounding NVA divisions.

I can still recall the day we got to Khe Sanh. It was a place that God forgot. You knew that death was around.
[Chuck Hoover, quoted in Valley of Decision, 1991]

On Easter Sunday morning, 14 April 1968, infantrymen from the 3rd Battalion, 26th Marines, attacked the last enemy bastion near Khe Sanh. The NVA fortress high atop Hill 881 North overlooked the Marine combat base. With fixed bayonets Marines swept through trenches and bunkers and routed NVA defenders. A battle-scarred infantryman then shinnied up a tree, whose limbs had been scythed away by prep fires, and affixed the Stars and Stripes. A Marine veteran would explain 28 years later in the book, *Bonnie-Sue.*

The red, white, and blue flag of the United States of America triumphantly fluttered in the stiff breeze atop Hill 881 North, deep in the heart of Indochina.

=====================

2 May 1968: Fighting in Leatherneck Square had continued for two years. The 2nd Battalion, 4th Marines, whose troops had fought on the knoll on 8-9 August 1966, remained in the thick of the contest. In late April 1968 the 320th NVA Division bypassed Con Thien and Gio Linh and drove southward to the abandoned village of Dai Do. There they dug-in and massed for an assault on the Dong Ha combat base slightly over a mile to the southwest.

The 2nd Battalion, 4th Marines, had no choice. They attacked. One under-strength battalion battled a division. The struggle raged for three days until surviving North Vietnamese withdrew on 2 May 1968. The battered 2nd Battalion, 4th Marines, had prevailed. Never again would the NVA try to overrun a Marine combat base.

Despite their overwhelming numbers the enemy had not been able to get past Magnificent Bastards of the 2nd Battalion, 4th Marines, and attack the Marine combat base at Dong Ha.
[Mark Huffman, One Magnificent Bastard, 2013]

=====================

27 January 1973: North Vietnam had found that it could not defeat U.S. Marines on the battlefield. However, it had much better success at the conference table.

The parties undertake to maintain the cease-fire and to ensure a lasting and stable peace.
[Agreement on Ending the War and Restoring Peace in Vietnam (aka, Paris Peace Accords), 27 January 1973]

The last United States combat troops would leave Vietnam two months after the agreement. Sadly, genuine peace would be elusive.

=====================

13 February 1973: Jeremiah Denton, a native of Alabama, had been a POW in North Vietnam for eight years. On 13 February 1973 he was the senior officer in the first group of POWs to be repatriated. After a flight from Hanoi the USAF C-141 rolled to a stop at Clark Air Force Base in the Phillippines. Denton was the first man to exit the aircraft. With dozens of television cameras rolling he walked to a microphone on the tarmac, stood ramrod straight, and announced:

We are honored to have had the opportunity to serve our country under difficult circumstances. We are profoundly grateful to our Commander-in-Chief and to our nation for this day. God bless America!

=====================

3 October 1973: The Sikorsky H-34 initially had been the backbone of Marine vertical lift capability in Vietnam. In 1966 new and larger Boeing H-46s had begun to arrive. The next year giant Sikorsky H-53s had entered the fray. Yet, the venerable H-34s continued to fly combat missions throughout I-Corps.

The H-34 was to emerge as the mainstay of Marine Corps helicopters until 1968 and was to bear much of the brunt of combat in
southeast Asia for the first six years of the war.
[LtCol. William Fails, Marines and Helicopters, 1962-1973, 1978]

H-34s continued to fly in Vietnam until 20 August 1969 when the
final six combat veterans flew to Da Nang for shipment to the United
States. Two months later the last active duty H-34 squadron was
decommissioned, but H-34s continued to fly with reserve units. Yet,
gradually the old warhorses retired.

On 3 October 1973 a Marine H-34 flew from Norfolk, Virginia,
to MCAS New River, North Carolina. Upon arrival the helicopter,
Bureau Number 147191, was stricken from records and enshrined at
the main gate entrance. An era ended. Old "one-ninety-one" had
been the last operational Marine Corps H-34.

=====================

29 April 1975: United States field combat units all had left Vietnam.
Nonetheless, the guardpost at Tan Son Nhut Airport at Saigon was
manned by two Marines, Cpl. Charles McMahon Jr. and LCpl.
Darwin Judge. Three hours before daylight at 0358 Hours on 29
April 1975, eight Russian-made rockets whistled down onto the
airport. By chance, one rocket scored a direct hit on the guardpost.

Judge, D.L., LCpl.... 16Feb56... 29Apr75... Marshalltown, IA
McMahon, C., Cpl.. . 10May53... 29Apr75... Woburn, MA
[TME Publishing, Vietnam KIAs and MIAs, 1984]

McMahon was from Woburn, Massachusetts. Judge hailed from
Marshalltown, Iowa. They were the last U.S. Marines, and also the
last American servicemen, to die during the war in Vietnam.

=====================

30 April 1975: Around midday a Russian-built T-54 tank, No. 843,
rumbled unopposed down Cong Ly Boulevard toward Independence
Palace in Saigon.

By the end of April 1975 the NVA had close to 500 tanks and 250 pieces of 122*[mm]* and 130mm artillery in the South.
[Michael Lanning et al, Inside the VC and the NVA, 1992]

The tank crashed through the steel gate and churned onto the green palace lawn. Nguyen Van Thieu, an NVA soldier, leaped off the tank and dashed up the palace steps. He turned and unfurled the National Liberation Front flag, blue and red with a bright yellow star. The long war in Vietnam was over.

======================

26 July 1976: Five minutes after midnight on 8-9 August 1966, Lt. Anthony Costa, a Huey copilot, had been shot down on the knoll. He had spent the rest of the night there and suffered only shrapnel wounds in his leg. Yet, tragedy would snare him 10 years later.

Camp Pendleton helicopter crash kills three Marines, injures two

[Headline, Page 6, The Stars and Stripes, July 1976]

On 26 July 1976, Costa piloted an H-53 on a training flight. As he neared Camp Pendleton, California, the tail rotor drive system failed. The helicopter rolled to the right and crashed. Two Marines aboard suffered crippling injuries, but they survived. Anthony Costa, age 35, and two more Marines died in the burning rubble.

======================

10 April 1977: During late 1966, 1967, and 1968 rolling hills in the coastal lowlands between Dong Ha and the DMZ had become known as Leatherneck Square. Marine infantry, artillery, and aviation units had squared off there against 35,000 invading North Vietnamese troops. The land and vegetation had been saturated with tons of chemical defoliants. The battlefields there had evolved into the most physically traumatized regions in Vietnam.

The place has a post-nuclear look to it.
[Morley Safer, <u>Flashbacks, On Returning to Vietnam</u>, 1990]

In former Leatherneck Square the Vietnamese government had begun building Truong Son Military Cemetery in 1975. It opened on 10 April 1977, and it is the largest military cemetery in Vietnam. The vast 202-acre burial ground lies eight miles northwest of Dong Ha. Each grave is marked by a flat memorial, and most of them are inscribed: "unknown." Graves are added when soldiers' remains are discovered nearby, and at last count the human remains (usually only *partial* remains) of over 13,000 NVA soldiers are interred there. The number grows as years roll by. Although grave markers are made from cheap masonry, the long rows are aligned exactly like those at Verdun and Arlington.

===================

8 December 1978: A motion picture, *The Deer Hunter*, debuted on 8 December 1978. This fictional screenplay was set in Vietnam and in Clairton, Pennsylvania. Three working-class steelworkers, all good friends, were the principal characters. At the Academy Awards the film would garner five Oscars including "Best Picture."

The final movie scene follows a wake for one of the characters who had lost his mind and his life during the war. As the film ends, surviving characters softly sing a cappella – *God Bless America*.

===================

13 November 1982: Funded solely by public donations, a Vietnam Veterans Memorial was erected on The Mall in Washington, DC. Names of 58,132 Americans (more names would be added later) had been etched into polished black granite panels. The memorial would become known as "The Wall," and its brief inscription explains:

The names of those who gave their lives and of those who remain missing are inscribed in the order they were taken from us.

On 13 November 1982 a vast throng gathered on The Mall for a dedication service. During the program a song began spontaneously in the rear of the crowd. Only a few sang at first, but others rapidly joined in. Their voices rose and rose until the whole crowd was singing, their 160,000 voices rolling out over the Potomac River. The official program was forgotten. The crowd dedicated The Wall with their song – *God Bless America*.

========================

17 May 1984: The U.S. Air Force had begun Operation Ranch Hand on 12 January 1962. During the next nine years 19 million gallons of defoliating herbicides had been sprayed onto jungle vegetation in Vietnam to expose enemy troops, supply roads, and weapons caches. The deadly mist looked *white* when sprayed from Fairchild C-123 spray-planes. The term "Agent Orange" would be derived from orange-striped steel barrels in which the defoliant was shipped.

It was chemical warfare, pure and simple. Its defenders had the arrogance to maintain that what killed trees would not hurt people, or American people anyway. We knew it was dirty work from the beginning.
[*Morley Safer, Flashbacks: On Returning to Vietnam, 1990*]

Agent Orange was a time bomb that would kill and maim Marines for decades to come. The defoliant contained *dioxin*, a known and highly toxic carcinogen. On 17 May 1984 a federal court approved a $180 million out-of-court settlement against nine chemical manufacturers. Meanwhile the time bomb continued its deadly rampage. By 1990 the Veterans Administration would be treating hundreds-of-thousands of surviving veterans for illnesses – primarily cancer – attributed to the lethal defoliant. In 1991 the U.S. Congress would pass the Agent Orange Act, making specified illnesses "presumptive" to Agent Orange exposure.

========================

8 November 1986: Public donations funded erection of the Vietnam Memorial in Columbia, South Carolina. Loosely modeled after the national memorial in Washington, its 70 tons of gray Carolina granite are inscribed with names of 980 South Carolinians killed or missing during the long war in Vietnam. It also is inscribed with words of Lawrence Binyon:

They shall grow not old as we that are left grow old. Age shall not weary them, nor the years condemn. At the going down of the sun and in the morning we will remember them.

Richard Riley, the governor of South Carolina, presided at the dedication ceremony on 8 November 1986. Then an enormous crowd converged on the granite wall. Lewis Kirk, age 37, a Marine Corps veteran from Easley, South Carolina, found the name for which he was searching: Don K. Ledford. Kirk softly remarked that he had been standing by Ledford, his close friend, when he was killed. When asked how his friend died, Kirk shrugged his shoulders and seemed at a loss for words. Prodded by a newspaper reporter, he finally tried to explain:

> I don't know – we just got hit by sniper fire – things like that just happen . . . .

Cpl. Don K. Ledford, USMC, had been killed-in-action on 25 May 1968. His home of record was tiny Marietta, South Carolina.

=====================

30 May 1987: For the Marines who had fought at the knoll on 8-9 August 1966, Air America was no secret. Its silver C-46s, C-47s, and Hueys had shuttled through the Dong Ha airstrip daily and headed westward into Laos, Cambodia, and God only knows where else. Some of the Air America pilots and cargo-kickers were old comrades of Marines at Dong Ha. They had been *sheep-dipped*. They had vanished from the Corps and had morphed into civilian mercenaries working for the U.S. Central Intelligence Agency (CIA).

Born in China in 1947 and growing during the 1950s, 1960s, and early 1970s, Air America had become the largest airline in the world. The shadowy airline *spooks* had unlimited financial backing because the CIA funded the entire operation.

> Air America is a company incorporated in Delaware, but it is also a generic name used to describe all the CIA air activities.
> *[Christopher Robbins, The Invisible Air Force: The Explosive True Story of the CIA's Secret Airlines, 1979]*

Air America had faded into history after the Vietnam War ended in 1975. However, 12 years later on 30 May 1987 the Air America Memorial was dedicated at the University of Texas campus at Dallas. Beginning with the name Robert P. Abrams, the bronze memorial lists 242 *civilians* who were killed while flying for Air America in Asia. William Colby, former CIA Director, was the keynote speaker. He was followed by William Clements, governor of Texas. Ronald Reagan, U.S. President, could not attend, but he sent a personally signed letter to each survivor:

> . . . The unique service you shared in defense of freedom forged a bond of brotherhood that time and distance cannot break. Unsung and unrecognized, each of you confronted danger and endured terrible hardships, and each of you rose to the challenge; you never faltered. Although free people everywhere owe you more than we can hope to repay, our greatest debt is to your companions who gave their last full measure of devotion. Just as their names are inscribed on this memorial, so their memories are inscribed on our hearts. We will never forget them or their families. God bless you, and God bless America.   *[signed] Ronald Reagan*

======================

26 June 1987: The critically acclaimed movie, *Full Metal Jacket*, premiered on 26 June 1987. The film began by depicting life in Marine Corps boot camp. Although fictional, the main character was a Drill Instructor portrayed by actor R. Lee Ermey. In real life, Ermey is a Marine Corps veteran and former Drill Instructor. His verbiage in the film was borrowed from his Marine Corps experience. In the movie he addressed new Marines as they completed boot camp.

> Marines Die! That's what we're here for! But your Marine Corps lives forever! And that means YOU will live forever!
> *[R. Lee Ermey, speaking in Full Metal Jacket, 1987]*

======================

11 May 1994: Lewis B. "Chesty" Puller Sr. (1898-1971) is a legend. He is the private who became a lieutenant general, the Marine who *loved* to fight, the most decorated Marine in history (example, *five* Navy Cross awards). Every Marine knows about Chesty, but some may not know about his son.

Lewis B. Puller Jr. (1945-1994) grew up in the shadow of his famous father. On 11 October 1968, Lt. Puller was a platoon commander in Vietnam when he triggered a booby-trapped howitzer shell. He lingered near death for months. He had lost his right leg at the hip, most of his left leg, his right hand, most of his left hand, and parts of his buttocks and stomach. His weight dropped to an infantile, almost unbelievable, 55 pounds.

Yet, Puller survived. He would not walk again, of course. He was confined to a wheelchair, but he fought back. He earned a law degree and struggled to rebuild his world. His acclaimed and searing book memoir, *Fortunate Son*, was published in 1991 and earned a Pulitzer Prize for literature the next year.

His book is a haunting tribute to all the names on the Vietnam Veterans Memorial.
[Editorial, The New York Times, 1992]

Yet, the war had taken its toll. Puller struggled against despair, dependency, and incapacitation. He needed ever-increasing doses of painkillers to combat excruciating agony from his wounds and from shrapnel that doctors could not remove. He died on 11 May 1994. The gunshot wound was self-inflicted. With full military honors he would be laid to rest in Arlington National Cemetery.

======================

12 July 1995: In his youth, Bill Clinton had been a fiery opponent of the war in Vietnam, and he managed to avoid military service there. He later became President of the United States and began a 30 month campaign to "prepare the nation" for full diplomatic relations with Vietnam. The Vietnamese government, eager to curry favor with Clinton, offered him *bargaining chips* to expedite the process. The high value bargaining chips were skeletal remains of 29 American servicemen.

President Clinton turned the page on an ugly chapter in American history by normalizing diplomatic relations with Vietnam.
[The State newspaper (in South Carolina), 12 July 1995]

========================

6 May 1997: Sgt. Herbert Murff had been the crew chief in the first H-46 that had tried to land at the knoll on 8 August 1966. He had been shot in the lower abdomen. After lengthy hospitalization in Vietnam, and later in the Phillippines, he had been sent to the U.S. Naval Hospital at Memphis, Tennessee. His treatment had been long, for his intestinal tract had been ripped apart. Among other things, surgeons had to remove his damaged spleen.

WIA – Hostile – Missile penetrating abdomen.
[Cas.Card, Sgt. Herbert Murff, USMC, 8 August 1966]

Murff survived for 13 years, but then he contracted bronchial pneumonia. His spleen had been removed, so his body could not effectively fight the ailment. He died on 31 March 1979. On 6 May 1997, 18 years after his death, The Pentagon stipulated that Murff died due to the "aftermath of wounds suffered in combat." Therefore, his name was dutifully added to the Vietnam Veterans Memorial in Washington, DC – Herbert Sterling Murff, Panel 10E, Line 16.

========================

7 June 1998: Thirty-two years after the Groucho Marx Battle, nine Americans would trek to the knoll on 7 June 1998. Among them were seven Marine veterans, one of whom had been wounded at the knoll on 8 August 1966. The group left Dong Ha by vehicle and drove westward along Route 9, a narrow one-lane dirt trail. Near the Rockpile the group left the road and began walking northward.

We wade across a stream atop a makeshift dam. The *[thatched huts]* behind us are the last sign of civilization. We have entered "Indian Country" where the Marines and North Vietnamese fought head-to-head for two years. We forge ahead *[toward the knoll]* through head-high undergrowth.
[photograph notation, 7 June 1998]

The small group used machetes to hack their way through brush and vines in Razorback Valley. After two hours they reached XD-986599 on their map, the tiny knoll for which they were searching. The fighting holes were still there, marking the site of the Marine perimeter atop the little hillock.

Each visitor was struck by the solemnity of the site. It seemed to be hallowed ground, a remote little hill where a fierce struggle had consumed the lives of so many combatants and maimed so many others. Before leaving the knoll one Marine veteran led the group in a prayer for the souls of all men who had struggled there for comrades and cause on 8-9 August 1966.

=========================

12 September 1999: 1stLt. Lanny Ingvoldstad had been one of the Huey gunship pilots flying over the knoll on the night of 8-9 August 1966. He had flown all night, stopping only to rearm and refuel. He had never met the Marine infantrymen on the knoll, but he had talked with them via radio and had come to know them as brothers. Years later on 12 September 1999 he reminisced:

> [*I remember*] feelings of helplessness, hopelessness, and frustration; of being alone [*via radio*] with the voice of the guy on the ground, just him and me in the dark . . . hearing his excited voice get calmer after getting wounded once – then twice – and then a new voice.
> *[Lanny Ingvoldstad, e-mail message, 12 September 1999]*

=========================

19 March to 15 April 2003: Richard Tompkins, a news reporter with United Press International, was embedded with a Marine battalion during the lengthy assault across the desert toward Baghdad, Iraq. For most of a month he witnessed the love, bond, loyalty, and camaraderie experienced by warriors in battle. After Baghdad fell his saga about Marines at war received international acclaim. The riveting story ended with three short sentences.

> They were U.S. Marines and Devil Dogs. Not hyphenated Marines, just Marines, the Few and the Proud. They are truly a band of

brothers.
[Richard Tompkins, <u>With the Marines in Iraq</u>, 2003]

=====================

10 November 2006: In 1999 the Marine Corps Heritage Foundation had begun plans for a national museum. A towering majestic steel and glass structure would be the centerpiece of a 135-acre Marine Corps Heritage Center. Construction had begun in 2003.

Located adjacent to the Marine base at Quantico, Virginia, the National Museum of the Marine Corps was completed three years later. On 10 November 2006, the 231st birthday of the Corps, the President of the United States was present to address thousands who attended the dedication ceremony.

Every Marine understands that the Corps' reputation for honor and courage is a sacred inheritance from Marines past, and a solemn trust to be passed on to Marines to come.
[George Bush, U.S. President, speaking at dedication of the National Museum of the Marine Corps, 10 November 2006]

The museum complex later would be expanded to include the Semper Fidelis Memorial Park, wherein monuments and memorials are erected on an ongoing basis. The park would include a nondenominational Semper Fidelis Memorial Chapel.

=====================

2 May 2009: Infantrymen who had fought on the knoll on 8-9 August 1966 were part of the 2nd Battalion, 4th Marines, the "Magnificent Bastards." Years later battalion veterans designed a monument to honor all who served in that famed fighting battalion. The polished black granite structure was dedicated on 2 May 2009.

Second Battalion, 4th Marines
"THE MAGNIFICENT BASTARDS"
In Every Clime And Place
[Inscription on the front side of the memorial]

Gen. Paul Kelly, a former 2/4 battalion commander and former

Commandant of the Marine Corps, was the guest speaker. The monument stands in Semper Fidelis Memorial Park adjacent to the National Museum of the Marine Corps at Quantico, Virginia.

====================

1 August 2015: H-46 helicopters had first worn Marine Corps green in 1964. Those versatile tandem rotor flying machines had hauled Marines and their tools of war for the remainder of the millennium and beyond. As new V-22 Ospreys had begun to debut in 2006 the old "forty-sixes" gradually had begun to retire.

> The primary mission of the H-46 is to rapidly disperse combat troops, support equipment, and supplies . . . under all weather conditions, day or night . . . .
> [*NATOPS Flight Manual*, CH-46D/UH-46D, October 1966]

On 1 August 2015 an H-46 warhorse, Bureau No. 153369, took off from Norfolk, Virginia, and flew to the Smithsonian National Air & Space Museum near Washington, DC. It was the symbolic final flight of a Marine Corps H-46. A long era came to an end.

During the elaborate retirement ceremony, Boeing H-46s were honored for their 51 years of military service in the Corps. Amid the pageantry the Marine Corps transferred Bureau No. 153369 – the last Marine H-46 – to the Smithsonian.

====================

16 October 2015: One-hundred years earlier in 1915 the Marine Corps had established a first-of-its-kind recruit training facility, the MCRD Parris Island, adjacent to the South Carolina coast. Although a recruit training base at San Diego would come years later, the depot at famous Parris Island was the first.

> The South Carolina General Assembly, by this Resolution, honors and congratulates the Marine Corps Recruit Depot at Parris Island on the occasion of its one-hundredth anniversary.
> [*Resolution of the South Carolina legislature, adopted 17 March 2015*]

Beginning in April 2015 the Parris Island recruit depot had begun a centennial celebration that had lasted for six months. Festivities concluded on 16 October 2015. That day thousands of attendees witnessed rededication of two monuments; the premier of a new movie, *100 Years of Making Marines*; and graduation of Charlie and Oscar recruit companies. When the young men graduated they were no longer recruits. On that October morning they had become newly minted United States Marines.

It's what you wear on your collar – the Eagle, Globe, and Anchor – that puts you in the Brotherhood of Marines. *[BGen. Carl Mundy Jr., USMC (later, Commandant of the Marine Corps), 10 November 1984]*

Waiting for a troop lift in the rain, Marines have covered themselves with ponchos (photo courtesy of U.S. Marine Corps).

Marine infantrymen from 2/4 probe through the ruins of Dai Do village on 3 May 1968 (photo courtesy of U.S. Marine Corps).

A Marine infantryman from 2/5 takes a cigarette break before a patrol (photo courtesy of U.S. Marine Corps).

A corporal from 1/9 fires his M-79 at NVA troops in the rolling hills around Con Thien (photo courtesy of U.S. Marine Corps).

A Sikorsky H-34 from HMM-163 undergoes preventive maintenance on the flight line at Marble Mountain (photo by the author).

Dr. Bernard Fall, the famous French military historian and author, accompanies Marines of 1/9 on 20 February 1967. The next day north of Hue on patrol with the Marines, Fall was killed when he triggered a buried mine (photo courtesy of U.S. Marine Corps).

Marines fire a 105mm howitzer. Note the mountains visible in the background (photo courtesy of U.S. Marine Corps).

Accompanied by a tank, Marines of 2/9 battle North Vietnamese troops north of Cam Lo as an H-46 (center background) arrives to evacuate two wounded men (photo courtesy of U.S. Marine Corps).

A lance corporal from 1/5 takes a cigarette break while on patrol with his comrades (photo courtesy of U.S. Marine Corps).

A tank from the 3rd Tank Battalion fires its 90mm gun at North Vietnamese fortifications (photo courtesy of U.S. Marine Corps).

Geared-up Marines from 2/9 relax while waiting for the order to move out on patrol (photo courtesy of U.S. Marine Corps).

A mortarman from 1/5 carries his 60mm mortar tube while on patrol in the barren and hostile "Arizona Territory" southwest of Da Nang (photo courtesy of U.S. Marine Corps).

H-34s from HMM-261 and HMM-362 drop Marines in an LZ in the coastal lowlands (photo courtesy of U.S. Marine Corps).

On 3 May 1968, Marines from 2/4 patrol near the village of Dai Do northeast of Dong Ha (photo courtesy of U.S. Marine Corps).

Mail call for Marines of the 2nd Battalion, 4th Marines, at a secure fire base in August 1969 (photo courtesy of U.S. Marine Corps).

A corpsman attached to 3/26 looks at terrain that he and Marines will have to cover (photo courtesy of U.S. Marine Corps).

A mountaintop fire base (photo courtesy of U.S. Marine Corps).

SLF troops from the 26th Marines patrol through the rice paddies, fresh-water marshes, and waterways south of Da Nang in February 1968 (photo courtesy of U.S. Marine Corps).

H-34 helicopter pilots from HMM-263 pose for the camera at Dong Ha during the summer of 1966 (photo courtesy of Tom Holmes).

Near a small village in Quang Tri Province, women have been given a construction job. Construction jobs for women were common in Vietnam, and the work often lasted all day (photo by the author).

While taking a break during a patrol on 6 November 1967, a Marine corporal tries to strike a deal on an equitable price for a pineapple (photo courtesy of U.S. Marine Corps).

Faced with a need to launch immediately, the commanding officer of HMM-361 conducts an impromptu briefing for affected pilots and aircrewmen on 4 July 1966 (photo courtesy of U.S. Marine Corps).

1st Reconnaissance Battalion Memorial. It stands in Semper Fidelis Memorial Park adjacent to the National Museum of the Marine Corps at Quantico, Virginia (photo by the author).

2nd Battalion, 4th Marines, Memorial. It stands in Semper Fidelis Memorial Park adjacent to the National Museum of the Marine Corps at Quantico, Virginia (photo by the author).

Marine Corps War Memorial. The memorial is based upon the photograph taken by Joe Rosenthal, depicting five Marines and a Navy corpsman raising the American flag on top of Mount Suribachi, Iwo Jima, during World War II. The picture earned a Pulitzer Prize and is considered the world's most famous photograph.

In 1947 the U.S. Congress authorized a war memorial based upon the photograph. Construction was completed seven years later. Burnished into the base of polished Swedish granite, in gold letters, are the words of Adm. Chester Nimitz: "Uncommon Valor Was A Common Virtue." Also inscribed in gold are these words:

In Honor And Memory Of The Men Of The United States Marine Corps Who Have Given Their Lives To Their Country Since 10 November 1775

The memorial features the largest bronze castings in the world. They weigh over 100 tons. Dwight Eisenhower, U.S. President, dedicated the memorial on 10 November 1954, the 179th birthday of the Corps. The memorial honors United States Marines of all eras who have fallen in battle (photo courtesy of U.S. Marine Corps).

The Return to the Knoll

Let us solemnly remember the sacrifices of all those who fought so valiantly . . . and let us reconsecrate ourselves to the task of promoting an enduring peace so that their efforts shall not have been in vain.
[Dwight Eisenhower, U.S. President, speaking on Veterans Day, 11 November 1954]

Return to Vietnam: Thirty-two years after the struggle on the knoll a tiny group of United States military veterans returned to Vietnam. Their expedition was organized by Military Historical Tours of Woodbridge, Virginia, and billed as the Marine I-Corps Tour. The tourists left Los Angeles International Airport on 1 June 1998 for a 14-hour Cathay Pacific flight to Hong Kong. After a layover they flew southward and landed at Noi Bai Airport in Hanoi, capital city of the Socialist Republic of Vietnam.

Socialism is a philosophy of failure, the creed of ignorance, and the gospel of envy. . . . Its inherent vice is equal sharing of misery.
[Winston Churchill, British Prime Minister, 28 May 1948]

In this contingent of nine veterans, former military rank ranged from lance corporal to lieutenant general. One veteran was the tour director from Military Historical Tours. Another had taken part in the battle at the knoll on 8-9 August 1966. In addition to these men, one adventurous non-veteran spouse accompanied the group.

The Vietnam to which they returned had changed. The country was not at war in 1998. Population had increased to roughly 82 million people, making Vietnam the 13th most populous country in the world. The government espoused communism and maintained the world's sixth largest army. Those who worked for the government lived comfortably in cities. There was no middle class worthy of the name. Most citizens lived in the countryside, where they eked out a living by fishing or growing rice. They were among the most impoverished people on Earth.

Nonetheless, there were signs of progress. The former Colonial Route 1 highway, running south to north through the length of the country, was open and heavily traveled in many places. There were small buses, three-wheel cars, oxcarts, hundreds of motor scooters, and bicycles. The railroad that parallels the highway had been totally shut down during the war, but in 1998 it was operative once again. Trains rumbled along the route several times each day.

The Vietnamese use old locomotives built decades ago in Czechoslovakia, under contract for the Russians.
[veteran's photo caption]

Electricity was available in many rural areas, and high voltage wires were attached to a combination of bamboo poles, trees, and regular utility poles. In rural villages the veterans sometimes could see television antennas protruding from tops of thatched roofs.

The veterans had not returned to Vietnam to participate in a fancy highbrow tour. They had come to travel through the countryside and visit old battlefields. True, they spent some time in cities, but most of their days were spent in rural areas. They were up at dawn each morning and rode from place to place in a Japanese minibus. Getting stranded in the middle of nowhere without communications ability was always a possibility. Consequently, crates of bottled water and hundreds of granola bars were kept in the bus for emergency use.

Two Vietnamese nationals accompanied the group. One was the bus driver. He spoke no English and simply drove the bus. The other was a Vietnamese-English translator. He spoke perfect English, and group members engaged him in conversation as they rode along. Whenever the bus stopped at points of interest the amiable young translator would explain the site, offer background information, and answer questions.

Hanoi, the Vietnamese Capital City: The capital city, Hanoi, is a popular destination for Japanese tourists. They visit the War Museum complex, similar to the U.S. Smithsonian Museum, but on a slightly smaller scale. Separate museums are dedicated to the French War, the American War, the Chinese Wars, and to Heroic Mothers of the Revolution. Nearby the massive Ho Chi Minh Mausoleum held the embalmed body of the revered Marxist-Leninist revolutionary. The body could be viewed by the public. The translator opined that the mausoleum offered the best air-conditioning in Vietnam.

In Hanoi the government maintained the main entrance to the old French prison, the "Maison Centrale," as a tourist attraction. Barbed wire, electric wires, and broken glass embedded in concrete topped the prison walls. It was an exercise in bad taste. During the war the prison had become known to American POWs as the Hanoi Hilton.

This 95-year-old jail was built by the French, and it occupied an entire city block. Now, most of it has been torn down.
[veteran's photo caption]

The fabled "Marine House," a residence for seven U.S. Marines who guard the American Embassy in Hanoi, was in a nearby suburb. In the evenings off-duty Marine guards were eager to host Marine veterans who were visiting Hanoi. Veterans were treated like royalty, and the libations flowed freely. Also in the city the United States maintained the "Joint Task Force - Full Accounting" office. The staff was dedicated to a search for remains of United States servicemen who became missing-in-action during the war.

Da Nang and Coastal Lowlands: After a day in Hanoi the veterans flew southward to Da Nang, the Marine Corps headquarters during the war. By 1998, Da Nang had become the home of over 400,000 Vietnamese. The airport looked much like it did during the war, and vacant protective revetments for fighter planes lined the eastern side of the main runway. In the city the veterans spotted a former Marine Corps jeep parked in front of a shop. It still bore faded green military paint, and on the rear was stenciled: "625557 USMC" (the veterans joked that a Marine supply sergeant may still be looking for it). Two miles east of the city was the former Marine helicopter base named Marble Mountain. Veterans could not access the premises, for the site was occupied by the Vietnamese Army.

Two miles south of the former Marine helicopter base are the five stone formations called Marble Mountain. The rock massifs rise straight up from the sandy coastal plain. The largest massif contains a huge cavern that houses a Buddhist shrine. One could climb 200 feet up a wide stairway chiseled into the rock side of the mountain and then enter the shrine. It is adorned with paintings, statues, and Buddhas. Visiting the shrine were 20 to 25 Japanese tourists plus a dozen Vietnamese. The air was thick with burning incense. Outside at the base of the mountain, vendors hawked t-shirts, incense sticks, various trinkets, and dragon statuettes carved from marble.

> I rent a *[pedal-powered]* cyclo for two dollars, and I get to ride all afternoon. . . . My *[Vietnamese]* cyclo operator is friendly, and he gives the camera a "thumbs-up."
> *[veteran's photo caption]*

South of Da Nang on the coastal plain, an enemy hotbed during the war, the veterans visited numerous villages. With help from their translator they conversed with friendly and accommodating villagers of all ages. Many entrepreneurial villagers had canned soft drinks and packaged crackers for sale, although there was no refrigeration or ice for the drinks. Water buffalo cooled themselves in a nearby irrigation canal. Only their heads were visible above water.

The one-lane dirt road westward toward An Hoa was almost impassible. During two occasions the veterans had to get out of the bus and push it out of a muddy mire. During the war An Hoa had been the gateway into hostile "Arizona Territory," named for the barren badlands of the American Southwest. Marines had based a rifle company at An Hoa. Yet, when the veterans arrived there was nothing left except remains of a narrow asphalt runway. Cows grazed nearby, but no people were seen.

> We pass farmers planting rice. The water buffalo is still used, but these animals are slowly being replaced by manual labor. Water buffalo eat too much, and farmers cannot *[spare the land]* to plant fodder to feed them. All land must be used to grow rice . . . .
> *[veteran's photo caption]*

Veterans drove past temples built by the Chams over 1,000 years ago. North of An Hoa the bus stopped, and veterans walked up the gentle slope of Hill 55. The French Army had based a battalion there in the late 1940s and early 1950s, for the hill offers a commanding view of the rice basin south of Da Nang. One could see rugged Charlie Ridge to the west, An Hoa and Arizona Territory to the southwest, the Que Son Mountains to the south, and the South China Sea to the east. In the 1960s the Marines had based an infantry company on the hill. They had doused the red earth on the hilltop with tons of oil and defoliant to eliminate dust, kill vegetation, and ensure clear fields of fire. After the war the Vietnamese had built a 30-foot-tall war memorial on the hill to commemorate a supposed Viet Minh victory over a French Army battalion.

Hue and the "Street Without Joy": The city of Hue was the home of roughly 500,000 people. Veterans spent four nights in the Huong Guang Hotel, originally built by the French, but totally renovated and updated to attract Japanese tourists. From the hotel balcony one could look across the Perfume River and see the shanty-town on the other side. It would rival the infamous Black Hole of Calcutta. On the street outside were beggars looking for a handout. Five-year-old children were desperate to sell postcards for 1,000 Vietnamese Dong, equivalent to about seven cents. Conversely, near Hue one could charter a tour motorboat and cruise six miles upriver to the enormous royal tomb complex. It is regal beyond description.

> *[Except for]* the Vietnamese dragons painted on it, *[the boat we chartered]* would be a dead ringer for "The African Queen." The old wheezing steam engine sounded like The African Queen too. I think we made about four knots, top speed.
> *[veteran's photo caption]*

In Hue tourists could access a masonry bridge, cross over a moat, and enter Hue Citadel. It was built as a military fortress. Inside the citadel one could cross over another moat and enter the Forbidden City, home of the former Vietnamese emperors. Inside the Forbidden City the Imperial Palace, modeled after the palace in Peking, had been ravaged during the war. It later had been rebuilt and restored to its former glory. Tourists could walk through all rooms in the palace and take photographs in any room except the throne room.

North of Hue the veterans visited dozens of villages in the coastal "Street Without Joy" chronicled by the French historian, Dr. Bernard

Fall. Farmers, fishermen, and their families lived a hand-to-mouth existence there, but they welcomed visitors into their homes. A few old men spoke English well enough to communicate, and they talked of the "American War" with no animosity. Yet, first they made sure that the veterans were not Russians. They *despise* the Russians.

At many prominent roadway intersections the government had erected 10-foot-tall public health billboards. They promoted AIDS prevention. For those who could not read, the graphic human images left nothing to one's imagination.

Dong Ha and Nearby Battlegrounds: During the war Dong Ha had been a sleepy village six miles below the DMZ. During the first half of the 1900s, a half-mile south of the village, the French had built a dirt airstrip on the coastal plain. In the summer of 1966 the Marines had established Dong Ha combat base at the little airstrip. The base had been the jumping-off place for combat in the rolling hills to the north, and in mountains and jungles to the west.

> *[This is]* the battleground where the third and fourth largest military machines on Earth clashed over a quarter-century ago.
> *[veteran's photo caption]*

North and west of Dong Ha in the former Leatherneck Square, Marines and North Vietnamese had squared-off during the war. The strategic hill, Con Thien, was the "Hill of Angels" in Vietnamese lore. However, any foolish angel who had dared to set foot there during the daily artillery duels in 1966-1968 would have been blown to bits. Yet, when veterans arrived and climbed the hill they found no evidence of the former Marine artillery compound. Only the concrete French Army command bunker remained.

> Atop Con Thien you have a grandstand viewpoint *[from which]* to observe the coastal plain in all directions, from the mountains to the sea, and from Dong Ha into *[the former]* North Vietnam.
> *[veteran's photo caption]*

The veterans found that Dong Ha village had grown, and crude homes had been built on what once was the airstrip. No traces of the former combat base were visible. The old Colonial Route 9 highway, a one-lane dirt road at best, once had extended westward from Dong Ha into Laos. During the war the route had been contested by the Marines and the North Vietnamese.

In 1998 the veterans found that the Vietnamese government had been modernizing the road, and it was a work-in-progress. Many sections were still narrow, unpaved, and muddy. Other sections had become a two-lane paved roadway. The 13-mile drive from Dong Ha westward to the Rockpile took 55 minutes. The huge geological freak, the famous 700-foot-high Rockpile, looked almost exactly as it had looked during the war. The only difference was on the northern slope. The government had been quarrying there to obtain crushed rock for the Route 9 highway improvement project.

In the northern part of Vietnam, this one-lane road is the only road leading from Vietnam into Laos.
[veteran's photo caption]

A mile northwest of the Rockpile the two-mile-long Razorback Ridge, over 1,000 feet high, forms the western extremity of Razorback Valley. The group drove farther west along Route 9 to Khe Sanh village, where thatched huts and shops lined the narrow road. Nearby the former Khe Sanh combat base was deserted. All traces of the titanic firestorm there in the spring of 1968 had vanished.

Yet farther west along Route 9 near Lang Vei the veterans looked across the Laotian border at the enormous and foreboding Co Roc Mountain. During the war North Vietnamese engineers had mounted 130mm artillery inside caves dug into the eastern rock face of the mountain. From that lofty stone bastion they had shelled Khe Sanh combat base six miles to the east.

The Return to The Knoll: The tour company had asked each veteran to list one place of interest, one site he wanted to visit if practical. The veteran who had taken part in the struggle at the knoll chose its map coordinates, XD-986599 in western Razorback Valley.

The veterans were thoroughly briefed before the attempt to reach the knoll. They were told that the trip through rough terrain would be brutal. They also were given a detailed description of the battle that had raged there on 8-9 August 1966. Only seven veterans elected to attempt the trek. The spunky spouse also agreed to tag along, and the Vietnamese translator also would go. Each was armed with several water bottles, and two carried 1:50,000 scale maps.

The veterans left Route 9 near the Rockpile and started walking. At first the attempt was easy. An oxcart trail led northward. They followed it, but soon the trail petered out. Guided by their maps, they pressed ahead. The huge Rockpile behind them to the south, the Razorback to the west, and Nui Cay Tre Ridge (aka, *Mutter Ridge*) to the north enabled them to remain oriented in the increasingly thick brush. Soon they were forced to slash their way with machetes.

> We forge ahead through head-high undergrowth. . . . I stop and point to unexploded ordnance, which litters the ground.
> *[veteran's photo caption]*

The group kept up a constant jovial chatter. Veterans and the plucky spouse joked about poisonous bamboo vipers, land-mines, Bengal tigers, leeches, and a host of real or imagined perils. Dense tangled undergrowth blocked visibility straight ahead, but peaks of the lofty Rockpile, Razorback, and Nui Cay Tre Ridge remained visible. After over two hours the maps and terrain confirmed their location. They had reached the little knoll.

On Top of the Knoll: The fighting holes were still there, but time and the elements had partially filled them with eroded soil and vegetation. Some were slightly over two feet deep, while others were much deeper. They marked the perimeter Marines had defended atop the little hill during the long afternoon and night 32 years earlier. During the battle in 1966 the knoll had been barren and denuded. No vegetation had blocked the defenders' view or their fields of fire. However, in 1998 the knoll was covered with vegetation. Much of it was substantially over head-high.

> I stand in one of the Marine fighting holes which still circle the summit of the knoll. The Marine perimeter *[had been]* only about 15 yards in diameter, judging by the layout of the fighting holes.
> *[veteran's photo caption]*

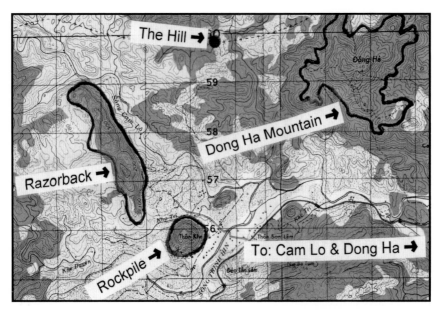

Part of the Series L-7014, Sheet 6342-I, map showing "The Hill" (top center) with the Razorback to the southwest, and the Rockpile to the south (map courtesy of U.S. Army Topographic Command).

Naturally the surrounding terrain had not changed. Deep ravines and gullies surrounded the knoll on all sides. They were filled with heavier vegetation which would have provided concealment for NVA infantrymen. The little "drop-off" on the eastern side of the knoll confirmed defenders' verbal accounts of the fighting there.

To the south the Rockpile peak was visible above the vegetation on the knoll. The long Razorback was visible to the southwest. Nui Cay Tre Ridge, the former NVA fortress, lay to the north. A few pieces of unexploded ordnance protruded above the red dirt on the hill. The veterans took photographs and pointed out each potential explosive threat to their peers, but they followed the cautionary look-but-do-not-touch doctrine.

Atop the hill, veterans and the spry spouse posed for a photograph with the Rockpile peak in the background. The translator snapped the picture. Other photographs quickly followed: veterans standing in fighting holes, veterans pointing to fighting holes, veterans kneeling and pointing to unexploded ordnance, veterans pointing to nearby terrain features, etc. Thirty minutes passed. Then an eerie silence slowly settled over the knoll. All conversation gradually ceased. No sound marred the summer afternoon. Cameras were put away. Veterans fell silent and reflected upon the struggle on the knoll 32 years in the past and their own experiences in Vietnam.

No sane person who has been to war wants to go to another.
[Col. Oliver North, USMC, 29 May 2003]

The little knoll was so tiny! For the veteran who had been there on 8-9 August 1966, it looked exactly like he had remembered it, exclusive of the new vegetation. So tiny! So small! The hill was perhaps a mere 40 feet high, and the perimeter had been only about 45 feet in diameter. It seemed inconceivable that so many men, both Marines and North Vietnamese, had struggled desperately there.

There was nothing left to do. No one spoke. Everyone knew that it was time to go, but no one wanted to be the first to say so. The little hill seemed to be hallowed ground, a brutal killing field where Asians and Americans had fought and sacrificed. One veteran finally broke the silence. He prayed for the souls of all men – whatever their nationality – who had fought and died at the hill for their comrades and the cause in which they believed.

The veterans, the spouse, and translator began the long arduous trek back to Route 9. The trip took two hours. Unlike the journey to the knoll, there was no joking or talking on the return trip. None of the veterans spoke until after they reached the bus.

Have you forgotten yet?
Look down, and swear by the slain of the War that you'll
      never forget.
[Siegfried Sassoon, Aftermath, 1919]

With the northern face of the 700-foot-high Rockpile in the background, the group of veterans (lower left) begins walking northward along an oxcart trail toward the knoll (photo by the author).

In the thick brush one veteran points to old ordnance imprinted with Chinese or Vietnamese markings (photo courtesy of the author).

About 300 meters before reaching the knoll the veterans saw an NVA 12.7mm heavy machinegun (equivalent to an American .50 caliber machinegun) firing pit. The 12.7mm gun can be used as an AAA weapon, and also it can be used against infantry. It is highly effective against helicopters and against light armor.

The ground all around the pit had been tamped down, and all grass and vegetation were gone. This indicated that the site recently had been discovered by local Vietnamese, who obviously had spent several days working there. Vietnamese have become skilled at salvaging weapons, ammunition, other ordnance, tools, and all material left behind by armies. In the instant case only the projectiles for the 12.7mm gun remained. In the photograph they can be seen littering the ground in and around the firing pit. The projectiles are virtually worthless to local Vietnamese. When they find ammunition, as they obviously did in this instance, they cut away and salvage the brass. They sell this valuable metal to scrap dealers.

Rural Vietnamese long ago rummaged through former Marine and NVA campsites. They salvaged concertina wire, metal matting, creosote poles, communications wire, hardware, and any other item of value. They sell most of it to scrap dealers, and they use the rest as building material (photo courtesy of the author).

On top of the knoll the group poses for the camera with the peak of the Rockpile in the background (photo courtesy of the author).

A member of the group walks across the knoll. In the background to the southwest the Razorback is visible (photo by the author).

On top of the knoll a veteran stands in one of the more shallow fighting holes (photo courtesy of the author).

One veteran (left) stands by a fighting hole. Two veterans stand in the hole, revealing its depth (photo courtesy of the author).

On top of the knoll five veterans explore fighting holes and look for unexploded ordnance (photo by the author).

This veteran has found an operative former Marine Corps jeep in front of a shop in Da Nang. He points to identification stenciled on the vehicle: "625557 USMC" (photo courtesy of the author).

A public health notice. The graphic artwork on many other such notices leaves nothing to the imagination (photo by the author).

A Buddhist shrine <u>inside a cavern</u> in the largest of the massifs known as Marble Mountain. It is two miles south of the former Marine Corps helicopter base, "Marble Mountain" (photo by the author).

To reach the shrine inside the largest of the Marble Mountain massifs, one first must climb up these steps. They are carved into the exterior stone side of the massif. After climbing 200 feet up the rock steps, one can enter the interior shrine by walking through a man-made tunnel carved through the rock (photo by the author).

Below the DMZ and on top of Con Thien (aka, "Hill of Angels"), site of the huge Marine artillery outpost during the war, a veteran stands by the old French Army command bunker (photo by the author).

On their last day in the countryside the veterans were met by children from a small village. The youngsters were curious. They were not beggars. The veterans gave their entire supply of emergency food, about 175 granola bars, to the children (photo by the author).

This huge war memorial structure stands on a hill west of the former Marine Corps airbase at Chu Lai. It is 55 feet in height. One can appreciate its size by comparing it with the three veterans standing to the left of its base (photo by the author).

This war memorial stands on Hill 55, which overlooks the rice basin south of Da Nang. The memorial commemorates a claimed victory over the French here in 1954 (photo courtesy of the author).

On the coastal plain north of Dong Ha, cows graze along the sides of Route 1, the Vietnamese version of I-95 (photo by the author).

At the former Marine combat base at An Hoa south of Da Nang, cattle graze by what is left of the asphalt runway. No other trace of the combat base remains (photo by the author).

Veterans stand in front of the Imperial Palace, former home of Vietnamese emperors. It is located inside the Forbidden City, which in turn is located inside the Hue Citadel (photo by the author).

This "cyclo," a three-wheel bicycle with a passenger seat in front, is the Vietnamese version of a Western World taxicab. In cities like Hue and Da Nang, one can hail a cyclo as one would hail a taxicab in America. For a two dollar fare one could ride all afternoon. In the photo, one of the veterans has rented a cyclo to visit points of interest in the city of Da Nang (photo by the author).

This pagoda stands along the Perfume River west of Hue. Monks who live in the adjacent complex make a living raising chickens. They sell eggs and chicken meat to families and local restaurants. Chicken, pork, and fish are the primary meats consumed by both Vietnamese and tourists (photo by the author).

A common sight in Vietnam. Two young water buffalo amble across Route 1 highway in Quang Tri Province (photo by the author).

In a village in front of two homes, a water buffalo - right center – cools himself in an irrigation canal (photo by the author).

This man and his wife have a roadside home that doubles as a restaurant. Customers could choose from bottled beer, bottled soft drinks, packaged crackers, and packaged cheese. The man and wife also offered a limited variety of cooked food. Fish, pork, and chicken sometimes were available. Their availability depended upon what could be caught and killed that day in the village.

With no refrigeration, caution was in order when eating local meat. Vegetables could be viewed to determine their freshness and desirability. Bottled water was available as a prudent alternative to water from local streams or wells (photo by the author).

Requiem

> I visited with three old friends recently at a park near my home. . . . I found Lance at Panel 54-W, Line 037; Lynn over at Panel 51-W, Line 032; and Vince at Panel 27-W, Line 103. I am especially proud of my friends, heroes who voluntarily and enthusiastically gave their all. . . . May their names, indelibly engraved on that memorial wall, likewise be found in the Book of Life.
>
> *[J.D. Wetterling, "Still the Noblest Calling" in* The Wall Street Journal, *May 1996]*

How many American servicemen *actually fought* in Vietnam? That is a loaded question. Statisticians love to quote numbers. They report that over 9,000,000 Americans served in the U.S. Armed Forces during the Vietnam era. However, they acknowledge that only about 3,403,000 served "in theater" (Vietnam, Laos, Cambodia, Thailand, and in waters of the South China Sea). About 2,594,000 of those set foot in Vietnam, some for a year or more, but many others for only a day or two. Many were among the hundreds-of-thousands in the supply chain that transported tools of war from the United States to coastal seaports or air terminals in Vietnam. So the question still remains: how many Americans *actually fought* in Vietnam?

> The structure of the U.S. Military in Vietnam was like a giant pyramid, with 80 percent of the troops at the bottom providing various services, so that the other 20 percent could fight.
>
> *[B.G. Burkett,* Stolen Valor, *1998]*

Since the days of Alexander and Caesar, armies in the field have been sustained by legions of armorers, builders, foragers, suppliers, administrators, and the like. The old axiom is correct: armies cannot fight without beans and bullets.

Modern armed forces have long administrative and logistic tails. The U.S. Armed Forces have the longest tails of all. In a hi-tech environment, those who fight are supported by swarms of planners, clerks, trainers, administrators, electricians, mechanics, technicians, logisticians, communicators, builders, etc. Such supporting forces are essential, and most rear echelon personnel are exemplary professionals. Their service is honorable, and it is necessary. They far outnumber those who close ranks with the enemy.

> The administrative non-combat jobs *[in Vietnam were]* as safe as any job in the states, their biggest complaint being bad coffee.
> *[Bud Willis, Marble Mountain, 2011]*

The statistical consensus is that only 521,000 to 874,000 men in the U.S. Armed Forces actually fought in Vietnam (the exact number depends upon one's definition of *fought*). Almost 59,000 died there, and another 303,704 were wounded.

Well intentioned pluralists refer to the "many" servicewomen killed in Vietnam. The U.S. Armed Forces did send some female volunteers to Vietnam. A few were administrators and clerks. Most were nurses in sprawling hospitals at big military bases. None saw combat in the field. One American servicewoman – only one – was killed by enemy action. Lt. Sharon Lane, U.S. Army, age 25, an Ohioan, died on 8 June 1969 when an enemy rocket slammed into the 312th Evacuation Hospital at Chu Lai, where she was a ward nurse. Seven more servicewomen died in Vietnam, but not in combat. One had a stroke (subarachnoid hemorrhage). Pneumonia killed another. The other five died in accidents. Once again the original question remains: how many Americans *actually fought* in Vietnam?

> War is a bloody, killing business. You've got to spill their blood, or they will spill yours. Rip them up the belly! Shoot them in the guts!
> *[Gen. George Patton, USA, 5 June 1944]*

How many American servicemen in Vietnam often slept in a hole half full of water? How many rushed into ongoing battles, into the belly of the beast, to bring ammunition or rescue wounded comrades under fire? How many lost arms or legs? How many were otherwise maimed, or escaped mutilation and attributed their good fortune to blind luck or divine intervention? How many daily went without food, without water, without sleep? How many endured leeches, swarming and stinging insects, immersion foot, and jungle-rot? How many lived with the exhaustion, the horror, the brutality, the hi-tech butchery of modern warfare? How many willingly sacrificed their lives so that their friends might live? Relatively few. Whatever the number, they are the men who *actually fought* in Vietnam.

=======================

Many-hundred-thousands of rear echelon servicemen returned to the United States after their time in Vietnam. They had never heard a shot fired in anger. Good for them. Most served with honor and distinction, and their duties were necessary. Yet, from their ranks a few *wannabes* delight in catching the ear of uninformed persons and weaving fabricated stories of their role in the war. They are joined by con artists who never wore a military uniform.

War phonies are ne'er-do-well losers. Left out of the mainstream of society, they crave attention. They get it by spinning scintillating tales of secret missions, inhuman atrocities, and combat bravado. They regale listeners with stories of military prowess and wartime shenanigans. These war phonies delight in claiming that records of their exploits are "still classified." For a prodigiously researched and authoritative account of high profile military phonies, fakers, and liars, the reader may consult the 692-page treatise, *Stolen Valor*, by B.G. Burkett, ISBN 0-96670-360-X.

Phony war heroes are not unique to the war in Vietnam. They have sprouted after every war: Revolutionary War, American Civil War, World War I, World War II, Korea, Vietnam, and recent wars in the Middle East. Wise adults can see through their charade.

Those who experienced close-combat are different. Many never came home at all, of course. Some who did return had lost legs, arms, or had invisible wounds that would not heal. Nonetheless, they got jobs, raised families, paid taxes, started businesses, voted, and joined the mainstream of American life. They do not try to explain the reality of close-combat, for an explanation is not possible.

The language failed us. The civilian-issue adjectives and nouns, verbs and adverbs, seemed made for a different universe. There were no metaphors that connected the war to everyday life.
[William Broyles Jr., in Esquire Magazine, November 1984]

Those who wish to romanticize close-combat are either naive, or they reject reality. For those who actually fought in Vietnam, the war was a timeless nightmare, an obscene neverland where they did things no civilized person can comprehend or sanction.

In your day-to-day life there is no one who understands, and because of that you just don't talk about it.
[Dave Jones, quoted in One Magnificent Bastard*, 2013]*

These men face a conundrum, a dilemma. The war was the most intense and utopian experience of their lives – and they have no way to tell anyone about it.

========================

In combat, men easily are motivated to kill other human beings. A combatant has no second thoughts and no regrets when he finds himself face-to-face with men who are trying to kill him. Survival instinct takes over. Kill, or be killed. Self-preservation is the most powerful human instinct. It transforms men into creatures who kill without reservation or remorse, all moral implications aside. The desire and will to kill become survival tools, and killing is easy.

War is not killing. Killing is the easiest part of the whole thing.
[Mark Baker, NAM*, 1981]*

For Marine infantrymen in a tropical jungle environment, war is not about killing. It is about exhaustion, thirst, hunger, immersion foot, jock-rot, malaria, ringworm, watching comrades drop from heatstroke, and trying to sleep soaking wet in the rain. War is about malaria, diarrhea, and trying to survive amid swarms of flying, buzzing, crawling, stinging, sucking insects that make days miserable and nights unbearable. It is about sweating all day and humping the hills in 100-plus degree heat, while praying for a firefight so everyone can stop walking for a while. A bath, a good night's sleep, clean sheets, and hot food are too remote to even dream about.

During combat in Vietnamese jungles, helicopter crewmen were characterized by one word: target. One historian wrote of the perils faced by Marine (and also, *U.S. Army*) helicopter crews.

Helicopter crews that survived an entire tour unscathed led charmed lives. Gunfire downed 1,777 helicopters during the first five years of the war, and others returned to base shot to splinters.
[Joseph Alexander, A Fellowship of Valor, 1997]

When Marine helicopters launched on a medevac mission, night ammunition resupply, emergency extraction, or Sparrow Hawk assault the crew expected to land amid an ongoing battle. They had no choice. They had to launch. Their infantry brothers needed them, depended upon them. Protective component armor and body armor helped. Yet, the thin aluminum skins of their craft offered no more protection from hostile fire than an empty aluminum beer can. There was nothing behind which a crewman could take cover. Nonetheless, duty demanded that they launch.

==========================

In recent years some people began acknowledging any and all armed forces personnel and veterans with a standard cliche: "Thank you for your service." Knee-jerk media whores adopted it, and the mindless phenomenon became universal and obligatory.

It's like saying "Hi" or "Hello." It's automatic, and it doesn't mean anything. It's fake. It's phony.
[Nicholas Tarzia, oral account, 11 February 2015]

Those orally offering such thanks often are well-intentioned and pregnant with desire to somehow acknowledge those who wore a military uniform. Yet, close-combat survivors plus many others in the U.S. Armed Forces are embarrassed by the trite little phrase. To them the copycat "thank-you-for-your-service" is shallow, hollow, crass, and insulting. Service? Service?

The automatic cliche perhaps would be suited for school mentors, soup kitchen volunteers, or someone who helps an elderly person cross a busy street. Such contributions to society are worthy of some acknowledgment. Any mindless automaton can voice the automatic words. They are always the same, as though they were permanently digitized. They require no thought, no sincerity, nothing from the heart, no conversation, no variation. One size fits all.

One of the worst examples of the mindless "thanks" was captured on video at Dulles International Airport on 12 February 2013. A twenty-something lady brushed against a military triple amputee in his wheelchair. He had lost both legs above the knee plus one arm below the elbow. With a brilliant smile and a vibrant congratulatory tone the woman voiced the thoughtless words: "Thank you for your service!" Then she went merrily on her way, laughing and giggling with her friends.

Those who have not *been there* have no way to comprehend the unspeakable privations, horrors, and sacrifices of close-combat. For survivors who have been through the fire, plus those in the armed forces who are prepared to do so, the mindless "thank-you-for-your-service" is both demeaning and embarrassing. They look down or turn away. A meaningful response is not possible.

========================

Close-combat veterans can truthfully say they hated the war, and the reason is not a mystery. War's perils and privations are obvious. In war, death is not pretty and often not quick. A friend may be shot, burned, mortared, bayoneted, rocketed, bombed, blasted, or beaten to death. Men die on the ground from assorted causes. Men die in the air. Death does not discriminate, and men at war are tasked with becoming agents of death. Some men who survive have no visible wounds. Others are maimed and lose limbs or their minds.

Men who fought despised the war. To say anything different is not publicly acceptable. But deep down inside where no one else can see, these men share a dark secret. That secret is akin to the crazy uncle that families will not talk about in public. Although they hated the war, most close-combat survivors agree – they also loved it!

The line between love and hate was razor thin, as was the line between death and life.
[William Myers, Marines, Medals, and Vietnam, 2012]

Nothing else will come close to the intensity, the horrible ecstacy, of combat. War stops time. It is a game played for the highest stakes of all, your life. Men love competitive games. There are no do-overs in battle. The higher the stakes, the greater the thrill. Amid hardships and danger it is easy to become enthralled by the challenge. Combat can evolve into the ultimate turn-on, an obscene adventure.

To kill and kill and kill was the cry. Men heard the madness, and knew it for madness, and embraced it – some with fear, and some with joy. Kill or be killed. Survive or perish.
[Floyd Gibbons, The Red Knight of Germany, 1927]

Men relish the clarity of combat. There are few rules. Combat is simple. You live, or you die. You crash in flames, or you live to fly again another day. Those who survive bask in the unadulterated joy of being alive when so many around them are dead. For the moment such men are winning, and all competitive men admire a winner.

When you win, nothing hurts.
[Joe Namath, professional football player, 1969]

The crucible of mechanized warfare is dirty, ugly, and obscene. Yet, it also is beautiful. Nothing in civilian life can compare to the eerie ghostly dancing shadows cast by a descending parachute flare at night. Tracers arcing up to kill flyers at night are lethal, but they also are mesmerizing. White phosphorus, with its glowing red comets and billowing white plumes, is unsurpassed visual art. The power and splendor of a napalm strike is unforgettable. Watching an air-strike and a 155mm artillery barrage is akin to witnessing the end of the world. No civilian experiences on Earth can duplicate the haunting raw beauty and power of such sights.

=====================

Civilians attempting to *earn the title* face more than training in military arts. They are schooled in Corps legacy. They honor 10 November each year. They study the famed "halls of Montezuma" and the great triumph on "the shores of Tripoli." They learn that Devil Dogs were born in Belleau Wood. Battle legacies are drilled into each recruit and officer candidate. Iwo Jima. The frozen Chosin. Khe Sanh. The Iraqi wall of death. Fallujah in the new millennium. The world's largest bronze war memorial on hallowed ground.
Marines are all about fighting. That is who they are, and the

Marine warrior ethos is simple: prowess in combat.

There is a fellowship of valor that links all U.S. Marines, past,
present, and future.
[Joseph Alexander, A Fellowship of Valor, 1997]

Marines revere their tradition of duty and sacrifice. Young men
(and in recent years, women) do not simply *join* the Corps. Marine
recruiters ask each applicant: "What do you have to offer us?" From
selected candidates, those who complete Marine basic training
become part of a proud Brotherhood of Marines. Their strength lies
in the collective will of their brothers, their comrades-in-arms.

A Marine's most sought after privilege is to be able to fight for
another Marine.
[MGen. Mike Myatt, USMC, in Kuwait, 1991]

Despite modern-day mechanization, the most basic tenet of
Marine Corps doctrine remains the infantryman, the Marine Grunt.
Everything revolves around him. Tanks, artillery, attack jets, and
helicopters all exist to support him. To become a Marine Grunt is a
great honor. Grunts are the Marines behind the bayonet, the tip of the
spear, the gunfighters. In their elite Corps they are the best of the
best, modern-day American Samurai. To spend time with Marine
Grunts is to walk among military kings and giants.

========================

For the United States the war in Vietnam ended a long time ago.
It was America's longest war, longer than the American Civil War,
World War I, and World War II all lumped together. Unlike Europe's
so-called *civilized* wars, combat in Vietnamese jungles degenerated
into unbridled animalistic savagery. Subhuman cruelty and violent
death became survival tools. Each Marine struggled for his life and
the lives of his brothers-in-arms.

Such close-combat evokes emotions including terror, horror, rage,
confusion, desperation, madness, and ecstacy. They are temporary.
But there is an overriding emotion that lasts long after the cacophony
of battle has faded away. For those who have experienced close-

combat, the greatest emotion is love – true brotherly love.

I knew I would never experience a bond like I had with these men.
The only thing I really knew for certain was that I loved these guys.
[Bud Willis, Marble Mountain, 2011]

The battle at the little knoll on 8-9 August 1966 exemplifies the Marine mystique, the warrior ethos of the Corps. Marines at the small hill never lost faith in their comrades-in-arms, their brothers, their friends. Loyalty and love are the glue that held them together as they shared the searing emotions of close-combat.

Yet, the struggle on the knoll was not unique. There were many hundreds of knolls, mountains, valleys, and battlegrounds where Marines fought and sacrificed for honor and their brothers-in-arms. In each instance, loyalty and love sustained them. For survivors the experience had forged values, beliefs, pride, and a fraternal bond that would last for a lifetime. Most would never meet again after the war, but it did not matter. Although apart, they remained a family.

The enduring emotion of war, when everything else has faded, is
comradeship. A comrade in war is a man you can trust with anything, because you trusted him with your life.
[William Broyles Jr., in Esquire Magazine, November 1984]

In the Third Millennium the Marines who had fought in Vietnam and survived are elderly men. Some had considered themselves and their Corps to be a vital cog in United States foreign policy. Many others had been content with a more limited view. In either case, when duty called they had given selflessly of themselves. They were sustained by loyalty, love for their comrades, and the warrior culture of their Corps. Their motto, Semper Fidelis, was not simply another catchy Latin phrase. It was a solemn promise.

=====================

Close-combat veterans sometimes reunite. They do not gather to look at faded photographs. They do not meet to mourn or to tell tales of daring-do. They reunite to once again experience the love, the bond, the camaraderie forged in battle. They meet to bask in the company of old friends, good men among whom there were no secrets, no pretenses, no games, men who were willing to sacrifice their lives for each other. One Marine veteran explained it this way.

> I know them in a way I know no other men. I have never since given anyone such trust. They were willing to guard something more precious than my life. They would have carried my reputation, the memory of me. It was part of the bargain we all made, the reason we were so willing to die for one another.
> *[Michael Norman, These Good Men, 1989]*

Marines who experienced close-combat in Vietnam shared an irrevocable bond, a spiritual brotherhood within their Corps. Each Marine trusted his friends, his comrades-in-arms. When in peril, each knew that his Marine brothers would risk their lives to save him. They might fail, and they might lose their own lives in the attempt, but they would try. No man can ask for more than that. All for one, and one for all. Pride in their unity sustained them.

> We fought for each other, or to uphold the honor of the Corps. That was what mattered.
> *[Angus Deming, in Newsweek Magazine, 7 August 1995]*

Marines who fought in Vietnam were all equal, all brothers, all proud professionals. They experienced the passion, the bond, the trust, the incommunicable experience of Marines at war. Loyalty to comrades never faded. They shared a brotherly love that cannot be shattered by time, or misfortune, or declining health, or poverty, or by anything other than death. Their love transcended military rank, age, education, race, social status, financial standing, and the passing years. There is no greater love.

– finis –

About the Author

Marion Sturkey was a young Marine NCO when he was selected for flight training in 1963. Two years later he was commissioned and designated a Naval Aviator. He flew H-46 helicopters in Vietnam during 1966 and 1967. After release from active duty he became a commercial pilot for the oil and gas industry. He later held managerial positions at AT&T for 25 years and served as guest instructor at Bell Communications Research. This is his 13th book.

The author stands by his H-46 helicopter at Marble Mountain, Vietnam, during July 1966.

Index

Suggested Reading

Bowman, John S. The Vietnam War: An Almanac. New York, NY. Random House, 1985.

Bryan, C.D.B. Friendly Fire. New York, NY. Bantam Books, 1977.

Burkett, B.G., et al. Stolen Valor. Dallas, TX. Verity Press, 1998.

Caputo, Philip. A Rumor of War. New York, NY. Ballantine Books, 1977.

Chinnery, Philip D. Life on the Line. New York, NY. St. Martin's Press, 1988.

Dengler, Dieter. Escape from Laos. New York, NY. Kensington Publishing Co., 1979.

Denton, Jeremiah A. Jr. When Hell Was in Session. Clover, SC. Commission Press, 1976.

Doyle, Edward, et al. Setting the Stage. Boston, MA. Boston Publishing Co., 1981.

Doyle, Edward, et al. Passing the Torch. Boston, MA. Boston Publishing Co., 1981.

Fails, William R. Marines and Helicopters: 1962-1973. Washington, DC. U.S. Marine Corps, 1978.

Fall, Bernard B. Street Without Joy. Harrisburg, PA. The Telegraph Press, 1961.

Fall, Bernard B. Hell in a Very Small Place: The Siege of Dien Bien Phu. Philadelphia, PA. J.B. Lippincott Co., 1966.

Fall, Bernard B. Last Reflections on a War. Garden City, NJ. Doubleday & Company, 1967.

Gettleman, Marvin E. Vietnam: History, Documents, and Opinions on a Major World Crisis. New York, NY. Fawcett World Library, 1963.

Hammel, Eric. <u>The Siege of Khe Sanh: An Oral History</u>. New York, NY. Warner Books, 1989.

Herr, Michael. <u>Dispatches</u>. New York, NY. Avon Books, 1968.

Lanning, Micheal Lee, et al. <u>Inside Force Recon: Recon Marines in Vietnam</u>. New York, NY. Ballantine Books, 1989.

Lanning, Michael Lee, et al. <u>Inside the VC and the NVA: The Real Story of North Vietnam's Armed Forces</u>. New York, NY. Ivy Books, 1992.

Lowry, Timothy S. <u>Valor</u>. New York, NY. Berkley Books, 1989.

McConnell, Malcolm. <u>Inside Hanoi's Secret Archives: Solving the MIA Mystery</u>. New York, NY. Simon & Schuster, 1995.

McDonald, Peter. <u>Giap</u>. New York, NY. W.W. Norton & Company, 1993.

Myers, William L. <u>Marines, Medals, and Vietnam</u>. Lafayette, LA. Redoubt Press, 2012.

Norman, Michael. <u>These Good Men: Friendships Forged from War</u>. New York, NY. Crown Publishers, 1989.

Norton, Bruce H. <u>Stingray</u>. New York, NY. Ballantine Books, 2000.

Prados, John, et al. <u>Valley of Decision: The Siege of Khe Sanh</u>. New York, NY. Houghton Mifflin Co., 1991.

Pearson, Willard. <u>The War in the Northern Provinces, 1966-1968</u>. Washington, DC. U.S. Army, 1991.

Pisor, Robert. <u>The End of the Line: The Siege of Khe Sanh</u>. New York, NY. W.W. Norton & Company, 1982.

Ricks, Thomas E. <u>Making the Corps</u>. New York, NY. Simon & Schuster, 1997.

Puller, Lewis B. Jr. <u>Fortunate Son</u>. New York, NY. Grove Press, 1991.

Robbins, Christopher. <u>Air America: The Explosive True Story of the CIA's Secret Airlines</u>. New York, NY. G.P. Putnam, 1979.

Safer, Morley. Flashbacks: On Returning to Vietnam. New York, NY. St. Martin's Paperbacks, 1990.

Schell, Jonathan. The Real War. New York, NY. Pantheon Books, 1988.

Shore, Moyers S. III. The Battle for Khe Sanh. Washington, DC. U.S. Marine Corps, 1977.

Shulimson, Jack. U.S. Marines in Vietnam: An Expanding War, 1966. Washington, DC. U.S. Marine Corps, 1982.

Sturkey, Marion F. Bonnie-Sue: A Marine Corps Helicopter Squadron in Vietnam. Plum Branch, SC. Heritage Press Intl., 1996.

Sturkey, Marion F. Warrior Culture of the U.S. Marines. Plum Branch, SC. Heritage Press Intl., 2010.

Telfer, Gary L., et al. U.S. Marines in Vietnam: Fighting the North Vietnamese, 1967. Washington, DC. U.S. Marine Corps, 1984.

Vetter, Lawrence C. Jr. Never Without Heroes. New York, NY. Ivy Books, 1996.

West, Bing, et al. The March Up: Taking Baghdad with the 1st Marine Division. New York, NY. Bantam Books, 2003.

West, Francis J. Jr. Small Unit Action in Vietnam: Summer 1966. Washington, DC. U.S. Marine Corps, 1977.

Wood, David Bowne. A Sense of Values: American Marines in an Uncertain World. Kansas City, MO. Newhouse News Service, 1994.

Glossary

<u>A-1</u>: Douglas Skyraider. A ground-attack piston-powered aircraft.

<u>A-4</u>: Douglas Skyhawk. A subsonic ground-attack jet aircraft.

<u>AAA</u>: Anti-Aircraft Artillery. Often called, *Triple-A*. In common usage, AAA means (1) any weapon designed for use against aircraft, or (2) the fire from such a weapon.

<u>AAR</u>: After Action Report.

<u>ADF</u>: Automatic Direction Finder. A low frequency radio receiver and instrument display in an aircraft. ADF provides homing direction toward a selected ground station (also called, *bird dog*).

<u>Air America</u>: The airline funded and directed by the U.S. Central Intelligence Agency. Air America flew helicopters and fixed-wing aircraft throughout Asia from the late 1940s into the mid-1970s.

<u>AK-47</u>: Avtomat Kalashnikova, Model 1947, a 7.62mm assault rifle manufactured in Russia, China, and other countries. The standard rifle used by the North Vietnamese Army.

<u>Alpha-Med</u>: Field hospital at Phu Bai.

<u>APC</u>: Armored Personnel Carrier.

<u>Arc-Light</u>: Code name for a tactical bombing mission by groups of U.S. Air Force B-52 heavy bombers.

<u>Arty</u>: Slang term for artillery.

<u>ARVN</u>: Army of the Republic of Vietnam. In common usage it can be either singular or plural. It can refer to a single South Vietnamese soldier, or a South Vietnamese military unit.

<u>Automatic Weapon</u>: A belt or magazine fed weapon that will fire and reload the chamber – and continue to fire and reload – until (1) the trigger is released, or (2) all ammunition has been exhausted.

> *<u>Semi-Automatic Weapon</u>*: A weapon that will fire and reload the chamber – once – each time the trigger is pulled.

Autorotate/Autorotation: A rapid descending glide without engine power in a helicopter. In the descent, air flowing *upward* through the rotor system keeps the rotors turning. That inertia can be used to arrest the descent when the helicopter nears the ground.

BLT: Battalion Landing Team.

C-47: Douglas Skytrain. A piston-powered twin-engine transport aircraft.

C-130: Lockheed Hercules. A large four-engine turboprop transport aircraft.

Charlie-Med: Field hospital at Da Nang.

Chicom (also, *ChiCom*): Contraction for Chinese Communist.

CIA: Central Intelligence Agency.

CIDG: Civilian Irregular Defense Group. A South Vietnamese para-military force.

CMC: Commandant of the Marine Corps.

Collective: In a helicopter, the large lever operated by a pilot's left arm and hand. The lever controls simultaneous *collective* pitch (and thereby, *lifting power*) of all main rotor blades.

CONUS: Continental United States.

CP: Command Post.

C-Rations: Factory packaged individual military meals designed for consumption in the field.

CSA: Confederate States Army.

Cyclic: In a helicopter, the large lever operated by a pilot's right arm and hand. The lever controls *cyclic* pitch of all main rotor blades (and thereby, *lateral and fore-and-aft control* of the helicopter).

Delta-Med: Medical aid station at Dong Ha.

DME: Distance Measuring Equipment. In aircraft, a DME display provides slant-range distance, in nautical miles, to selected electronic ground stations.

<u>DMZ</u>: Demilitarized Zone along the Ben Hai River separating South Vietnam from North Vietnam. The DMZ was established as a buffer area during the Geneva Accords, which ended the French Indochina War in 1954. It was intended to prevent "any incident which might result in the resumption of hostilities." Yet, both the Marines and the North Vietnamese routinely attacked each other inside the DMZ.

<u>DOD</u>: U.S. Department of Defense.

<u>DOW</u>: Died of Wounds.

<u>F-8</u>: Vought Crusader. A supersonic jet fighter and ground-attack aircraft.

<u>FAC</u>: Forward Air Controller.

<u>Frag</u>: Slang term for Fragmentary Order.

<u>Grunt</u>: Slang term for an infantryman. A term of utmost respect.

<u>H-34</u>: Sikorsky Choctaw. A radial-engine powered helicopter used to transport troops and cargo (spoken, *thirty-four*, or *dog*).

<u>H-46</u>: Boeing Sea Knight. A twin-turbine powered helicopter used to transport troops and cargo (spoken, *forty-six*, or *frog*, or *phrog*).

<u>H-53</u>: Sikorsky Sea Stallion. A large twin-turbine transport helicopter (spoken, *fifty-three*).

<u>HE</u>: High Explosive.

<u>Helicopter Valley</u>: Common term for the Ngan River Valley in northern Quang Tri Province of South Vietnam. The valley gained its moniker due to the many Marine helicopters lost there.

<u>H&I</u>: Harassment & Interdiction fire from mortars or artillery.

<u>HMC</u>: Hospitalman Chief (military rank).

<u>Huey</u>: Slang term for a Bell UH-1E helicopter.

<u>Huey Gunship</u>: A Bell UH-1E helicopter equipped with (1) two 2.75-inch rocket pods, (2) four fixed forward-firing 7.62mm machineguns fired electrically by the pilot, and (3) two swivel-mounted 7.62mm machineguns fired by the crew chief and gunner.

I-Corps: First Corps (spoken, *eye-core*). The five northernmost provinces of South Vietnam. Military responsibility for these five provinces fell to the U.S. Marine Corps.

ICS: Internal Communications System.

IFR: Instrument Flight Rules.

VFR: Visual Flight Rules.

Indian Country: Slang military term for enemy territory.

JP-4: Fuel, essentially kerosene, used by turbine powered aircraft.

Ka-Bar: Fighting knife used by Marine infantrymen.

KIA: Killed-in-Action.

Knots: Speed expressed in nautical miles per hour (one knot equals 1.15 miles per hour).

LAW: Light Anti-tank Weapon. A disposable, single shot, open end, shoulder fired, 66mm weapon.

LCU: Landing Craft Utility. A boat used to transport cargo.

Leatherneck Square: Name given to a fiercely embattled region of northern Quang Tri Province contested by the Marines and North Vietnamese. Leatherneck Square was loosely bordered by (1) Dong Ha on the southeast, (2) Gio Linh on the northeast, (3) Con Thien on the northwest, and (4) Cam Lo on the southwest.

LZ: Landing Zone.

M-2: Belt fed, recoil operated, .50 caliber heavy machinegun. It is usually crew-served in the field due to its large size and weight. However, when mounted on a vehicle or in an aircraft it can be operated by one man. Often called, *Ma Deuce.*

M-14: Gas operated, magazine fed, 7.62mm shoulder weapon. A stock M-14 fires in semi-automatic mode. A "modified" M-14 can fire in either semi-automatic or fully automatic mode.

M-26: A hand grenade. A hand-launched miniature bomb.

M-60: Belt fed, gas operated, 7.62mm light machinegun.

M-79: Known as a "grenade launcher." A single shot, breach loaded, shoulder weapon that fires a 40mm explosive round.

M-1911A1: Single action, recoil operated, magazine fed, semi-automatic, .45 caliber pistol (called, *forty-five*).

MACV: Military Assistance Command in Vietnam.

MAG-16: Marine Air Group 16, headquartered at Marble Mountain.

MCAS: Marine Corps Air Station.

Medevac: Medical Evacuation. Refers to the injured or wounded person being taken to medical facilities, or to the air or ground vehicle used to transport the person.

MIA: Missing-in-Action.

mm: Contraction for, *millimeter*. The suffix used to specify the muzzle diameter of military weapons.

Mortar: Heavy muzzle loaded, smooth bore, single shot, high angle of fire weapon.

Mustang: A military officer with prior enlisted service.

NCO: Non-Commissioned Officer.

NSA: Naval Support Activity.

Nung: Chinese mercenary. Used by the CIA for reconnaissance and guerrilla warfare in Laos and elsewhere.

NVA: North Vietnamese Army. Singular or plural, may indicate a single North Vietnamese soldier, or a North Vietnamese Army unit.

POW: Prisoner-of-War.

Pri-Fly: Primary Flight Control. On an aircraft carrier, Pri-Fly is equivalent to an airport control tower.

Razorback Valley: A huge valley in northern Quang Tri Province of South Vietnam. The valley was named for its western extremity, Razorback Ridge, centered at map coordinates XD-964576.

Recon: A Marine uniquely trained for reconnaissance missions.

<u>Rockpile</u>: A steep 700-foot-high rock promontory in northern Quang Tri Province of South Vietnam at map coordinates XD-979558. The lofty peak is accessible by helicopter and was used as an observation post by Marines.

<u>RPG</u>: Rocket Propelled Grenade.

<u>PRC-25</u>: American man-portable and battery-powered radio used by a Marine "radioman" in the field.

<u>SAR</u>: Search and Rescue.

<u>SAS</u>: Stability Argumentation System.

<u>Shackle Code</u>: Changeable alphanumeric code used to encrypt voice radio messages to make them unintelligible to the enemy.

<u>SITREP (also, *SitRep*)</u>: Situation Report.

<u>SLF</u>: Special Landing Force.

<u>SOG</u>: Studies and Observation Group. SOG forces were assigned clandestine missions in Laos, Cambodia, and North Vietnam.

<u>Song</u>: Vietnamese language word meaning *river*, or *stream*.

<u>Sparrow Hawk</u>: Marine Corps term applied to a rapid reaction team of infantrymen designed to be flown by helicopter into the field to exploit contact with the enemy.

<u>TAC</u>: Tactical Air Controller.

<u>TAC(A)</u>: Tactical Air Controller, Airborne.

<u>TACAN</u>: Tactical Air Navigation (spoken, *tack-ann*). A UHF radio transceiver in an aircraft. TACAN provides continuous slant-range distance, in nautical miles, and bearing to a selected ground station.

<u>TAD</u>: Temporary Additional Duty.

<u>Translational Lift</u>: When a helicopter hovers, its rotors *bite* into the air and force the air downward, generating lift. Yet, this creates a partial vacuum above the rotor system, and rotors cannot get firm *bites* in this low-pressure air. Consequently it takes much more engine power to hover high above the ground. However, as a helicopter flies forward the rotors continuously get solid *bites* of

undisturbed air. Lifting power is increased. The increase is called Translational Lift.

<u>Turns</u>: Slang helicopter term for rotor RPM.

<u>UH-1E</u>: Bell Iroquois. A turbine-powered utility or ground-attack helicopter. The utility variant was called a *Huey*. The ground-attack variant was known as a *gunship*, or *Huey gunship*.

<u>UHF</u>: Ultra-High-Frequency radio transmission or equipment.

<u>USA</u>: United States Army.

<u>USAF</u>: United States Air Force.

<u>USMC</u>: United States Marine Corps.

<u>USN</u>: United States Navy.

<u>VC</u>: (see, *Viet Cong*).

<u>Viet Cong</u>: Contraction for Vietnamese Communist. An indigenous fighter, as opposed to a soldier of the North Vietnamese Army. In verbal use, Viet Cong often was shortened to (1) *VC*, or (2) *Charlie*.

<u>Viet Minh</u>: Contraction for Vietnam Doc Lap Nong Minh Hoi, the communist coalition that fought against (1) the Japanese Army during World War II, and later against (2) the French Army until 1954.

<u>WIA</u>: Wounded-in-Action.

<u>WP</u>: White Phosphorus. Often called, *Willie Pete*.

<u>2/4</u>: Marine abbreviation for 2nd Battalion, 4th Marine Regiment (3/5 is the abbreviation for 3rd Battalion, 5th Marine Regiment, etc.).